Artificial Intelligence and Conservation

With the increasing public interest in artificial intelligence (AI), there is also increasing interest in learning about the benefits that AI can deliver to society. This book focuses on research advances in AI that benefit the conservation of wildlife, forests, coral reefs, rivers, and other natural resources. It presents how the joint efforts of researchers in computer science, ecology, economics, and psychology help address the goals of the United Nations' 2030 Agenda for Sustainable Development.

Written at a level accessible to conservation professionals and AI researchers, the book offers both an overview of the field and an in-depth view of how AI is being used to understand patterns in wildlife poaching and to enhance patrol efforts in response, covering research advances, field tests, and real-world deployments. The book also features efforts in other major conservation directions, including protecting natural resources, ecosystem monitoring, and bio-invasion management through the use of game theory, machine learning, and optimization.

FEI FANG is Assistant Professor of Computer Science at Carnegie Mellon University. Her work has won the Innovative Application Award at the Conference on Innovative Applications of AI in 2016 and the Outstanding Paper Award in Computational Sustainability Track at the International Joint Conferences on AI in 2015.

MILIND TAMBE is Helen N. and Emmett H. Jones Professor of Engineering and Founding Co-Director of the University of Southern California Center for Artificial Intelligence in Society. He has received the IJCAI John McCarthy Award, the ACM/SIGAI Autonomous Agents Research Award, the Christopher Columbus Fellowship Foundation Homeland Security Award, and the INFORMS Wagner Prize in Operations Research. He is a fellow of the AAAI and ACM.

BISTRA DILKINA is Assistant Professor of Computer Science and Associate Director of the University of Southern California Center for AI in Society. Prior to that, she was an assistant professor at Georgia Tech and a co-director of the Data Science for Social Good Atlanta program. She has published at top AI conferences as well as in journals such as *Conservation Biology*.

ANDREW J. PLUMPTRE is Head of the Key Biodiversity Areas Secretariat, associated with the Conservation Science Group in the Zoology Department at Cambridge University. He previously was the Wildlife Conservation Society's senior scientist for Africa and managed a regional program of conservation in the Albertine Rift that supported conservation of some of Africa's most biodiverse sites.

Artificial Intelligence for Social Good

Artificial intelligence has a diversity of applications, many with social benefits. Books in this series will offer a multidisciplinary perspective on these applications, ranging from social work to health care to environmental sciences. Each book will survey the AI approaches to a particular societal problem and promising research directions, with case study examples.

OTHER BOOKS IN THIS SERIES:

Milind Tambe and Eric Rice, eds., *Artificial Intelligence and Social Work*

Artificial Intelligence and Conservation

Edited by

FEI FANG
Carnegie Mellon University

MILIND TAMBE
University of Southern California

BISTRA DILKINA
Georgia Institute of Technology

ANDREW J. PLUMPTRE
Key Biodiversity Areas Secretariat

CAMBRIDGE
UNIVERSITY PRESS

CAMBRIDGE
UNIVERSITY PRESS

University Printing House, Cambridge CB2 8BS, United Kingdom

One Liberty Plaza, 20th Floor, New York, NY 10006, USA

477 Williamstown Road, Port Melbourne, VIC 3207, Australia

314–321, 3rd Floor, Plot 3, Splendor Forum, Jasola District Centre,
New Delhi – 110025, India

79 Anson Road, #06–04/06, Singapore 079906

Cambridge University Press is part of the University of Cambridge.

It furthers the University's mission by disseminating knowledge in the pursuit of
education, learning, and research at the highest international levels of excellence.

www.cambridge.org
Information on this title: www.cambridge.org/9781316512920
DOI: 10.1017/9781108587792

First published 2019

Printed and bound in Great Britain by Clays Ltd, Elcograf S.p.A.

A catalogue record for this publication is available from the British Library.

Library of Congress Cataloging-in-Publication Data
Names: Fang, Fei, 1989– editor.
Title: Artificial intelligence and conservation / edited by Fei Fang, Carnegie Mellon University,
Pennsylvania, Milind Tambe, University of Southern California, Bistra Dilkina, Georgia Institute
of Technology, Andrew J. Plumptre, Key Biodiversity Areas Secretariat.
Description: Cambridge, United Kingdom ; New York, NY : Cambridge University Press, 2019. |
Series: Artificial intelligence for social good | Includes bibliographical references and index.
Identifiers: LCCN 2018040979 | ISBN 9781316512920 (hardback : alk. paper) |
ISBN 9781108464734 (paperback : alk. paper)
Subjects: LCSH: Wildlife conservation–Technological innovations. | Artificial intelligence.
Classification: LCC QL82 .A78 2019 | DDC 333.95/4–dc23
LC record available at https://lccn.loc.gov/2018040979

ISBN 978-1-316-51292-0 Hardback
ISBN 978-1-108-46473-4 Paperback

Contents

Contributors   *page* vii

1   Introduction   1
Fei Fang, Milind Tambe, Bistra Dilkina, and Andrew J. Plumptre

PART I   15

2   Law Enforcement for Wildlife Conservation   17
Andrew J. Plumptre

3   Wildlife Poaching Forecasting Based on Ranger-Collected Data and Evaluation through Field Tests   29
Shahrzad Gholami, Benjamin Ford, Debarun Kar, Fei Fang,
Andrew J. Plumptre, Milind Tambe, Margaret Driciru, Fred Wanyama,
Aggrey Rwetsiba, Mustapha Nsubuga, and Joshua Mabonga

4   Optimal Patrol Planning Against Black-Box Attackers   57
Haifeng Xu, Benjamin Ford, Fei Fang, Bistra Dilkina,
Andrew J. Plumptre, Milind Tambe, Margaret Driciru, Fred Wanyama,
Aggrey Rwetsiba, Mustapha Nsubuga, and Joshua Mabonga

5   Automatic Detection of Poachers and Wildlife with UAVs   77
Elizabeth Bondi, Fei Fang, Mark Hamilton, Debarun Kar,
Donnabell Dmello, Venil Noronha, Jongmoo Choi, Robert Hannaford,
Arvind Iyer, Lucas Joppa, Milind Tambe, and Ram Nevatia

PART II   101

6   Protecting Coral Reef Ecosystems via Efficient Patrols   103
Yue Yin and Bo An

7   Simultaneous Optimization of Strategic and Tactical
     Planning for Environmental Sustainability and
     Security   118
     Sara M. McCarthy, Milind Tambe, Christopher Kiekintveld,
     Meredith L. Gore, and Alex Killion

8   NECTAR: Enforcing Environmental Compliance through
     Strategically Randomized Factory Inspections   136
     Benjamin Ford, Matthew Brown, Amulya Yadav, Amandeep Singh,
     Arunesh Sinha, Biplav Srivastava, Christopher Kiekintveld, and
     Milind Tambe

9   Connecting Conservation Research and Implementation:
     Building a Wildfire Assistant   151
     Sean McGregor, Rachel M. Houtman, Ronald Metoyer,
     and Thomas G. Dietterich

10   Probabilistic Inference with Generating Functions
     for Animal Populations   177
     Daniel Sheldon, Kevin Winner, and Debora Sujono

11   Engaging Citizen Scientists in Data Collection
     for Conservation   194
     Yexiang Xue and Carla P. Gomes

12   Simulator-Defined Markov Decision Processes: A Case
     Study in Managing Bio-invasions   210
     H. Jo Albers, Thomas G. Dietterich, Kim Hall, Katherine D. Lee,
     and Majid A. Taleghan

     Glossary   231
     Index   235

Contributors

H. Jo Albers
University of Wyoming

Bo An
Nanyang Technological University

Elizabeth Bondi
University of Southern California

Matthew Brown
University of Southern California

Jongmoo Choi
University of Southern California

Thomas G. Dietterich
Oregon State University

Bistra Dilkina
University of Southern California

Margaret Driciru
Uganda Wildlife Authority

Donnabell Dmello
University of Southern California

Fei Fang
Carnegie Mellon University

Benjamin Ford
University of Southern California

Shahrzad Gholami
University of Southern California

Carla P. Gomes
Cornell University

Meredith L. Gore
Michigan State University

Kim Hall
Oregon State University

Mark Hamilton
Microsoft

Robert Hannaford
AirShepherd

Rachel M. Houtman
Oregon State University

Arvind Iyer
AirShepherd

Lucas Joppa
Microsoft

Debarun Kar
University of Southern California

Christopher Kiekintveld
University of Texas at El Paso

Alex Killion
Michigan State University

Katherine D. Lee
University of Idaho

Joshua Mabonga
Wildlife Conservation Society

Sara M. McCarthy
University of Southern California

Sean McGregor
Oregon State University

Ronald Metoyer
University of Notre Dame

Ram Nevatia
University of Southern California

Venil Noronha
University of Southern California

Mustapha Nsubuga
Wildlife Conservation Society

Andrew J. Plumptre
Key Biodiversity Areas Secretariat

Arunesh Sinha
University of Michigan

Amandeep Singh
Wharton Business School

Aggrey Rwetsiba
Uganda Wildlife Authority

Daniel Sheldon
University of Massachusetts Amherst

Biplav Srivastava
IBM Research

Debora Sujono
University of Massachusetts Amherst

Majid A. Taleghan
Oregon State University

Milind Tambe
University of Southern California

Fred Wanyama
Uganda Wildlife Authority

Kevin Winner
University of Massachusetts Amherst

Haifeng Xu
University of Southern California

Yexiang Xue
Cornell University

Amulya Yadav
University of Southern California

Yue Yin
University of Chinese Academy of Sciences

1

Introduction

Fei Fang, Milind Tambe, Bistra Dilkina, and Andrew J. Plumptre

Artificial intelligence (AI) has undoubtedly been integrated into our lives. It is hard to enumerate all the aspects of our personal lives that are influenced by AI. Nowadays, the most common way of using the internet, web search, is powered by AI. Almost all the recommender systems are powered by sophisticated AI algorithms that decide what advertisement we see when browsing a website, what items are suggested to us when shopping on Amazon or eBay, what videos, news, and posts are brought to our attention on YouTube, CNN, Facebook, and Twitter. As another example, facial recognition supported by AI techniques is being used in more and more situations to verify the identity of a person, including unlocking of smartphones, security screening at the airport, and verifying customers at the gate during the boarding of a flight. Similarly, speech recognition and synthesis techniques have been embedded into AI-powered home assistants, real-time speech-to-text translation or language translation tools, and automated customer service systems with which we frequently interact. Self-driving cars are no longer a dream.

In short, we are already in an era of AI with all these AI-powered tools and applications. Indeed, with the breakthroughs made in the past few decades, AI has taken over many tasks that have traditionally been completed by humans. This has led to transformation and evolution in many domains and industries, ranging from the IT industry to traditional industries such as finance (e.g., whether to approve a consumer loan, how much one should pay for insurance) and health care (e.g., analyzing medical images automatically).

With all of these rapid advances in the field of AI and the pervasive use of AI, many in both the scientific community and the lay public are increasingly interested in the impact that AI may have on society. Together with these changes brought about by AI, there is a series of concerns. One set of concerns is related to the significant potential for job loss. Another is related to the potential risk of using AI to make critical decisions and, in fact, ensuring

1

the safety of humans from a future powerful AI in charge of such decisions (perhaps similar to what has been depicted in Hollywood movies like *The Terminator*). Yet a third set of concerns focuses on the ethical, moral, and legal challenges that arise from the use of AI in our daily lives – life-and-death questions that come to the forefront when AI must interact with society, as in self-driving cars making choices in life-critical situations.

While these are no doubt legitimate concerns, this book continues with the emphasis in the Artificial Intelligence for Social Good – to push AI research to bring more beneficial results for society. The thrust of the current book series is that AI can be harnessed to address a wide range of social problems and make a significant positive impact. Indeed, the theme of AI for Social Good has been highlighted at different venues where researchers have presented a set of promising emerging applications to promote social good. However, a comprehensive book series that organizes these applications into different topics has so far been missing. Accordingly, each book in our series focuses on how AI could work with a particular field and the social good that could be achieved in that field. The first book in this series, *AI and Social Work*, focused on the fields of AI and social work to address societal problems requiring intervention in social interactions, particularly with low-resource communities (e.g., homeless youth). Topics included HIV prevention, substance abuse prevention, suicide prevention, and others.

This book is the second in this series, taking on a very different domain of impact. In this book we focus on how AI researchers can work with conservation scientists and others in the field of conservation to assist in handling challenges related to the conservation of wildlife, forests, fisheries, rivers, and our environment. The book provides an introduction to this rich and yet new area of research, and outlines key challenges and opportunities. There is tremendous and growing interest in this area, and it is important for us to understand how the significant progress recently achieved in AI could be used to benefit conservation.

The book showcases the interdisciplinary collaboration among many different disciplines in allowing the fields of AI and conservation to partner. We, the editors of this book, are indeed part of this interdisciplinary collaboration, as AI researchers who have spent significant research effort in applying AI to address challenges in conservation (Fang, Tambe, Dilkina) collaborating with a conservation scientist and practitioner who has guided and sought AI efforts for conservation (Plumptre). The book provides an in-depth view of a key thrust of our joint research over the past five years – in this joint work, we have focused on the use of AI in the service of wildlife conservation, specifically how AI can be used to better understand patterns in wildlife poaching and enhance security to combat poaching. The joint effort in this key thrust has led to an important application tool named Protection Assistant for Wildlife Security, or PAWS (Yang et al., 2014; Fang et al., 2016), which has been tested and deployed in countries around the world, including Malaysia, Uganda, and Botswana. The book also features some chapters from key teams of AI researchers partnering with conservation scientists, covering other directions and showcasing various challenges in environmental conservation and how they could be tackled by AI. In these chapters, the book presents work resulting from interdisciplinary collaborations among researchers in computer science, ecology, economics, and psychology.

This book aims to inspire new AI research that can help address conservation challenges. These advances in AI research can bring benefits to the conservation of key natural resources, and help us advance toward the goals listed in the United Nations's 2030 Agenda for Sustainable Development. Simultaneously, the book is intended for conservation scientists who may be interested in using AI approaches and techniques; the variety of examples in the book may yield clues as to how AI could be used, and the strengths and limitations of current AI tools. Accordingly, the intended audience for the book is: (1) researchers in computer science who are interested in AI and social good and in particular applications of AI in conservation; (2) researchers and practitioners in conservation and related scientific fields who are interested in how AI techniques can be used for conservation; and (3) other researchers interested in both computer science and conservation who may be interested in starting research in this area.

Since this book aims to speak to multiple different audiences, including conservation and AI researchers, a brief overview of these two disciplines is warranted. Unfortunately, a few paragraphs on these topics can hardly hope to do each area much justice. Moreover, such a short treatment will inevitably be biased – reflecting our own personal biases within our respective disciplines. That said, we hope these next few paragraphs help you, our readers, to be grounded to some extent in the work of these two fields.

What Is Conservation Science?

Conservation Biology

Conservation biology is about the management of nature, the maintenance, loss, and restoration of biodiversity on the earth with the aim of protecting species, their habitats, and ecosystems from excessive rates of extinction and the erosion of biotic interactions (Soule, 1980, 1985). The extinction of species, the loss of habitat, and the decline of biodiversity and biological systems around the world raises significant concerns about the sustainable well-being of human society; together they may contribute to poverty, starvation, and will even reset the course of evolution on this planet. Conservation biologists study these causes, trends, and their impacts, as well as action plans to combat undesired change (Groom et al., 2006).

Conservation biology started as a scientific discipline in the mid-1970s during the First International Conference on Research in Conservation Biology, held at the University of California, San Diego Douglas, 1978. The field of conservation biology and the concept of biodiversity emerged together, helping to crystallize the modern era of conservation science and policy, and bridging the gap between theory in ecology and evolutionary genetics and conservation policy and practice. It has grown rapidly to include many subdisciplines, such as conservation genetics, conservation planning, conservation social science, conservation physiology, ex-situ and in-situ conservation, restoration science, and many others. It is an interdisciplinary subject drawing on natural and social sciences and the practice of natural resource management. Conservation biology is closely connected to ecology, biology, and economy, among other related disciplines (Van Dyke, 2008).

Conservation of Natural Resources

The conservation of natural resources is a topic for both research and practice. The practice of natural resource conservation exists in history in different cultures (Kala, 2005; Murphree, 2009). Within conservation biology, the research on conservation of natural resources can be further classified based on the type of natural resources being considered, such as water conservation, energy conservation, marine conservation, wildlife conservation, habitat conservation, soil conservation, forest conservation, wetland conservation, etc. In this book, the work we discuss will cover several of these topics – including wildlife conservation, forest conservation, water conservation, and marine conservation – but our emphasis will be on wildlife conservation.

Managing Conservation Areas

Since the establishment of the first national park, Yellowstone National Park in the USA, in 1872 there has been a need to manage protected areas both for their wildlife and also for the people living around them. Initially, these areas were established to conserve wilderness and areas for recreation, but over time there has been an increasing focus on the conservation of biodiversity and the richness of life on earth. Over the years, the percentage of the planet covered by protected areas has increased to about 15 percent on land, and about 10 percent of coastal areas together with 4 percent of global ocean areas. The Aichi targets of the Convention on Biological Diversity (CBD) set a goal of 17 percent of terrestrial and 10 percent of marine areas for conservation by 2020, but these targets are already being reassessed as the area required to conserve all species on the planet will need to be larger than this.

With the growth of conservation areas, there has also been incredible growth in the human population, from about 1.2 billion in 1872 to 7.4 billion today. This has changed the nature of conservation, as the demand for land has greatly increased, causing fragmentation and loss of habitat, together with the increasingly unsustainable use of natural resources. The challenges a protected area manager has to tackle today are very different to those of 145 years ago, and are increasingly complex and often involve tradeoffs between various management options. Many of the management practices in conservation improve with the experience of the manager as they learn how to negotiate the issues they face. There is a need to improve the ability of managers to make wise decisions, and conservation science aims to provide answers to improve management and conservation. Conservation science aims to help identify questions, such as where to conserve, when to conserve, and how to conserve.

What Is AI?

From the Turing Test to National Strategies

Many people have heard about the Turing Test, proposed by Alan Turing in 1950 (Turing, 1950). The Turing Test is designed to answer the question "Can the machine think?" Briefly, the test consists of a human judge conversing with a human and a machine via text. The judge needs to identify the machine reliably, while the machine's objective is to mimic a human as closely as possible in an attempt to fool the judge. This test is highly influential yet widely criticized. Even if a machine can do well in this game, can we claim the machine has intelligence? This relates to the question of how AI should be defined. Indeed, there is no accepted definition of AI, but generally speaking we will consider AI to include computer systems (including robots) that perform tasks that require intelligence.

Since the creation of the Turing Test, research in AI has continued to advance with the design of new algorithms and tools. AI progressed from being an academic discipline that few had heard about, to a discipline that is often in the news, to a discipline that is now mentioned in national research strategies in multiple countries, including the USA and UK.

History of AI

The discipline of AI was founded in the 1950s. Four scientists are generally considered to be founding fathers: Allen Newell and Herbert Simon of Carnegie Mellon University, John McCarthy of Stanford University, and Marvin Minsky of Massachusetts Institute of Technology. They had the optimistic vision that "aspects of intelligence can be so precisely described that a machine can be made to simulate it" (McCarthy et al., 1955). Since then, AI has experienced optimism and disappointment. The early years of optimism in AI were based on computer programs performing tasks that could be considered difficult for humans, such as playing chess, proving theorems, and solving puzzles. In these tasks, interacting with the outside world was not a priority and uncertainty was not a major concern. For example, statements are either true or false; chess moves are deterministic. Furthermore, without the need to rapidly interact with the outside world, a program could reason about a situation in depth and then react. Indeed, early progress in AI was dominated by the use of logic and symbolic systems, heuristic reasoning, and search algorithms, which did not involve probabilistic reasoning or uncertainty.

In the 1980s, this optimism about AI research led to integrated AI systems that could combine machine learning to autonomously learn from interactions of the AI system with the world, automated reasoning and planning to act in the world, possibly speech and dialogue in natural language to interact with the world, social interactions with humans and other entities, and so on. Such integrated intelligent agents included robots, but also avatars in virtual worlds. This vision of AI involved gathering data from the world and using machine learning to build a predictive model of how the world would evolve. However, it did not stop only at making predictions but also included planning and reasoning from first principles, that is, providing prescriptions and taking actions in the world.

This early optimism was followed by the AI winter around 1990, when outsiders criticized AI research for not living up to its promises, and this led to a general reduction in funding and interest in AI. Researchers realized that what was easy for humans (e.g., recognizing objects in images, understanding human speech as English words) turned out to be difficult for AI systems.

As AI systems started interacting with the real world, an entirely new set of tools was needed to handle reasoning with uncertainty and for quick reactions to unanticipated events. These difficulties led to new quantitative tools from decision theory, optimization, and game theory being brought into AI. This period also coincided with an emphasis on fast, reactive reasoning (rather than purely in-depth reasoning) in AI, particularly for robots interacting with the world. Despite the criticism and difficulties, AI researchers continued working hard and making progress in various aspects of AI. Encouraging news started flowing again to slowly lift research out of the AI winter, including the famous victory of IBM supercomputer Deep Blue over the world chess champion, Garry Kasparov.

New Era of AI

We are now in a new era of AI. The increasing computing power and the ability to gather and store large quantities of data has led to promising new tools and approaches. Machine learning using deep neural networks has led to significant new successes in tasks such as recognizing objects in images and natural language understanding. The computer program AlphaGo defeating world champions at the game Go was viewed as another milestone of AI – the game of Go, a classic strategy board game for two players, was considered to be a very complex game that required a high level of intelligence to play.

This new era has brought significant new interest and investment from industry due to the use of AI in commercial applications, from ad auctions to the search, recommendation, verification, and translation tools that are used by millions of people. It has also led to some misunderstanding in the general public that AI is only about machine learning and prediction, and that unless there are vast quantities of data, AI cannot function. Often not well understood is AI's ability to provide prescriptions or to plan intervention in the world by reasoning through millions of possibilities – for example, using millions of simulations from first principles of how entities may interact in the world, and, more importantly, how such interventions can be integrated with machine learning to accomplish more complex tasks. In our work described in Part I of this book, and the other chapters outlined in Part II, we will often focus on this ability to plan interventions and their integration.

Subfields of AI

As can be seen from the development of AI, AI research has been divided into subfields, including machine learning, multi-agent systems, natural language processing, computer vision, planning and scheduling, reasoning under uncertainty, search and constraint satisfaction, heuristic search and optimization, knowledge representation and reasoning, and others. Nonetheless, AI systems in the real world may require integration of research from several subfields.

Partnership of AI and Conservation Science

Despite the obvious differences in AI and conservation science, they also complement each other in important ways, which makes the partnership of AI and conservation science a productive one. The shared interest of AI and conservation science are centered around a few major topics. First, measuring and monitoring the ecosystem often requires statistical inference, for which machine learning models and algorithms can be developed and applied. For example, the problem of estimating the distribution of wildlife species or poaching activities based on occurrence data can be viewed as predicting the probability distribution given a set of training data, which is naturally addressed in the AI subfield of machine learning.

Second, the conservation and management of natural resources often involves planning, scheduling, and optimization, which are the focus of study in several subfields of AI. For example, to manage invasive species, a land manager must decide how and where to fight the invasion – for example, she may choose a location to eradicate invasive plants or plant more native plants. Finding the optimal location and treatment is an optimization problem that may exceed the capability of a human manager, but can be addressed through developing Markov decision process-based models and algorithms which are heavily studied in AI. In fact, the partnership of AI and conservation science dates back to 1989, when a conservation planning problem in South Australia was modeled as an optimization problem, and mathematical programming was first used to solve the problem (Cocks and Baird, 1989). This solution approach was followed by Marxan, a decision support software for conservation planning developed in 2005 that is widely used across the globe.

Third, conservation of natural resources often involves understanding how multiple agents interact. For example, conservation agencies send rangers to protected areas to detect and deter poaching activities conducted by poachers, and both parties behave in ways that are best for themselves, leading to strategic interplay. Similarly, conservation may also require understanding the conflict between humans and wildlife. Such interactions are modeled via a multi-agent system, the focus of a key subfield in AI. Therefore, frameworks and approaches in multi-agent systems become a natural fit to understand and analyze the interactions as well as to optimize the actions of some agents (e.g., planning the patrol routes for the rangers) to achieve the conservation goal.

This productive collaboration between AI and conservation is a new intellectual space that empowers new research for both fields. It goes beyond just taking a problem in conservation biology and applying existing AI techniques to solve it. Instead, it creates new challenges for both sides and fosters innovative science in AI and conservation biology, with general applications. Take our work on predicting poaching threat, described later in this book, as an illustrative example. The data collected from previous patrols provide information about where snares (a common poaching tool) were found and how often different regions in the protected area have been patrolled; the question to be answered is where the poachers will place snares in the future. From the perspective of AI, predicting the distribution of poaching activity introduced several new challenges for which existing algorithms could not be directly applied. First, the level of poaching threat varies spatially and temporally, and poachers may adapt to how the rangers patrol by circumventing areas that have been heavily patrolled in the past. Second, unlike many other domains that have a tremendous amount of data, the anti-poaching domain often has a training dataset that is highly imbalanced, biased, and noisy. The imbalances come from the fact that patrollers patrol vast areas, but they often find actual poaching signs or snares in small parts of the areas they patrol. Furthermore, since the patrollers cannot cover all the regions in a protected area and the selection of patrol routes is decided by the site manager, the data collected suffer significantly from sampling bias. Finally, the noisiness comes from imperfect detection. When a patroller does not find any poaching activity in a region, it is possible that poaching activity actually occurred but the patroller failed to detect it because the poaching signs remain well hidden in the forest. Thus, we had to propose new algorithms to address these research challenges, advancing the techniques in machine learning from limited labeled data. From the perspective of conservation, while conservation tools such as SMART (Spatial Monitoring And Reporting Tool) have been used to record and analyze the coverage of patrols and distribution of poaching activities found, there is not much work on predicting future poaching threats using machine learning models. Such predictive models radically shift the view of conservation site management from summarizing historical poaching activities and patrols to predicting the future and proactively planning patrols.

The interdisciplinary space also leads to challenges that have been underexplored in these two disciplines. One set of challenges is how to integrate AI with human insight and knowledge. For example, how to elicit valuable prior knowledge from conservation researchers and practitioners when building an AI tool. Practitioners working on conservation often have a much better understanding of the domain than what is recorded in a dataset. In predicting poaching threat, the dataset only contains where the rangers went and what they found, but the rangers know more than that. They may know which features make a region attractive to poachers, which villages the poachers come from, what external factors make the overall level of poaching threat increase or decrease, and so on. Such prior knowledge, if used properly, may significantly boost the performance of the machine learning algorithm, but there is a lack of research on how to make proper use of it. Also, it is important to build tools so that human experts can provide iterative inputs to improve the performance of an algorithm. Another example is how to interpret solutions to conservation challenges provided by AI tools. For AI researchers, the research questions include how to provide explainable solutions and effectively convey the solutions to conservation researchers and practitioners. For conservation science researchers, the research question is how to interpret the solution to provide conservation insights.

In addition to the challenges in knowledge elicitation and interpretation, another set of challenges center on the validation and evaluation of prediction or planning tools. While evaluating predictions on a readily available test set (dataset in the lab) is a more traditional approach to evaluating predictive models, an important method of evaluating a predictive model in this interdisciplinary space is to test it in the real world. However, it is difficult to conduct tests under perfectly controlled conditions in the real world. These difficulties also extend to the evaluation of planning tools. For example, to evaluate a patrol planning tool, ideally one would have two identical portions of a protected area, with one running the planning tool and one not; but finding such identical areas is difficult. Furthermore, improved patrolling could lead to an increase in the numbers of captures of poaching tools such as snares, but it may also cause poachers to reduce poaching and thus a reduction of the numbers of snares found. Finally, there may also be contamination in the experiment because poachers may shift poaching activities from one area to another precisely because of improved patrolling in a neighboring area. Many of these challenges are still open questions, forming important directions for future research in how to evaluate AI algorithms in the field.

In fact, AI and conservation is one of the key research thrusts in the broader research field of computational sustainability (Gomes, 2009), which focuses on ways that computational models, methods, and tools can help solve some of the key sustainability challenges that our planet and society face. This growing interdisciplinary research area provides a two-way street of benefits, by harnessing the power of computing and specifically AI for real-world impact on the path to sustainable development, and at the same time enriching the field of computer science with novel computational techniques and models developed in the process of addressing these challenging problems. In addition to AI and conservation, computational sustainability covers other important themes, with research efforts on developing computational methods to analyze, predict, or optimize various aspects related to sustainability, including the discovery of new renewable materials (Xue et al., 2017), predicting poverty based on satellite imagery (Jean et al., 2016), finding optimized sustainable building designs (Safarzadegan Gilan et al., 2016), and livestock disease management (Teose et al., 2011), among many others.

AI and conservation is thus an active area of collaborative research, with many challenges awaiting solutions. This book features collaborative work between AI and conservation scientists for the conservation of wildlife, forests, fisheries, and rivers, with solutions that show promise; but more effort is certainly needed toward full solutions. Besides the work introduced in this book, there are other lines of important work in AI and conservation, including but not limited to bioacoustic monitoring (Salamon et al., 2016), predicting individual wildlife locations through collective movement (Farine et al., 2016), protecting fisheries from overfishing (Haskell et al., 2014), protecting forest land from excessive fuelwood extraction (Johnson et al., 2012), and analyzing the effect of reduced ship strike on the North Atlantic right whale (Conn and Silber, 2013). Beyond the existing work, there are many more directions to be explored, including the protection and management of land, habitat, ocean and sea resources, and the management of soil to prevent erosion, depletion, and contamination. The purpose of this book is to start to make conservation practitioners and AI scientists more aware of where synergies could be developed. We encourage researchers in AI and conservation science to participate in this area of research and contribute to it.

The Structure of the Book

This book has two sections following this introductory chapter which defines the collaboration between AI and conservation. Hopefully by now you have a better understanding of how AI and conservation scientists can collaborate, how AI can be useful for addressing conservation challenges, what new challenges may arise in AI techniques themselves, and so on.

Part I focuses on our ongoing interdisciplinary research specifically around anti-poaching. We show how we develop and harness advanced AI techniques to assist patrol resources such as human patrollers and conservation drones to combat wildlife poaching, a key challenge in wildlife conservation. We start with an introduction to law enforcement for environment conservation, and then focus on the development of a set of AI-based analytical, predictive, and prescriptive tools that have been developed for anti-poaching efforts. Importantly, we present how the tools are deployed and evaluated in the field worldwide. Some of this work has been published in a series of papers at various international AI conferences. The work provides an example of close collaboration of AI and conservation scientists by illustrating how AI algorithms can be used to understand and curb illegal wildlife poaching, through predicting poaching hotspots, analyzing poacher behavior from past poaching data and video streams taken by conservation drones, and designing effective patrol routes. This work has been deployed in multiple countries and has received a significant number of awards, including the Innovative Application Award at IAAI in 2016 (Fang et al., 2016) and the Outstanding Paper Award in Computational Sustainability Track at IJCAI in 2015 (Fang et al., 2015). We attempt to present this work in a fashion that is more accessible to an interdisciplinary audience rather than a purely AI audience, especially readers in relevant communities such as conservation biology and ecology.

Part II of the book features other major directions of current work on AI and conservation, including protecting natural resources, ecosystem monitoring, and bio-invasion management. These chapters are written by leading teams working in these areas and showcase various challenges in environmental conservation and how they could be tackled by AI. The AI work includes techniques such as robust optimization, dynamic optimization, and sequential planning under uncertainty.

At the end of the book, we provide a glossary of terms together with a brief introduction to the AI techniques used in this book in natural language. One of the challenges that researchers and practitioners with AI or conservation backgrounds face is the "language barrier" when they try to foster joint efforts. Over years of collaboration, we have learned the vocabulary in both areas and the most confusing terminologies, and we would like to share with you our lessons learned.

References

Cocks, K. D., & Baird, I. A. (1989). Using mathematical programming to address the multiple reserve selection problem: an example from the Eyre Peninsula, South Australia. *Biological Conservation*, *49*(2), 113–130.

Conn, P. B., & Silber, G. K. (2013). Vessel speed restrictions reduce risk of collision-related mortality for North Atlantic right whales. *Ecosphere*, *4*(4), 1–16.

Douglas, J. (1978). Biologists urge US endowment for conservation. *Nature, 275,* 82–83.

Fang, F., Stone, P., & Tambe, M. (2015). When security games go green: designing defender strategies to prevent poaching and illegal fishing. In *Proceedings of the 24th International Conference on Artificial Intelligence* (pp. 2589–2595). AAAI Press.

Fang, F., Nguyen, T. H., Pickles, R. et al. (2016). Deploying PAWS: field optimization of the Protection Assistant for Wildlife Security. In *Twenty-Eighth IAAI Conference* (pp. 3966–3973). AAAI Press.

Farine, D. R., Strandburg-Peshkin, A., Berger-Wolf, T. et al. (2016). Both nearest neighbours and long-term affiliates predict individual locations during collective movement in wild baboons. *Scientific Reports, 6.* DOI: 10.1038/srep27704

Gomes, C. P. (2009). Computational sustainability: computational methods for a sustainable environment, economy, and society. *The Bridge, 39*(4), 5–13.

Groom, M. J., Meffe, G. K., & Carroll, C. R. (2006). *Principles of conservation biology.* Sunderland, MA: Sinauer Associates.

Haskell, W. B., Kar, D., Fang, F. et al. (2014). Robust protection of fisheries with COmPASS. In *Proceedings of the Twenty-Sixth Annual Conference on Innovative Applications of Artificial Intelligence* (pp. 2978–2983). AAAI Press.

Jean, N., Burke, M., Xie, M. et al. (2016). Combining satellite imagery and machine learning to predict poverty. *Science, 353*(6301), 790–794.

Johnson, M. P., Fang, F., & Tambe, M. (2012). Patrol strategies to maximize pristine forest area. In Proceedings of the Twenty-Sixth AAAI Conference on Artificial Intelligence. AAAI Press.

Kala, C. P. (2005). Indigenous uses, population density, and conservation of threatened medicinal plants in protected areas of the Indian Himalayas. *Conservation Biology, 19*(2), 368–378.

McCarthy, J., Minsky, M. L., Rochester, N., & Shannon, C. E. (1955). A proposal for the Dartmouth summer research project on artificial intelligence, August 31, 1955. *AI Magazine, 27*(4), 12.

Murphree, M. W. (2009). The strategic pillars of communal natural resource management: benefit, empowerment and conservation. *Biodiversity and Conservation, 18*(10), 2551–2562.

Safarzadegan Gilans, Goyal, N., & Dilkina, B. (2016). Active learning in multi-objective evolutionary algorithms for sustainable building design. In *Proceedings of the Genetic and Evolutionary Computation Conference 2016.* ACM.

Salamon, J., Bello, J. P., Farnsworth, A. et al. (2016). Towards the automatic classification of avian flight calls for bioacoustic monitoring. *PloS One, 11*(11), e0166866.

Soule, M. E. (1980). *Conservation biology: an evolutionary-ecological perspective* Sunderland, MA: Sinauer Associates.

Soulé, M. E. (1985). What is conservation biology? *BioScience, 35*(11), 727–734.

Teose, M., Ahmadizadeh, K., O'Mahony, E. et al. (2011). Embedding system dynamics in agent based models for complex adaptive systems. In *Proceedings: International Joint Conference on Artificial Intelligence* (Vol. 22, No. 3, p. 2531). AAAI Press.

Turing, A. M. (1950). Computing machinery and intelligence. *Mind, 59*(236), 433–460.

Van Dyke, F. (2008). *Conservation biology: foundations, concepts, applications.* New York: Springer Science & Business Media.

Xue, Y., Bai, J., Le Bras, R., et al. (2017). Phase-Mapper: an AI platform to accelerate high throughput materials discovery. In *Twenty-Ninth IAAI Conference* (pp. 4635–4643). AAAI Press.

Yang, R., Ford, B., Tambe, M., & Lemieux, A. (2014). Adaptive resource allocation for wildlife protection against illegal poachers. In *Proceedings of the 2014 International Conference on Autonomous Agents and Multi-Agent Systems* (pp. 453–460). International Foundation for Autonomous Agents and Multiagent Systems.

PART I

2

Law Enforcement for Wildlife Conservation

Andrew J. Plumptre

Introduction

Prior to the colonial period in Africa, wildlife was relatively plentiful and the human population relatively small, so that hunting of wildlife for bushmeat and trophies was mostly sustainable. Colonialization brought in roads, improved access to medical care, and improved agricultural methods, which led to rapid growth in the human population and the loss of large mammals in particular. It was at this point that the colonial administrations started to set aside land for the protection of large mammals, initially for sport hunting as a means of generating income, but then as parks and wildlife reserves as tourism started to develop and flights to the continent from Europe and the USA became affordable (Jachmann, 1998). Africa's first park, Virunga National Park in eastern Democratic Republic of Congo, was established in 1925 to protect the dwindling numbers of mountain gorillas and then was expanded to include the savannah and forest to the north to protect elephants, hippopotamuses, and the rich biodiversity of the region.

One of the key strategies used by any manager of protected areas is to implement law enforcement at a site. Whether it is a national park in the USA, policing visitors or quad bike users; a rare orchid site in the UK that has to be protected from collectors; or a large savannah park in Africa which needs to protect its wildlife from poaching, each site has to employ some form of protection strategy. In Africa in particular, law enforcement activities form a major component of a protected area authority's budget because of the employment of many rangers to enforce the law. This strategy is also used in Asia and Latin America, but can only really be effective where wages are relatively low and many staff can be employed as a result. Law enforcement has been used as a tool to manage protected areas for nearly a century, but until recently assessments over whether the strategies used are effective or how they

17

might be improved have been rare. This chapter reviews how law enforcement is undertaken in an African context and summarizes some of the ways in which AI is starting to be used to help make patrolling more efficient and effective.

Law Enforcement Practice in Africa: An Example from Uganda

Law enforcement in Africa is primarily carried out with a ranger force that patrols a protected area, from patrol posts, on a daily basis. Most protected areas will have several patrol posts and will require 3–4 rangers to be based at those posts at a minimum, because one person will have to protect the post while the other three make *daily patrols*. In places where rangers are targeted by poachers and can be potentially killed, the ranger force has to be larger (10–20 rangers) at each post and several members are left to protect the patrol post.

Overnight/camping patrols are also made from patrol posts with the aim of traveling further and covering more ground. These patrols require camping equipment and rations for the rangers and therefore cost more than the daily patrols. Where intelligence information is obtained that poachers may enter a protected area, then rangers may also organize an *ambush patrol* in which they lie in wait in the general area where the poachers plan to operate. In savannah parks there can be a *mobile ranger unit* that is taken out from the park head-quarters or a satellite base in vehicles and then dropped off to make foot patrols in more remote areas. In some parks there is also the use of technical equipment such as drones, and there will be a dedicated ranger team that operates this equipment.

The costs of patrolling vary depending on the types of patrolling that occur and the size of the ranger force. In the 1980s a figure of about \$200/km^2 was proposed as an estimate of an appropriate investment in savannah parks (Cumming et al., 1984; Leader-Williams, 1993; Leader-Williams and Albon, 1988) which would be equivalent to about \$450/km^2 today using an online inflation cost calculator (https://inflationdata.com/Inflation/ Inflation_Calculators/Inflation_Rate_Calculator.asp). Data from Uganda show the 2008/2009 costs of personnel as a proportion of the overall budget for the different parks and wildlife reserves in the country (Table 2.1), are on average 66 percent of the costs of managing a site. The figures given in Table 2.1 only give the costs of personnel and benefits and do not include other costs of law enforcement such as vehicle costs, uniforms, boots, or camping equipment.

Table 2.1. *Costs of management of parks and wildlife reserves in Uganda 2008–2009.*

Site	Protected area	Area (km^2)	Operating costs (US$)	Personnel costs (US$)	Percentage ranger costs	Costs/area (US$/km^2)
Murchison Falls	Park	5,025	1,165,609	752,046	64.52	231.96
Queen Elizabeth	Park	2,475	799,320	485,402	60.73	322.96
Mt. Elgon	Park	1,110	826,810	449,920	54.42	744.87
Kidepo	Park	1,430	516,059	335,334	64.98	360.88
Bwindi	Park	327	535,567	352,565	65.83	1,637.82
Mgahinga	Park	38	139,505	91,779	65.79	3,671.20
Lake Mburo	Park	370	482,646	252,716	52.36	1,304.45
Kibale Forest	Park	766	679,541	304,395	44.79	887.13
Rwenzori	Park	995	281,779	160,799	57.07	283.20
Semuliki	Park	220	97,596	66,862	68.51	443.62
Semliki	Wildlife reserve	542	118,824	83,382	70.17	219.23
Katonga	Wildlife reserve	210	72,684	43,468	59.80	346.12
Pian-Upe	Wildlife reserve	2,304	82,253	75,436	91.71	35.70
Ajai	Wildlife reserve	148	37,225	28,429	76.37	251.52
Kabwoya	Wildlife reserve	87	48,268	32,439	67.21	554.80
Matheniko	Wildlife reserve	1,757	68,593	63,438	92.49	39.04
Average			372,018	223,651	66.05	708.00

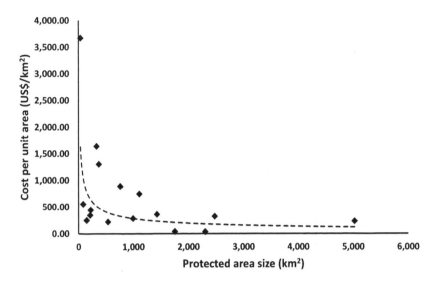

Figure 2.1 Relationship between annual operating costs and size of a site in Uganda.

Total law enforcement costs will therefore form a larger percentage of the budget overall.

The sites receiving most funding per unit area are the two with mountain gorillas (Bwindi Impenetrable, and Mgahinga Gorilla National Parks) and Lake Mburo National Park, which has many problems with cattle encroachment. In general, costs per unit area decrease with the size of the site (Figure 2.1) because most illegal activities tend to occur near the edge of protected areas and the larger the size of a site the smaller the perimeter/area ratio. There is therefore relatively less perimeter to patrol with large sites, particularly if they tend to be closer to a circular shape rather than a long rectangular shape.

These results show that Uganda is achieving the proposed investment of $450/km^2 for savannah protected areas across many of their sites, particularly the smaller sites, but that the larger sites are at a lower level of investment (although the investment in law enforcement will be higher if vehicle costs and equipment are included). Currently, animal populations are growing within the larger sites such as Murchison Falls and Queen Elizabeth National Parks, so the lower levels of investment are reducing poaching to sustainable levels and possibly such large sites do not need as much investment per unit area as has been proposed in the past. An assessment of the law enforcement costs per unit area required to stop elephant poaching in the Luangwa Valley in Zambia, an area of 14,000 km^2, was as low as $82/km^2 in the mid-1990s

(Jachmann, 1998), which would be about $130/km^2$ today. Uganda therefore appears to be able to invest in law enforcement adequately for most of the protected areas it manages. However, are the funds being spent wisely and could law enforcement be improved?

The Practice of Ranger Patrolling

Ranger patrols act to provide a deterrence to poachers who want to enter a protected area and obtain bushmeat, animal trophies (e.g., ivory), timber, charcoal, or medicinal plants and other non-timber forest products. In some sites, poachers also take fish from rivers or lakes illegally. Rangers also deter the loss of land/habitat to illegal grazing of domestic animals or to cultivation and general encroachment for settlement. It is evident that where there is investment in law enforcement in ranger patrols, there is an impact on the wildlife and integrity of sites (Tranquilli et al., 2012) compared with "paper parks" where there is little investment in law enforcement. However, over much of the history of ranger patrolling in Africa there has been little consistent monitoring of where patrols go and what they find. As a result, it was very hard to assess how effective the ranger patrols were and whether they could be improved.

In the 1990s some South African sites started to develop methods to record data on where rangers were moving and what they were finding in terms of illegal activities. These were paper reporting methods which were compiled and synthesized at a park headquarters on a monthly basis to produce patrol reports. Around the same time, Louis Liebenberg started to develop *Cybertracker*, an app that could be loaded on a portable device and used to capture georeferenced data on sightings of animals or illegal activities (www.cybertracker.org). Although initially aimed at helping capture data from the bushmen in the Kalahari, a system that would allow illiterate hunters to record data, it has expanded greatly over the years to become an app that can be customized and used to collect any georeferenced data. However, it was not until the late 1990s that the Uganda Wildlife Authority (UWA), together with GTZ, developed a software package to capture and manage georeferenced ranger patrol data with the ability to map observations of sightings of illegal activities or key species, as well as where the patrols had visited. This Management Information System (MIST) was developed specifically to manage ranger-collected data and was designed so that rangers could enter the data and make basic analyses. Rangers would take GPS locations of every sighting of illegal activities as well as certain key species (the rarely observed ones such as large carnivores or elephants). If nothing was observed within a 30-minute period, then rangers would take a patrol positon point so that an assessment of their route taken could be made.

The Wildlife Conservation Society (WCS) helped UWA roll out MIST across the protected area network in Uganda and then took it to other countries in Africa and the rest of the world, where it was successfully used to map patrol coverage in particular, which could be used to target ranger patrols. As a result, patrol coverage by rangers greatly improved in most places where MIST was implemented, and the mapping of where illegal activities were most common was used to orient patrols at monthly patrol planning meetings (Plumptre et al., 2014a). MIST was adopted by the CITES Monitoring of the Illegal Killing of Elephants (MIKE) program and taken to all the MIKE sites in Africa and Asia. By the end of the 2000s it became clear that it would be useful to be able to make more complex analyses of the ranger-collected data, in particular include the ability to assess the abundance of illegal activities per unit effort (patrol day or per kilometer of patrol walked) on a grid basis across a protected area. It is important to correct for patrol effort by rangers, as they tend to patrol more frequently around patrol posts and in areas where past experience has led them to suspect poachers to operate. The patrol coverage is therefore biased to where rangers expect to find illegal activities. MIST was able to make an assessment of the abundance per unit effort across the whole protected area, but not to map concentrations of relative abundance of threats. A consortium of non-governmental organizations (NGOs) came together to form a partnership to develop a new database for managing ranger-collected data, the Spatial Monitoring and Reporting Tool (SMART).

The SMART partnership (http://smartconservationtools.org) includes eight core partners with 18 associate institutions who have rolled out SMART across tropical Africa, Southeast Asia, and Central and South America. It is now the most widespread tool used to manage ranger patrol data and provides a greater variety of options for analysis of the data. Those sites that had adopted MIST have for the most part now migrated their data into SMART because of its added benefits. SMART is open source in theory and plugin options are being developed to better analyze or manage different types of data, such as intelligence data and biological survey data, as well as the ability to collect data on a handheld smartphone in Cybertracker and then download it to SMART automatically. This last plugin allows much faster collection and processing of the data; previously it could take 1–2 months to enter the ranger patrol data from datasheets they completed when on patrol. SMART can also be managed in the Cloud (SMART Connect) so that patrols can be uploaded over a telephone or radio network to the main database and rangers can even be tracked in real time while on patrol.

Uganda has migrated all of its MIST data into SMART for its ten national parks and 14 wildlife reserves. This provides one of the longest datasets of ranger patrolling of a protected area network in the world, and as such is useful to analyze for exploring ways to make ranger patrolling more effective.

Making Ranger Patrols More Effective

Analyzing ranger patrol data is complex because of the biased way rangers patrol. Rangers target sites where they believe illegal activities are occurring and where they think they may detect poachers operating. They do not patrol in a random manner allowing the use of normal statistical analyses. In addition, rangers can patrol a site and may detect an illegal activity if it is present, or they may not detect it. Therefore, the probability that a specific activity is detected is less than 1.0 (certainty) for almost all sightings. Consequently, if something is not recorded at a site it may be because it was not there or because it was there but was not detected.

Using data from the Queen Elizabeth National Park and subsequently other sites, researchers at York University developed a method, using Bayesian analyses, to map hotspots in illegal activities across a protected area (Critchlow et al., 2015). This method takes the mapping of encounter rate per unit of patrol effort that SMART can calculate to estimate a probability of occurrence of an illegal activity within a grid cell. It also makes extrapolations to the whole park (even areas where rangers have not patrolled) using covariables that are good predictors of illegal activities where patrolling does take place. This method also incorporates an estimate of the probability of detection of an illegal activity, assuming that it increases as effort increases.

An example of two types of illegal activity distributions from Queen Elizabeth National Park shows that the sites where snares are set for bushmeat are very different to sites where large mammals (elephant, hippos, and buffalos) are killed for meat or ivory (Figure 2.2). It is important to recognize that different threats occur in different places in protected areas and this consequently has an impact on planning of ranger patrols, because not all threats are of equal importance. One way to rank the relative importance of threats is to make a pairwise comparison through an analytical hierarchy process (Saaty, 1990), which ensures that the comparisons are consistent across all pairs. We asked wardens and rangers in Queen Elizabeth and Murchison Falls National Parks in Uganda to make pairwise comparisons of six main threats to their sites (Table 2.2): snaring, commercial hunting of large mammals, fishing, timber harvesting and charcoal production, illegal grazing

Table 2.2. *Results of pairwise comparisons of threats in two savannah parks in Uganda. Values are the desired percentage allocation of ranger time to tackle each threat*

Threat	Queen Elizabeth	Murchison Falls
Snaring	14.9	18.2
Commercial hunting	47.7	59.8
Fishing	3.7	5.9
Timber and charcoal production	8.2	5.1
Grazing	21.7	11.1
Non-timber forest product collection	3.7	5.9

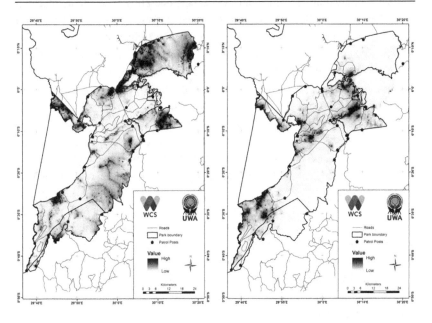

Figure 2.2 Hotspots of snaring (left) and sites where large mammals are killed (right) in Queen Elizabeth National Park, Uganda.

of livestock, and collection of non-timber forest products. The results estimated the relative importance of each threat and the percentage allocation of time by ranger patrols to tackle each threat. In both parks, commercial hunting of large mammals was ranked as the most serious threat because of elephant poaching for ivory, followed by illegal grazing and then snaring.

Any method to allocate ranger patrol effort needs to undertake these types of analyses to effectively weight how much effort is directed to each type of threat when planning where to send patrols. Note, however, that this weighting is a measure of how wardens and rangers perceive the threat's importance and not how effective ranger patrols would be at tackling the threat. This must be thought about also when allocating weights to the different threats. It is not surprising that poaching is weighted highly by the rangers and wardens; an assessment of wildlife crime in Uganda found that bushmeat hunting was the most common threat in the protected areas (Harrison et al., 2015).

A test has been made of the Bayesian probability maps for predicting snaring where rangers did not patrol frequently. This showed that these maps could be useful for predicting snaring hotspots (Critchlow et al., 2016). By actively sending ranger patrols to areas predicted to have high probabilities of snares, the test managed to double the detection of snares by the rangers over a three-month period.

Another study comparing the length of overnight patrolling in Kafue National Park in Zambia also showed that rangers were more effective by undertaking 2–8-day overnight patrols but that they became less effective with longer patrols (Nyirenda and Chomba, 2012). The number of encounters with poachers tended to increase up to about seven days of patrol, but then declined either through a deterrence effect or because rangers became tired and less motivated. Given that overnight patrols cost more than regular daily surveillance patrols, it is important to know that they become less effective when prolonged.

Occupancy methods have also been used to assess where patrolling is having an impact on snaring in the Nyungwe National Park in Rwanda based on data from MIST (Moore et al., 2018). This analysis showed that snares were greatly reduced where rangers patrolled frequently and suggested therefore that ranger presence was having a deterrence effect. The paper proposed establishing some new ranger posts in areas where illegal activities were high. However, there is an issue with interpreting the results as a deterrence effect in that the rangers remove snares as they are detected, which will reduce the probability of occupancy of snares. The probability of detection of snares in this densely forested habitat was 6–13 percent, showing how few snares are detected on any one visit compared to what may be there, although detection probability increased over time, suggesting the rangers became more effective at detecting snares.

Another approach to better target patrolling that has been used is to model the cost and benefits for poaching to better understand where poachers may undertake poaching. This has been applied to the Serengeti (Hofer et al., 2000) and showed that the model best predicted poaching in the north and west of the park, where travel costs were lower and ranger patrols less frequent. The model results mapped well with where animals were snared.

AI and Improving the Effectiveness of Ranger Patrols

Conservation planning approaches have used AI through *simulated annealing* algorithms to try to identify optimal conservation of a number of species across sites (Possingham et al., 2000). Plumptre et al. (2014b) applied this type of approach to the allocation of law enforcement resources to conserve target species and habitats within the Greater Virunga Landscape (GVL), a network of 13 interconnected protected areas that includes the Queen Elizabeth National Park. This approach identified the important areas for species and habitats within the landscape and where the threats to these species occurred (based on MIST data), and then looked at where patrolling costs could be minimized while maximizing protection of the conservation targets. It showed that the costs of patrolling could be reduced to about 15–20 percent of the current costs by targeting areas where the species of conservation concern or threatened habitats occur in the landscape. However, the method made several assumptions about the frequency of visitation by rangers to have a deterrence effect which have yet to be tested.

Other, more advanced, AI approaches are described in more detail in subsequent chapters and therefore are not detailed here. Various algorithms have been applied to best predict where poachers will operate based on prior data from MIST/SMART in Uganda. Specific field tests across Queen Elizabeth National Park have been made to assess how well the best models predict snaring, the most comprehensive tests of any of the methods to date (Gholami et al., 2017). Given their success, these are being started in Murchison Falls National Park to assess how well the models can be used at other sites.

AI approaches have the benefit of taking these analyses further and producing applications that can be used to plan for future patrolling and ultimately to direct rangers to specific areas within a protected area on a daily basis, using past data they have collected. The approaches used to date have been relatively static in that they assume that poachers will behave on average as they have behaved in the recent past. In order to generate predictions from the AI, Bayesian, or occupancy approaches, there is a need for a fair amount of data to make accurate predictions and the assumptions are that poachers do not change much where they operate during this time period. Critchlow et al. (2015) showed that in Queen Elizabeth National Park this assumption held in that where poaching occurred in one year was a good predictor of where it occurred in subsequent years. This might indicate that ranger patrols are not acting as a very effective deterrence if poachers are not changing their behaviors, but it might also be due to the costs of poaching and being caught precluding changing behavior to operate at another site. AI approaches have the potential to look at more dynamic modeling, where predictions about how poachers may respond to the re-deployment of rangers can be made and incorporated in planned patrolling to adjust the patrol routes to account for these predicted changes in poachers' behaviors.

Conclusions

Recent work interviewing local people around both Queen Elizabeth and Murchison Falls National Parks has shown that a large percentage of the population admits to hunting in the park. Between 40 and 50 percent of households around these parks were involved in hunting in 2014. Most people are doing this for emergency cash for school fees or medical bills, but there are some "professional" hunters who tend to be relatively wealthy in their communities (Travers et al., 2017). The impacts of this hunting on ungulates in these parks is therefore likely to be considerable and may explain the fluctuations in numbers of animals such as Uganda kob (*Kobus kob thomasi*) in these two parks, seen in aerial surveys. It is unlikely that more resources can be put into funding patrolling in Uganda, given the already large proportion of the budget (Table 2.1), and therefore finding ways to make ranger patrolling more effective for the same cost is critically important.

Ultimately what needs to be assessed is the deterrence effect and how best to maximize this. Deterrence will be affected by the probability of getting caught, the cost in terms of prison sentences or fines if caught, as well as the probability of benefiting by undertaking poaching. Understanding this is critical to identifying methods to tackle poaching, but to date we still do not understand what makes effective deterrence anywhere in Africa. It is hoped that using these AI models to manipulate ranger behavior and collecting the data to assess how poaching changes will enable us to get a better handle on what makes effective deterrence at a site.

References

Critchlow, R., Plumptre, A.J., Driciru, M., et al. (2015) Spatiotemporal trends of illegal activities from ranger-collected data in a Ugandan national park. *Conservation Biology*, 29, 1458–1470.

Critchlow, R., Plumptre, A.J., Andira, B., et al. (2016). Improving law enforcement effectiveness and efficiency in protected areas using ranger-collected monitoring data. *Conservation Letters* 10, 572–580.

Cumming, D.H.M., Martin, R.B., and Taylor, R.D. (1984) *The status and conservation of Africa's elephants and rhinos*. IUCN, Gland.

Gholami, S., Ford, B., Fang, F., et al. (2017). Taking it for a test drive: a hybrid spatio-temporal model for wildlife poaching prediction evaluated through a controlled field test. In *Proc. of the European Conference on Machine Learning & Principles and Practice of Knowledge Discovery in Databases*.

Harrison, M., Roe, D., Baker, J., et al. (2015) *Wildlife crime: a review of the evidence on drivers and impacts in Uganda*. IIED, London.

Hofer, H., Campbell, K.L.I., East, M.L., and Huish, S.A. (2000). Modeling the spatial distribution of the economic costs and benefits of illegal game meat hunting in the Serengeti. *Natural Resource Modeling*, 13, 151–177.

Jachmann, H. (1998) *Monitoring illegal wildlife use and law enforcement in African savanna rangelands*. Wildlife Monitoring Unit, Lusaka.

Leader-Williams, N. (1993) The cost of conserving elephant. *Pachyderm*, 17, 30–34.

Leader-Williams, N. & Albon, S.D. (1988) Allocation of resources for conservation. *Nature*, 336, 533–535.

Moore, J.F., Mulindahabi, F., Masozera, M.K., et al. (2018) Are ranger patrols effective in reducing poaching-related threats within protected areas? *Journal of Applied Ecology*, 55, 99–107.

Nyirenda, V.R., and Chomba, C. (2012) Field foot patrol effectiveness in Kafue National Park, Zambia. *Journal of Ecology and the Natural Environment*, 4, 163–172.

Plumptre, A.J., Kujirakwinja, D., Rwetsiba, A., et al. (2014a) *Law enforcement monitoring: lessons learned over fifteen years in the Albertine Rift Region of Africa*. WCS, Sydney.

Plumptre, A.J., Fuller, R.A., Rwetsiba, A., et al. (2014b) Efficiently targeting resources to deter illegal activities in protected areas. *Journal of Applied Ecology*, 51, 714–725.

Possingham, H.P., Ball, I.R., and Andelman, S. (2000) Mathematical methods for identifying representative reserve networks. *Quantitative methods for conservation biology* (Eds. S. Ferson and M. Burgman), pp. 291–305. Springer-Verlag, New York.

Saaty, T.L. (1990) How to make a decision: the analytic hierarchy process, *European Journal of Operational Research*, 48, 9–26.

Tranquilli, S., Abedi-Lartey, M., Amsini, F., et al. (2012) Lack of conservation effort rapidly increases African great ape extinction risk. *Conservation Letters*, 5, 48–55.

Travers, H., Mwedde, G., Archer, L., et al. (2017). *Taking action against wildlife crime in Uganda*. IIED, London.

3

Wildlife Poaching Forecasting Based on Ranger-Collected Data and Evaluation through Field Tests

Shahrzad Gholami, Benjamin Ford, Debarun Kar, Fei Fang,
Andrew J. Plumptre, Milind Tambe, Margaret Driciru, Fred Wanyama,
Aggrey Rwetsiba, Mustapha Nsubuga, and Joshua Mabonga

Worldwide, conservation agencies employ rangers to protect conservation areas from poachers. However, agencies lack the manpower to have rangers effectively patrol these vast areas frequently. While past work has modeled poachers' behavior so as to aid rangers in planning future patrols, those models' predictions were not validated by extensive field tests. In this chapter, we present a hybrid spatiotemporal model that predicts poaching threat levels and results from a five-month field test of our model in Uganda's Queen Elizabeth Protected Area (QEPA). To our knowledge, this is the first time that a predictive model has been evaluated through such an extensive field test in this domain. We present two major contributions. First, our hybrid model consists of two components: (1) an ensemble model that can work with the limited data common to this domain and (2) a spatiotemporal model to boost the ensemble's predictions when sufficient data are available. When evaluated on real-world historical data from QEPA, our hybrid model achieves significantly better performance than previous approaches with either temporally aware dynamic Bayesian networks or an ensemble of spatially aware models. Second, in collaboration with the Wildlife Conservation Society and Uganda Wildlife Authority, we present results from a five-month controlled experiment in which *rangers patrolled over 450* km^2 *across QEPA*. We demonstrate that our model successfully predicted (1) where snaring activity would occur and (2) where it would not occur. In areas where we predicted a high rate of snaring activity, rangers found more snares and snared animals than in areas of lower predicted activity. These findings demonstrate that (1) our model's predictions are selective; (2) our model's superior laboratory performance extends to the real world; and (3) these predictive models can aid rangers in focusing their efforts to prevent wildlife poaching and save animals.

Introduction

Wildlife poaching continues to be a global problem as key species are hunted toward extinction. For example, the latest African census showed a 30 percent decline in elephant populations between 2007 and 2014 (Convention on International Trade in Endangered Species of Wild Fauna and Flora 2016; Great Elephant Census 2016). Wildlife conservation areas have been established to protect these species from poachers, and these areas are protected by park rangers. These areas are vast, and rangers do not have sufficient resources to patrol everywhere with high intensity and frequency.

At many sites now, rangers patrol the protected areas and collect data related to snares they confiscate, poachers they arrest, and other observations. Given rangers' resource constraints, patrol managers could benefit from tools that analyze these data and provide future poaching predictions. However, this domain presents unique challenges. First, this domain's real-world data are few, extremely noisy, and incomplete. To illustrate, one of the rangers' primary patrol goals is to find wire snares, which are deployed by poachers to catch animals. However, these snares are usually well-hidden (e.g., in dense grass), and thus rangers may not find them and so (incorrectly) label an area as not having any snares. Second, poaching activity changes over time, and predictive models must account for this temporal component. Third, because poaching happens in the real world, there are mutual spatial and neighborhood effects that influence poaching activity. Finally, while field tests are crucial in determining a model's efficacy in the world, the difficulties involved in organizing and executing field tests often preclude them.

Previous work in this domain has modeled poaching behavior with data from simulated games and human subject experiments (Gholami et al. 2016) or real-world historical data. Based on a dataset from the QEPA, Nguyen et al. (2016) introduced a two-layered temporal graphical model (named CAPTURE) and Kar et al. (2017) constructed an ensemble of decision trees (named INTERCEPT) that accounted for spatial relationships. However, these works did not (1) account for both spatial and temporal components or (2) validate their models via extensive field testing. In this chapter, we will discuss the INTERCEPT model and the field tests in detail.

In this chapter, (1) we introduce a new hybrid model that enhances an ensemble's broad predictive power with a spatiotemporal model's adaptive capabilities. Because spatiotemporal models require a lot of data, this model works in two stages. First, predictions are made with an ensemble of decision trees. Second, in areas where there are sufficient data, the ensemble's prediction is boosted via a spatiotemporal model. (2) In collaboration with the

Wildlife Conservation Society and the Uganda Wildlife Authority, we designed and deployed a large, controlled experiment to QEPA. Across 27 areas we designated across QEPA, rangers patrolled approximately 452 km^2 over the course of five months; to our knowledge, this is the largest controlled experiment and field test of machine learning-based predictive models in this domain. In this experiment, we tested our model's selectiveness: is our model able to differentiate between areas of high and low poaching activity?

In experimental results, we demonstrate our model's superior performance over the state-of-the-art mdoels of Kar et al. (2017) and thus the importance of spatiotemporal modeling. During our field test, rangers found over three times more snaring activity in areas where we predicted higher poaching activity. When accounting for differences in patrol effort, there was a 12-fold increase in the level of detection by rangers per kilometer walked in those areas. These results demonstrate that (1) our model is selective in its predictions and (2) our model's superior predictive performance in the laboratory extends to the real world (Gholami et al. 2017).

Background and Related Work

Spatiotemporal models have been used for prediction tasks in image and video processing. Markov random fields (MRF) were used by Solberg et al. (1996) and Yin and Collins (2007) to capture spatiotemporal dependencies in remotely sensed data and moving object detection, respectively.

Critchlow et al. (2015) analyzed spatiotemporal patterns in illegal activity in Uganda's QEPA using Bayesian hierarchical models. With real-world data, they demonstrated the importance of considering the spatial and temporal changes that occur in illegal activities. However, in this work and other similar works with spatiotemporal models (Rashidi et al. 2015, 2016), no standard metrics were provided to evaluate the models' predictive performance (e.g., precision, recall). As such, it is impossible to compare our predictive model's performance to these models. While Critchlow et al. (2016) was a field test of Critchlow et al.'s (2015) work, Rashidi et al. (2015, 2016) did not conduct field tests to validate their predictions in the real world.

In the machine learning literature, Nguyen et al. (2016) introduced a two-layered temporal Bayesian network predictive model (CAPTURE) that was also evaluated on real-world data from QEPA. CAPTURE, however, assumes one global set of parameters for all of QEPA, which ignores local differences in poachers' behavior. Additionally, the first layer, which predicts poaching attacks, relies on the current year's patrolling effort, which makes it impossible to predict future attacks (since patrols haven't happened yet). While CAPTURE includes temporal elements in its model, it does not include spatial components and thus cannot capture neighborhood-specific phenomena.

It is vital to validate predictive models in the real world. Critchlow et al. (2016) conducted field tests in QEPA by selecting three areas for rangers to patrol. Their goal was to maximize the number of observations sighted per kilometer walked by the rangers. Their test successfully demonstrated a significant increase in illegal activity detection at two of the areas, but they did not provide comparable evaluation metrics for their predictive model. Also, our field test was much larger in scale, involving 27 patrol posts compared to their nine posts.

Wildlife Crime Dataset: Features and Challenges

This study's wildlife crime dataset is from Uganda's QEPA, an area containing a wildlife conservation park and two wildlife reserves, which spans about 2,520 km^2. There are 37 patrol posts situated across QEPA, from which Uganda Wildlife Authority rangers conduct patrols to apprehend poachers, remove any snares or traps, monitor wildlife, and record signs of illegal activity. Along with the amount of patrolling effort in each area, the dataset contains 14 years (2003–2016) of the information on type, location, and date of wildlife crime activities.

Rangers lack the manpower to patrol everywhere all the time, and thus illegal activity may be undetected in unpatrolled areas. Patrolling is an imperfect process, and there is considerable uncertainty in the dataset's negative data points (i.e., areas being labeled as having no illegal activity); rangers may patrol an area and label it as having no snares when, in fact, a snare was well-hidden and undetected. These factors contribute to the dataset's already large class imbalance; there are many more negative data points than positive points (crime detected). It is thus necessary to consider models that estimate hidden variables (e.g., whether an area has been attacked) and also to evaluate predictive models with metrics that account for this uncertainty, such as those in the positive and unlabeled learning (PU learning) literature (Lee and Liu 2003). We divide QEPA into 1 km^2 grid cells (a total of 2,522 cells; Figure 3.1), and we refer to these cells as targets (Figure 3.1). Each target is associated with several static geospatial features such as terrain (e.g., slope), distance values (e.g., distance to border), and animal density. Each target is also associated with dynamic features such as how often an area has been patrolled (i.e., coverage) and observed illegal activities (e.g., snares).

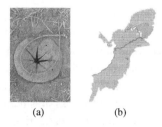

(a)   (b)

Figure 3.1 (a) A snare; (b) the QEPA grid. Photo credit: UWA ranger.

INTERCEPT Model

The attempts to use the best previous model, CAPTURE, and the more complex variants of CAPTURE (proposed to address the limitations of the original CAPTURE) all resulted in poor attackability prediction performance, as shown in the next section. The natural progression then would have been to pursue more complex models in this behavioral game theory family of models with the expectation that they would improve performance on our real-world data. However, as reported by Nguyen et al. (2016), complex models such as CAPTURE and its variants incur heavy computational costs; it takes approximately six hours for these models to complete execution. In addition, these models become more difficult to interpret when the dimensionality of the feature space increases (e.g., more numerical values to simultaneously account for in a single interpretation). We wanted to use models that would address all of these shortcomings by not only significantly reducing computational costs so as to be usable by rangers with limited computing power in Uganda, but also remain interpretable to domain experts as the feature space dimensionality increases. All of these factors led us away from using more complex behavioral models. Therefore, we break from the current trend in behavior modeling in security games and instead model adversary behavior in terms of decision tree-based behavior models, even though we were initially skeptical about the predictive capabilities of this approach. Surprisingly, this simpler approach led to significant improvements in performance over the prior state-of-the-art (i.e., CAPTURE).

BoostIT

A binary decision tree D is trained on a set Θ of independent variables x (the domain features), a dependent variable o (attack observations), and outputs a binary classification D_i for each target i: {not attacked ($D_i = 0$), attacked

$(D_i = 1)$}. A decision tree's negative predictions for a test set Ψ are denoted by $P_\Psi^-(D)$ and positive predictions by $P_\Psi^+(D)$ (i.e., vectors of binary predictions).

Crime hotspots are part of a well-known theory in criminology (Eck et al. 2005) that views crime as an uneven distribution; i.e., crime is likely to be concentrated in particular areas called hotspots. If a particular geographic area has a high concentration of predicted attacks, it is reasonable to interpret these predictions as a hotspot prediction (i.e., predicting a high concentration of crime). While CAPTURE explicitly models attacks as a probability distribution decided by a linear combination of feature values and thus can implicitly represent the hotspots with soft boundaries in geographic space, decision tree rules with hard boundaries in the feature space would lead to fine-grained segmentations in the geographic space and are thus less capable of representing hotspots. As such, we designed the **Boost**ed decision tree with an **I**terative learning algorithm (henceforth referred to as BoostIT) (Algorithm 3.1), where proximity to a predicted hotspot is encoded as an additional input feature.

Algorithm 3.1 BoostIT

$D^0 \leftarrow$ LEARNDECISIONTREE(Θ^0)

repeat

$\quad h^\Theta \leftarrow$ CALCHOTSPOTPROXIMITY$(P_{\Theta^{m-1}}(D^{m-1}), \alpha)$

$\quad h^\Psi \leftarrow$ CALCHOTSPOTPROXIMITY$(P_{\Psi^{m-1}}(D^{m-1}), \alpha)$

$\quad \Theta^m \leftarrow$ ADDFEATURE(Θ^0, h_Θ)

$\quad \Psi^m \leftarrow$ ADDFEATURE(Ψ^0, h_Ψ)

$\quad D^m \leftarrow$ LEARNDECISIONTREE(Θ^m)

$\quad m = m + 1$

until iterationStoppingLevelReached

return P

D^0 is the initial decision tree learned without the hotspot proximity feature h, and Θ^0 and Ψ^0 correspond to the initial training and test sets, respectively. For each level of iteration m, a feature h^Θ (and h^Ψ) is computed for each target $i \in I$ that corresponds to whether that target is close to a predicted hotspot in the training (and test) sets; for example, if a target $i \in P_{\Theta^{m-1}}(D^{m-1})$ is adjacent to α or more targets in $P_{\Theta^{m-1}}^+(D^{m-1})$ (i.e., targets that are predicted to be positive), then $h_i^\Theta = 1$. We then re-learn the decision tree at each iteration m with a feature-augmented dataset Θ^m. As an example, BoostIT may add a feature to a target i that i is near a hotspot if there are two adjacent targets that are predicted to be attackable. In the next iteration, this new feature ("near a hotspot") will get used in learning about predicting attacks on i. This continues until an iteration criterion is reached. Note that the test set Ψ is not used while learning new decision trees (only training data Θ are used) and is only used to update the test set prediction P_Ψ. In the rest of the chapter, we will refer to BoostIT with an α as BoostIT-αNearestNeighbors (or BoostIT-αNN). With this algorithm, the final decision tree D^m would generally predict more positive predictions with concentrated areas (i.e., hotspots) compared to D^0, but the set of predictions of D^m is not necessarily a superset of the set of predictions of D^0.

Although we are primarily interested in predicting attackability, we can also predict where patrollers would observe attacks by cascading attackability predictions with the LB observation layer. We convert the unconditional observation probability, derived from the cascaded model to binary predictions by classifying samples as observed/not observed based on whether they are above or below the mean respectively.

INTERCEPT: Ensemble of Experts

We investigated the predictions of the traditional decision tree and BoostIT and observed that they are diverse in terms of their predictions. Here, by diversity, we mean that prediction of attacks over targets varies across models. Therefore, while one model may fail to correctly classify a particular target as attacked, another model may succeed. This indicates the ability of different models to correctly learn and predict on different regions of the feature space. For example, let us consider the following three models: (1) DecisionTree, (2) BoostIT-3NN, and (3) BoostIT-2NN. While computing pairwise disagreement between the models' attackability predictions, we observed that: (1) DecisionTree and BoostIT-3NN disagree on 105 out of 2,211 target samples; (2) DecisionTree and BoostIT-2NN disagree on 97 out of 2,211 samples; and (3) BoostIT-3NN and BoostIT-2NN disagree on 118 out of 2,211 samples. This observation led us to consider combining the best decision tree- and BoostIT-based models, thus forming INTERCEPT, an ensemble of experts.

Because of uncertainty in negative labels, INTERCEPT considers not only decision tree models with the standard false positive (FP) cost of 1, but also decision trees with various FP costs. For a decision tree with FP cost of 0.6, during the learning process the decision tree will not receive the full penalty of 1 but will instead receive a penalty of 0.6 for each FP prediction it makes.

In INTERCEPT, each expert model voted for the final attack prediction on a particular target. We considered three types of voting rules to determine whether a target should be predicted to be attacked by the ensemble: (1) majority of the experts predict an attack; (2) all experts predict an attack; and (3) any one expert predicts an attack. INTERCEPT uses the best voting rule: majority.

We considered ensembles with three and five experts. Having at most five experts makes the ensemble easily interpretable. In other words, the final prediction at a target is due to only five decision rules at a maximum, and it is easy to walk the human domain experts through the five rules in a way that the logic is easily verified.

Evaluation of INTERCEPT

Evaluation Metrics

To evaluate all the models, we first prepared two separate train/test splits on the dataset. For one dataset we trained on data from 2003–2013 and evaluated our models on data from 2014, and for the other dataset we trained on data from 2003–2014 and evaluated on data from 2015. Prior to discussing the evaluation results, we briefly discuss the metrics we used for computing our performance on predicting attackability and observed attacks.

Any metric to evaluate targets' *attackability* in domains such as wildlife poaching must account for the uncertainty in negative class labels. Therefore, in addition to standard metrics (precision, recall, and F1-score) that are used to evaluate models on datasets where there is no uncertainty in the underlying ground truth, we also evaluate our models with a metric that accounts for the uncertainty present in our dataset. The metric introduced by Lee and Liu (2003), henceforth referred to as L&L, is an appropriate metric since it is specifically designed for models learned on PU datasets (i.e., datasets with uncertain negative labels). L&L is defined in equation 3.1, where r denotes the recall and $\Pr[f(Te) = 1]$ denotes the probability of a classifier f making a positive class label prediction. We compute $\Pr[f(Te) = 1]$ as the percentage of positive predictions made by our model on a given test set:

$$\text{L\&L}(D, Te) = \frac{r^2}{\Pr[f(Te) = 1]}. \tag{3.1}$$

As we are certain about the positive samples in our dataset, L&L rewards a classifier more for correctly predicting where attacks have occurred (i.e., positive labels). However, it also prevents models from predicting attacks everywhere, via its denominator, and ensures that the model is selective in its positive predictions.

We also evaluate the models in terms of *observation* predictions. Here, we report standard metrics (precision, recall, and F1-score). We also compute the area under the precision–recall curve (PR-AUC). PR-AUC is a more appropriate metric for evaluating models on datasets with severe class imbalance compared to the area under the ROC curve. When there are many more negative points than positive points, the model can make many FP predictions and the FP rate would still be low, and thus the ROC curve becomes less informative. In contrast, precision better captures how well the model is making correct positive predictions given a small number of positive examples. L&L is no longer used to evaluate the observation probability model as there is no uncertainty in terms of the observations, i.e., we either observed or did not observe an attack, and we are measuring the model's ability to predict whether we will observe attacks at already attacked targets.

To compare INTERCEPT with its competitors, we conducted a thorough investigation of the performance of 41 different models and 193 variants. This is one of the largest evaluation efforts on a real-world dataset in the wildlife crime domain, and we compared INTERCEPT against the previous best model, CAPTURE, its variants, and other machine learning approaches such as support vector machines (SVM), AdaBoosted decision trees, and logistic regression.[1] All the numbers highlighted in **bold** in the tables that follow indicate the results of the best performing models in that table. The best performing INTERCEPT system is an ensemble of five decision trees with majority voting. The five decision trees are: a standard decision tree, two BoostIT decision trees ($m = 1$) with $\alpha = 2$ and $\alpha = 3$ respectively, and two decision trees with modified FP costs of 0.6 and 0.9 respectively. Note that, due to data collection methodology changes in 2015, the distribution of attack data in 2015 is significantly different to all previous years; 2015 is a difficult dataset to test on when the training dataset of 2003–2014 represents a different distribution of attack data, and we will demonstrate this impact in the following evaluation.

Attackability Prediction Results

In Tables 3.1 and 3.2, we show a comparison of the performance between our best INTERCEPT system (the five-decision tree ensemble with majority voting), the current state-of-the-art CAPTURE, its variants, and other baseline models toward accurately predicting the attackability of targets in QENP for 2014 and 2015, respectively. The PositiveBaseline corresponds to a model that predicts every target to be attacked ($p(a_{t,i}) = 1; \forall i, t$), and the UniformRandom corresponds to the baseline where each target is predicted to be attacked or not attacked with equal probability. Note that, in this subsection, when evaluating

---

[1] Note that due to data confidentiality agreements, we are unable to show an example decision tree in this chapter.

Table 3.1. *Attackability prediction results on 2014 test data*

Classifier Type	F1	L&L	Precision	Recall
PositiveBaseline	0.06	1	0.03	1
UniformRandom	0.05	0.51	0.03	0.50
CAPTURE	0.31	3.52	0.25	0.39
CAPTURE-PCov	0.13	1.29	0.08	0.48
CAPTURE-PCov-LB	0.08	0.87	0.04	0.58
CAPTURE-DKHO	0.10	1.05	0.06	0.67
INTERCEPT	**0.41**	**5.83**	0.37	0.45

Table 3.2. *Attackability prediction results on 2015 test data*

Classifier Type	F1	L&L	Precision	Recall
PositiveBaseline	0.14	1	0.07	1
UniformRandom	0.19	0.50	0.11	0.50
CAPTURE	0.21	1.08	0.13	0.63
CAPTURE-PCov	0.19	0.87	0.11	0.57
CAPTURE-PCov-LB	0.18	0.69	0.11	0.46
CAPTURE-DKHO	0.20	0.71	0.12	0.5
INTERCEPT	**0.49**	**3.46**	0.63	0.41

two-layered models such as CAPTURE and its variants, we are examining the performance of just the attackability layer output, and we defer the evaluation of the observation predictions to the next subsection. Since we evaluate the attackability predictions of our models on metrics for binary classification, the real-valued output of the attackability layer of CAPTURE and its variants were converted to a binary classification where probabilities greater than or equal to the mean attack probability were classified as positive.

We make the following observations from these tables: First, INTERCEPT completely outperforms the previous best model, CAPTURE, and its variants, as well as other baseline models in terms of L&L and F1 scores. For 2014, INTERCEPT outperforms CAPTURE in terms of precision, recall, F1, and L&L score. For 2015 test data, INTERCEPT represents an even larger performance increase by approximately 3.50 times (L&L score of 3.46 versus 1.08) over CAPTURE and even more so for CAPTURE-PCov (L&L score of 3.46 versus 0.87). CAPTURE-PCov doesn't even outperform the positive baseline. Second, CAPTURE performs better on the 2014 dataset (when the training and testing data were similarly distributed) than on the 2015 dataset. In contrast, INTERCEPT remained flexible enough to perform well on the difficult 2015 testing set. However, CAPTURE-PCov, the more realistic variant of CAPTURE that can actually be used for forecasting, fails to make meaningful predictions about the attackability of targets. Its similar performance to PositiveBaseline demonstrates the need for models to learn the attackability of targets independently of observation probability to avoid learning models that make incorrect inferences about the attackability of the park (e.g., the entire park can be attacked). This is particularly important in the wildlife poaching domain because, due to the limited number of security resources, rangers cannot patrol every target all the time. Therefore, the attack probability model's predictions need to be extremely precise (high precision) while also being useful indicators of poaching activities throughout the park (high recall). Third, CAPTURE-PCov-LB performs even worse than CAPTURE-PCov in terms of L&L score for these attackability predictions, although the only difference between the two models is the observation layer. This occurs because the attackability prediction layer and the observation layer are not independent of one another; with the EM algorithm, the parameters are being learned for both layers simultaneously. In addition, by incorporating domain knowledge and penalizing the unattractive areas, CAPTURE-DKHO unfortunately does not lead to a significant improvement in performance. Fourth, INTERCEPT's precision values are significantly better compared to CAPTURE-PCov in 2014 and both CAPTURE and CAPTURE-PCov in 2015, with only modest losses of recall, indicating a significant reduction in the number of FP predictions made throughout the park.

In Tables 3.3 and 3.4, we also compare INTERCEPT with other models, including: (1) a decision tree in which each sample was weighted based on the patrol intensity for the corresponding target (weighted decision tree); (2) the best performing SVM; (3) logistic regression (which predicted no attacks and thus metrics could not be computed); and (4) the best-performing AdaBoosted decision tree. INTERCEPT provides significantly better performance than these other models as well.

Table 3.3. *Additional attackability prediction results on 2014 test data*

Classifier Type	F1	L&L	Precision	Recall
Weighted decision tree	0.11	1.01	0.06	0.48
SVM-BestFPCost-0.3	0.13	1.18	0.46	0.45
Logistic regression	–	–	–	0
AdaBoostDecisionTree-BestFPCost-0.2	0.13	1.22	0.07	0.48
INTERCEPT	**0.41**	**5.83**	0.37	0.45

Table 3.4. *Additional attackability prediction results on 2015 test data*

Classifier Type	F1	L&L	Precision	Recall
Weighted decision tree	0.25	1.42	0.15	0.69
SVM-BestFPCost-0.25	0.19	0.72	0.12	0.43
Logistic regression	–	–	–	0
AdaBoost-DT-BestFPCost-0.15	0.21	0.86	0.13	0.49
INTERCEPT	**0.49**	**3.46**	0.63	0.41

Table 3.5. *Observation prediction results on 2014 test data*

Classifier Type	F1	Precision	Recall	PR-AUC
PositiveBaseline	0.13	0.07	0.79	0.12
UniformRandom	0.09	0.05	0.46	0.07
CAPTURE	0.14	0.08	0.73	0.33
CAPTURE-PCov	0.12	0.07	0.61	0.31
CAPTURE-PCov-LB	0.13	0.08	0.48	0.36
CAPTURE-DKHO	0.16	0.09	0.72	0.33
INTERCEPT	**0.36**	0.32	0.89	**0.45**

Table 3.6. *Observation prediction results on 2015 test data*

Classifier Type	F1	Precision	Recall	PR-AUC
PositiveBaseline	0.26	0.16	0.66	0.20
UniformRandom	0.19	0.12	0.45	0.14
CAPTURE	0.29	0.18	0.70	0.29
CAPTURE-PCov	0.29	0.18	0.70	0.29
CAPTURE-PCov-LB	0.34	0.21	0.85	0.32
CAPTURE-DKHO	0.36	0.24	0.79	0.32
INTERCEPT	**0.50**	0.65	0.41	**0.49**

Observation Prediction Results

Tables 3.5 and 3.6 correspond to how accurately each model predicted the observations in our test datasets. For a fair comparison, we also cascade the attackability predictions of the PositiveBaseline and UniformRandom baselines with an LB observation layer, and convert those unconditional observation probabilities to binary predictions with a mean threshold, as was done for CAPTURE's attackability predictions. We observe the following. First, incorporating the observation model improved the PR-AUC score of

CAPTURE in both test datasets (for 2014, 0.36 versus 0.33; for 2015, 0.32 versus 0.29). Second, INTERCEPT outperforms the other models by a large margin, both in terms of F1 and PR-AUC, for both test datasets. Combined with the attackability results, these results demonstrate the benefit of learning more precise attackability models in order to better predict observation probability.

Impact of Ensemble and Voting Rules

INTERCEPT consists of five experts with a majority voting rule. We now investigate the impact of combining different decision trees into an ensemble, and the impact of different voting rules. Tables 3.7 and 3.8 show that constructing an ensemble, INTERCEPT, significantly improves the performance of the system as a whole, compared to the performance of its individual decision tree and BoostIT members. The standard decision tree is more conservative as it predicts fewer FPs, leading to higher precision, but suffers from low recall.

Table 3.9 shows the impact that a voting rule has on performance on 2015 test data (due to space, we omit the 2014 test data as it exhibits the same trends). We evaluate the performances of the best ensemble compositions, with

Table 3.7. *Attackability prediction results for decision tree models on 2014 test data*

Classifier Type	F1	L&L	Precision	Recall
PositiveBaseline	0.06	1	0.03	1
DecisionTree	0.2	1.8	0.14	0.36
BoostIT-1NN	0.19	2.23	0.12	0.55
BoostIT-2NN	0.21	2.13	0.13	0.45
BoostIT-3NN	0.2	2.01	0.13	0.45
INTERCEPT	**0.41**	**5.83**	0.37	0.45

Table 3.8. *Attackability prediction results for decision tree models on 2015 test data*

Classifier Type	F1	L&L	Precision	Recall
PositiveBaseline	0.14	1	0.07	1
DecisionTree	0.39	2.01	0.39	0.38
BoostIT-1NN	0.39	2.16	0.32	0.50
BoostIT-2NN	0.37	2.00	0.30	0.50
BoostIT-3NN	0.42	2.45	0.35	0.52
INTERCEPT	**0.49**	**3.46**	0.63	0.41

Table 3.9. *Attackability prediction results for different ensembles on 2015 test data*

Classifier Type	F1	L&L	Precision	Recall
BoostIT-3Experts-Any	0.36	2.11	0.26	0.59
BoostIT-5Experts-Any	0.34	2.13	0.23	0.68
BoostIT-3Experts-All	0.36	2.68	0.88	0.22
BoostIT-5Experts-All	0.28	1.97	0.89	0.16
BoostIT-3Experts-Maj	**0.49**	3.34	0.58	0.43
INTERCEPT	**0.49**	**3.46**	0.63	0.41

three and five experts for each voting rule. We observe that: (1) ensembles which predict an attack if any one expert predicts an attack (*Any*) are significantly better in terms of recall (0.68), but do poorly in terms of precision (0.23). This is because such ensembles are more generous in terms of predicting an attack, and this leads to a significantly higher number of FPs; (2) ensembles with a voting rule in which all experts have to agree (*All*) perform worse in terms of recall (0.16), but do best in terms of precision (0.89) as it makes fewer positive predictions (both true positives [TPs] as well as FPs). This would mean that it would miss a lot of attacks in our domain, however; (3) the majority voting based ensembles (*Maj*), used by INTERCEPT, provide an important balance between precision (0.63) and recall (0.41) as they are neither extremely conservative nor generous in terms of their predictions and therefore outperform other voting rules significantly (L&L of 3.46).

This analysis provides important guidance for selecting ensembles depending on the requirements of the domain. For example, if it is extremely crucial to predict as many TPs as possible and a high number of FPs is acceptable, then using an *Any* voting method would be beneficial. However, in our wildlife poaching prediction problem, we have limited security resources and therefore cannot send patrols to every target all the time. Therefore, we not only wish to limit the number of FPs, but also increase the number of correct poaching predictions. The majority voting rule provides this important balance in our domain.

Hybrid Model

In the following subsections, we discuss a graphical modeling approach to improve poaching activity prediction. We propose a hybrid spatiotemporal model and discuss its components in detail.

Prediction by Graphical models

Markov Random Field (MRF)

To predict poaching activity, each target, at time step $t \in \{t_1, \ldots, t_m\}$, is represented by coordinates i and j within the boundary of QEPA. In Figure 3.2(a), we demonstrate a three-dimensional network for spatiotemporal modeling of poaching events over all targets. Connections between nodes represent the mutual spatial influence of neighboring targets and also the temporal dependence between recurring poaching incidents at a target. $a_{i,j}^t$ represents poaching incidents at time step t and target i, j. Mutual spatial influences are modeled through first-order neighbors (i.e., $a_{i,j}^t$ connects to $a_{i\pm1,j}^t$, $a_{i,j\pm1}^t$, and $a_{i,j}^{t-1}$) and second-order neighbors (i.e., $a_{i,j}^t$ connects to $a_{i\pm1,j\pm1}^t$); for simplicity, the latter is not shown on the model's lattice. Each random variable takes a value in its state space; in this chapter, $\mathcal{L} = \{0, 1\}$.

To avoid index overload, henceforth, nodes are indexed by serial numbers, $S = \{1, 2, \ldots, N\}$ when we refer to the three-dimensional network. We introduce two random fields, indexed by S, with their configurations: $\mathcal{A} = \{a = (a_1, \ldots, a_N) | a_i \in \mathcal{L}, i \in S\}$, which indicates an *actual* poaching attack occurred at targets over the period of study, and $\mathcal{O} = \{o = (o_1, \ldots, o_N) | o_i \in \mathcal{L}, i \in S\}$ indicates a *detected* poaching attack at targets over the period of study. Due to the imperfect detection of poaching activities, the former represents the hidden variables, and the latter is the known observed data collected by rangers, shown by the gray-filled nodes in Figure 3.2(a). Targets are related to one another via a neighborhood system, $\mathcal{N}_n$, which is the set of nodes neighboring n and $n \notin \mathcal{N}_n$. This neighborhood system considers all spatial and temporal neighbors. We define neighborhood attackability as the fraction of neighbors that the model predicts to be attacked: $u_{\mathcal{N}_n} = \sum_{n \in \mathcal{N}_n} a_n / |\mathcal{N}_n|$.

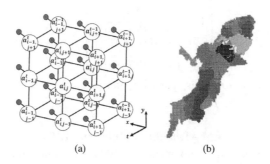

(a) (b)

Figure 3.2 Geo-clusters and graphical model graph. (a) Spatiotemporal model; (b) geo-clusters.

The probability, $P(a_i|u_{\mathcal{N}_n}, \alpha)$, of a poaching incident at each target n at time step t is represented in equation 3.2, where α is a vector of parameters weighting the most important variables that influence poaching; Z represents the vector of time-invariant ecological covariates associated with each target (e.g., animal density, slope, forest cover, net primary productivity, distance from patrol post, town and rivers (Critchlow et al. 2015; O'Kelly 2013). The model's temporal dimension is reflected through not only the backward dependence of each a_n, which influences the computation of $u_{\mathcal{N}_n}$, but also in the past patrol coverage at target n, denoted by c_n^{t-1}, which models the delayed deterrence effect of patrolling efforts:

$$p(a_n = 1|u_{\mathcal{N}_n}, \alpha) = \frac{e^{-\alpha[Z, u_{\mathcal{N}_n}, c_n^{t-1}, 1]^\mathsf{T}}}{1 + e^{-\alpha[Z, u_{\mathcal{N}_n}, c_n^{t-1}, 1]^\mathsf{T}}}. \tag{3.2}$$

Given a_n, o_n follows a conditional probability distribution proposed in equation 3.3, which represents the probability of rangers detecting a poaching attack at target n. The first column of the matrix denotes the probability of not detecting or detecting attacks if an attack has not happened, which is constrained to 1 or 0 respectively. In other words, it is impossible to detect an attack when an attack has not happened. The second column of the matrix represents the probability of not detecting or detecting attacks in the form of a logistic function if an attack has happened. Since it is less rational for poachers to place snares close to patrol posts and more convenient for rangers to detect poaching signs near the patrol posts, we assumed dp_n (distance from patrol post) and c_n^t (patrol coverage devoted to target n at time t) are the major variables influencing rangers' detection capabilities. Detectability at each target is represented in equation 3.3, where β is a vector of parameters that weight these variables:

$$p(o_n|a_n) = \begin{bmatrix} p(o_n = 0|a_n = 0) & p(o_n = 0|a_n = 1, \beta) \\ p(o_n = 1|a_n = 0) & p(o_n = 1|a_n = 1, \beta) \end{bmatrix}$$

$$= \begin{bmatrix} 1, & \dfrac{1}{1 + e^{-\beta[dp_n, c_n^t, 1]^\mathsf{T}}} \\ 0, & \dfrac{e^{-\beta[dp_n, c_n^t, 1]^\mathsf{T}}}{1 + e^{-\beta[dp_n, c_n^t, 1]^\mathsf{T}}} \end{bmatrix}. \tag{3.3}$$

We assume that (o, a) is pairwise independent, meaning $p(o, a) = \prod_{n \in \mathcal{S}} p(o_n, a_n)$.

EM Algorithm to Infer on MRF

We use the expectation-maximization (EM) algorithm (Bishop 2006) to estimate the MRF model's parameters $\theta = \{\alpha, \beta\}$. For completeness, we provide details about how we apply the EM algorithm to our model. Given a joint distribution $p(o, a|\theta)$ over observed variables o and hidden variables a, governed by parameters θ, EM aims to maximize the likelihood function $p(o|\theta)$ with respect to θ. To start the algorithm, an initial setting for the parameters θ^{old} is chosen. At E-step, $p(a|o, \theta^{old})$ is evaluated for each node in the MRF model:

$$p(a_n|o_n, \theta^{old}) = \frac{p(o_n|a_n, \beta^{old}).p(a_n|u_{\mathcal{N}_n}^{old}, \alpha^{old})}{p(o_n)}. \tag{3.4}$$

M-step calculates θ^{new}, according to the expectation of the complete log likelihood, $\log p(o, a|\theta)$, given in equation 3.5.

$$\theta^{new} = \arg\max_{\theta} \sum_{a_n \in \mathcal{L}} p(a|o, \theta^{old}).\log p(o, a|\theta) \tag{3.5}$$

To facilitate calculation of the log of the joint probability distribution, $\log p(o, a|\theta)$, we introduce an approximation that makes use of $u_{\mathcal{N}_n}^{old}$, represented in equation 3.6:

$$\log p(o, a|\theta) = \sum_{n \in \mathcal{S}} \sum_{a_n \in \mathcal{L}} \log p(o_n|a_n, \beta) + \log p(a_n|u_{\mathcal{N}_n}^{old}, \alpha). \tag{3.6}$$

Then, if convergence of the log likelihood is not satisfied, $\theta^{old} \leftarrow \theta^{new}$, and repeat.

Dataset Preparation for MRF

To split the data into training and test sets, we divided the real-world dataset into year-long time steps. We trained the model's parameters $\theta = \{\alpha, \beta\}$ on historical data sampled through time steps $(t_1, \ldots, t_m)$ for all targets within the boundary. These parameters were used to predict poaching activity at time step t_{m+1}, which represents the test set for evaluation purposes. The trade-off between adding years' data (performance) versus computational costs led us to use three years ($m = 3$). The model was thus trained over targets that were patrolled throughout the training time period (t_1, t_2, t_3). We examined three training sets: 2011–2013, 2012–2014, and 2013–2015, for which the test sets are from 2014, 2015, and 2016, respectively.

Capturing temporal trends requires a sufficient amount of data to be collected regularly across time steps for each target. Due to the large amount of missing inspections and uncertainty in the collected data, this model focuses on learning poaching activity only over regions that have been continually monitored in the past, according to Definition 3.1. We denote this subset of targets as $\mathcal{S}_c$.

Definition 3.1   Continually versus occasionally monitoring: a target i, j is continually monitored if all elements of the coverage sequence are positive; $c_{i,j}^{t_k} > 0, \forall k = 1, \ldots, m$ where m is the number of time steps. Otherwise, it is occasionally monitored.

Experiments with MRF were conducted in various ways on each dataset. We refer to (1) a *global* model with spatial effects as **GLB-SP**, which consists of a single set of parameters θ for the whole QEPA, and (2) a *global* model without spatial effects (i.e., the parameter that corresponds to $u_{\mathcal{N}_n}$ is set to 0) as **GLB**. The spatiotemporal model is designed to account for temporal and spatial trends in poaching activities. However, since learning those trends and capturing spatial effects are impacted by the variance in local poachers' behaviors, we also examined (3) a *geo-clustered* model which consists of multiple sets of local parameters throughout QEPA with spatial effects, referred to as **GCL-SP**, and also (4) a *geo-clustered* model without spatial effects (i.e., the parameter that corresponds to $u_{\mathcal{N}_n}$ is set to 0) referred to as **GCL**.

Figure 3.2(b) shows the geo-clusters generated by Gaussian mixture models (GMMs), which classifies the targets based on the geo-spatial features, $\mathbf{Z}$, along with the targets' coordinates, $(x_{i,j}, y_{i,j})$, into 22 clusters. The number of geo-clusters, 22, are intended to be close to the number of patrol posts in QEPA such that each cluster contains one or two nearby patrol posts. Not only are local poachers' behaviors described by a distinct set of parameters, but also the data collection conditions, over the targets within each cluster, are maintained to be nearly uniform.

Prediction by Ensemble Models

A **Bagging ensemble model** or **B**ootstrap **agg**regation technique, called Bagging, is a type of ensemble learning that bags some weak learners, such as decision trees, on a dataset by generating many bootstrap duplicates of the dataset and learning decision trees on them. Each of the bootstrap duplicates are obtained by randomly choosing M observations out of M with replacement, where M denotes the training dataset size. Finally, the predicted response of the ensemble is computed by taking an average over predictions from its individual decision trees. To learn a Bagging ensemble, we used the *fitensemble* function of MATLAB. **Dataset preparation** for the Bagging ensemble model is designed to find the targets that are liable to be attacked (Kar et al. 2017). A target is assumed to be attackable if it has ever been attacked; if any observations occurred in the entire training period for a given target, that target is labeled as attackable. For this model, the best training period contained five years of data.

Hybrid of MRF and Bagging Ensemble

Since the amount and regularity of data collected by rangers varies across regions of QEPA, predictive models perform differently in different regions. As such, we propose using different models to predict over them; first, we used a Bagging ensemble model, and then improved the predictions in some regions using the spatiotemporal model. For global models, we used MRF for all continually monitored targets. However, for geo-clustered models, for targets in the continually monitored subset, $\mathcal{S}_c^q$, (where temporally aware models can be used practically), the MRF model's performance varied widely across geo-clusters according to our experiments. q indicates clusters and $1 \leq q \leq 22$. Thus, for each q, if the average catch per unit effort (CPUE), outlined in Definition 3.2, is relatively large, we use the MRF model for $\mathcal{S}_c^q$. In conservation biology, CPUE is an indirect measure of poaching activity abundance. A larger average CPUE for each cluster corresponds to more frequent poaching activity and thus more data for that cluster. Consequently, using more complex spatiotemporal models in those clusters becomes more reasonable.

Definition 3.2 **Average CPUE** is $\sum_{n \in \mathcal{S}_c^q} o_n / \sum_{n \in \mathcal{S}_c^q} c_n^t$ in cluster q.

To compute CPUE, effort corresponds to the amount of coverage (i.e., 1 unit = 1 km walked) in a given target, and catch corresponds to the number of observations. Hence, for $1 \leq q \leq 22$, we will boost selectively according to the average CPUE value; some clusters may not be boosted by MRF, and we would only use Bagging ensemble model for making predictions on them. Experiments on historical data show that selecting 15 percent of the geo-clusters with the highest average CPUE results in the best performance for the entire hybrid model (discussed in the evaluation section).

Evaluations of Hybrid Model

Experiments with Real-World Data

Evaluation of models' attack predictions are demonstrated in Tables 3.10–3.15. To compare models' performances, we used several baseline methods: (1) PositiveBaseline, **PB**, a model that predicts poaching attacks to occur in all targets (1×1 km cells); (2) RandomBaseline, **RB**, a model which flips a coin to decide its prediction; (3) Training Label Baseline, **TL**, a model which predicts a target as attacked if it has ever been attacked in the training data. We also present the results for support vector machines, **SVM**, and AdaBoost methods,

Table 3.10. *Comparing all models' performances with the best-performing BG-G model*

Test set			2014		
Models	PB	RB	TL	SVM	BG-G*
Precision	0.06	0.05	0.26	0.24	**0.65**
Recall	1.00	0.46	0.86	0.3	**0.54**
F1	0.10	0.09	0.4	0.27	**0.59**
L&L	1.00	0.43	4.09	1.33	**6.44**
Models	RUS	AD	BG	INT	BG-G*
Precision	0.12	0.33	0.62	0.37	**0.65**
Recall	0.51	0.47	0.54	0.45	**0.54**
F1	0.19	0.39	0.58	0.41	**0.59**
L&L	1.12	2.86	6.18	5.83	**6.44**

Table 3.11. *Comparing all models' performances with the best-performing BG-G model*

Test set			2015		
Models	PB	RB	TL	SVM	BG-G*
Precision	0.10	0.08	0.39	0.4	**0.69**
Recall	1.00	0.43	0.78	0.15	**0.62**
F1	0.18	0.14	0.52	0.22	**0.65**
L&L	1.00	0.37	3.05	0.62	**4.32**
Models	RUS	AD	BG	INT	BG-G*
Precision	0.2	0.52	0.71	0.63	**0.69**
Recall	0.51	0.5	0.53	0.41	**0.62**
F1	0.29	0.51	0.61	0.49	**0.65**
L&L	1.03	2.61	3.83	3.46	**4.32**

AD, which are well-known machine learning techniques, along with results for the best-performing predictive model on the QEPA dataset, INTERCEPT, **INT** (Kar et al. 2017). Results for the Bagging ensemble technique, **BG**, and RUSBoost, **RUS**, a hybrid sampling/boosting algorithm for learning from datasets with class imbalance (Seiffert et al. 2010), are also presented. In all tables, **BG-G*** stands for the best-performing model among all variations of the hybrid model, which will be discussed in detail later. Tables 3.13–3.15 demonstrate that **BG-G*** outperformed all other existing models in terms of L&L and also F1.

Table 3.12. *Comparing all models' performances with the best-performing BG-G model*

Test Set			2016		
Models	PB	RB	TL	SVM	BG-G*
Precision	0.10	0.09	0.45	0.45	**0.74**
Recall	1.00	0.44	0.75	0.23	**0.66**
F1	0.18	0.14	0.56	0.30	**0.69**
L&L	1.00	0.38	3.4	1.03	**4.88**
Models	RUS	AD	BG	INT	BG-G*
Precision	0.19	0.53	0.76	0.40	**0.74**
Recall	0.65	0.54	0.62	0.66	**0.66**
F1	0.29	0.53	0.68	0.51	**0.69**
L&L	1.25	2.84	4.75	2.23	**4.88**

Table 3.13. *Performances of hybrid models with variations of MRF (BG-G models)*

Test Set		2014		
MRF models	GLB	GLB-SP	GCL	GCL-SP
Precision	0.12	0.12	0.63	0.65
Recall	0.58	0.65	0.54	0.54
F1	0.20	0.20	0.58	0.59
L&L	1.28	1.44	6.31	6.44

Table 3.14. *Performances of hybrid models with variations of MRF (BG-G models)*

Test Set		2015		
MRF models	GLB	GLB-SP	GCL	GCL-SP
Precision	0.19	0.19	0.69	0.69
Recall	0.52	0.58	0.65	0.62
F1	0.28	0.29	0.65	0.65
L&L	0.99	1.14	4.32	4.32

Tables 3.13–3.15 provide a detailed comparison of all variations of our hybrid models, **BG-G** (i.e., when different MRF models are used). When **GCL-SP** is used, we get the best-performing model in terms of L&L score, which is denoted as **BG-G***. The poor results of learning a global set of

Table 3.15. *Performances of hybrid models with variations of MRF (BG-G models)*

Test Set	2016			
MRF Models	GLB	GLB-SP	GCL	GCL-SP
Precision	0.18	0.19	0.72	0.74
Recall	0.50	0.46	0.66	0.66
F1	0.27	0.27	0.69	0.69
L&L	0.91	0.91	4.79	4.88

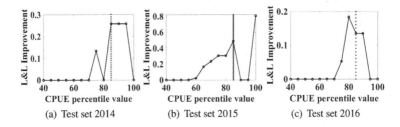

(a) Test set 2014   (b) Test set 2015   (c) Test set 2016

Figure 3.3 L&L improvement versus CPUE percentile value; BG-G* compared to BG.

parameters emphasize the fact that poachers' behaviors and patterns are not identical throughout QEPA and should be modeled accordingly.

Our experiments demonstrated that the performance of the MRF model within $\mathcal{S}_c^q$ varies across different geo-clusters and is related to the CPUE value for each cluster, q. Figure 3.3(a) displays an improvement in L&L score for the **BG-G*** model compared to **BG** versus varying the percentile of geo-clusters used for boosting. Experiments with the 2014 test set show that choosing the 85th percentile of geo-clusters for boosting with MRF, according to CPUE, (i.e., selecting 15 percent of the geo-clusters with highest CPUE), results in the best prediction performance. The 85th percentile is shown by vertical lines in figures where the **BG-G*** model outperformed the **BG** model. We used a similar percentile value for conducting experiments with the MRF model on test sets of 2015 and 2016. Figures 3.3(b) and 3.3(c) confirm the efficiency of choosing an 85th percentile value for those test sets as well. Also, Tables 3.13–3.15 demonstrate that for **BG-G*** recall increased up to almost 10 percent for the 2015 test set, which would result in marking roughly 10 percent more vulnerable targets as attacked and thus protecting more endangered animals.

QEPA Field Test

One-Month Test

After development and evaluation of the model on historical data, INTER-CEPT was deployed to the field. Based on the predictions, two patrol areas were chosen for QENP rangers to patrol for one month. These areas were selected (approximately 9 km^2 each) such that they were (1) predicted to have multiple attacks and (2) previously infrequently patrolled as rangers did not consider these as important as other areas (and thus are good areas to test the model predictions). After providing the rangers with GPS coordinates of particular points in these areas, they patrolled these areas on foot and utilized their expert knowledge to determine where exactly in these areas they were most likely to find snares and other signs of illegal human activity (e.g., salt licks, watering holes). On each patrol, in addition to their other duties, rangers recorded their observations of animal sightings (21 animals were sighted in one month) and illegal human activity. The key findings are demonstrated in Tables 3.16 and 3.17, and a selection of photos taken by park rangers are shown in Figures 3.4(a) and 3.4(b). The most noteworthy findings of these patrols are those related to elephant poaching; rangers, unfortunately, found one poached elephant with its tusks removed. However, this result demonstrates that poachers find this area, predicted by the model, attractive for poaching but they had not patrolled the area regularly in the past. On a more positive note, the model's predictions led rangers to find many snares before they caught any animals: one large roll of elephant snares, one active wire snare, and one cache of ten antelope snares. In fact, the machine learning model predictions assisted rangers' efforts in potentially saving the lives of multiple animals, including elephants.

In addition to wildlife signs, which represent areas of interest to poachers, the findings of trespassing (e.g., litter, ashes) are significant as these represent areas of the park where humans were able to enter illegally and leave without being detected; if we can continue to patrol areas where poachers are

Table 3.16. *Base rate comparison: hits per month*

Crime type	**INT**	Average	Percentile
AnimalCom	1	0.16	89
AnimalNoncom	3	0.73	91
Fishing	1	0.73	79
PlantNoncom	1	0.46	76
Trespassing	19	0.20	100
Total	25	2.28	

Table 3.17. *Real-world patrol results: illegal activity*

Week#	Illegal Activity	Count
2	Trespassing	19
3	Active snares	1
	Plant harvesting	1
4	Poached elephants	1
	Elephant snare roll	1
	Antelope snares	10
	Fish roasting racks	2

(a)   (b)

Figure 3.4 Elephant snare roll found by rangers directed by the model. Photo credit: Uganda Wildlife Authority.

visiting, rangers will eventually encounter the poachers themselves. To provide additional context for these results, a set of base rates are presented in Table 3.16. These base rates, computed in and around the proposed patrol areas, correspond to the average number of observed crimes per month from 2003 to 2015. Animal commercial (AnimalCom) crimes correspond to elephant, buffalo, and hippopotamus poaching; animal noncommercial (AnimalNoncom) corresponds to all other poaching and poaching via snares; and plant noncommercial (PlantNoncom) corresponds to illegal harvesting of non-timber forest products (e.g., honey). The percentile rank corresponds to the number of months in which the deployed patrols recorded more observations than in the historical data. For animal noncommercial crime, there was an average of 0.73 attacks observed monthly; for the deployed patrols, there were three separate observations (such as a roll of elephant snares), and in 91 percent of the months from 2003 to 2015, two or fewer observations were recorded.

Eight-Month Tests

While our model demonstrated superior predictive performance on historical data, it is important to test these models in the field. The initial field test we conducted (Kar et al. 2017) in collaboration with the Wildlife Conservation Society (WCS) and the Uganda Wildlife Authority (UWA) was the first of its kind in the machine learning community and showed promising improvements over previous patrolling regimes. Due to the difficulty of organizing such a field test, its implications were limited: only two 9 km^2 areas (18 km^2) of QEPA were patrolled by rangers over a month. Because of its success, however, WCS and UWA graciously agreed to a larger-scale, controlled experiment: also in 9 km^2 areas, but rangers patrolled 27 of these areas (243 km^2, spread across QEPA) over five months. This is the largest to-date field test of machine learning-based predictive models in this domain. We show the areas in Figure 3.5(a). Note that rangers patrolled these areas in addition to other areas of QEPA as part of their normal duties.

This experiment's goal was to determine the selectiveness of our model's snare attack predictions: Does our model correctly predict both where there are and are not snare attacks? We define attack prediction rate as the proportion of targets (a 1 km by 1 km cell) in a patrol area (3 by 3 cells) that are predicted to be attacked. We considered two experiment groups that corresponded to our model's attack prediction rates from November 2016 to March 2017: high (group 1) and low (group 2). Areas that had an attack prediction rate of 50 percent or greater were considered to be in a high area (group 1); areas with a lower rate were in group 2. For example, if the model predicted five out of nine targets to be attacked in an area, that area was in group 1. Due to the importance of QEPA for elephant conservation, we do not show which areas belong to which experiment group in Figure 3.5(a) so that we do not provide data to ivory poachers.

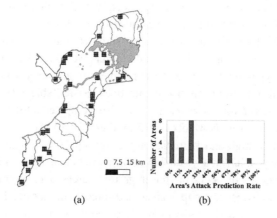

(a)   (b)

Figure 3.5 Patrol area statistics: (a) patrolled areas; (b) prediction rates.

Table 3.18. *Patrol area group memberships*

Experiment Group	Exhaustive Patrol Areas	Final Patrol Areas
High (1)	50 (9%)	5 (19%)
Low (2)	494 (91%)	22 (81%)

To start, we exhaustively generated all patrol areas such that (1) each patrol area was 3×3 km^2, (2) no point in the patrol area was more than 5 km away from the nearest ranger patrol post, and (3) no patrol area was patrolled too frequently or infrequently in past years (to ensure that the training data associated with all areas were of similar quality); in all, 544 areas were generated across QEPA. Then, using the model's attack predictions, each area was assigned to an experiment group. Because we were not able to test all 544 areas, we selected a subset such that no two areas overlapped with each other and no more than two areas were selected for each patrol post (due to manpower constraints). In total, five areas in group 1 and 22 areas in group 2 were chosen. Note that this composition arose due to the preponderance of group 2 areas (see Table 3.18). We provide a breakdown of the areas' exact attack prediction rates in Figure 3.5(a); areas with rates below 56 percent (5/9) were in group 2, and, for example, there were eight areas in group 2 with a rate of 22 percent (2/9). Finally, when we provided patrols to the rangers, *experiment group memberships were hidden to prevent effects where knowledge of predicted poaching activity would influence their patrolling patterns and detection rates*.

The field test data we received were in the same format as the historical data. However, because rangers needed to physically walk to these patrol areas, we received additional data that we have omitted from this analysis; observations made outside of a designated patrol area were not counted. Because we only predicted where snaring activity would occur, we have also omitted other observation types made during the experiment (e.g., illegal cattle grazing). We present results from this five-month field test in Table 3.19. To provide additional context for these results, we also computed QEPA's park-wide historical CPUE (from November 2015 to March 2016): 0.04.

Areas with a high attack prediction rate (group 1) had significantly more snare sightings than areas with low attack prediction rates (15 versus 4). This is despite there being far fewer group 1 areas than group 2 areas (5 versus 22); on average, group 1 areas had three snare observations whereas group 2 areas had 0.18 observations. It is worth noting the large standard deviation for the mean observation counts; the standard deviation of 5.2, for the mean of 3, signifies that not all areas had snare observations. Indeed,

Table 3.19. *Field test results: observations*

Exp. Group	Obs. Count (%)	Mean Count (std)	Effort (%)	CPUE
High (1)	15 (79)	3 (5.20)	129.54 (29)	0.12
Low (2)	4 (21)	0.18 (0.50)	322.33 (71)	0.01

two out of five areas in group 1 had snare observations. However, this also applies to group 2 areas, where only three out of 22 areas had snare observations.

We present CPUE results in Table 3.19. When accounting for differences in areas' effort, group 1 areas had a CPUE that was over ten times that of group 2 areas. Moreover, when compared to QEPA's park-wide historical CPUE of 0.04, it is clear that our model successfully differentiated between areas of high and low snaring activity. The results of this large-scale field test, the first of its kind for machine learning models in this domain, demonstrated that our model's superior predictive performance in the laboratory extends to the real world.

Conclusion

In this chapter, we presented a hybrid spatiotemporal model to predict wildlife poaching threat levels. Additionally, we validated our model via an extensive five-month field test in QEPA, where rangers patrolled over 450 km^2 across QEPA – the largest field-test-to-date of machine learning-based models in this domain. On real-world historical data from QEPA, our hybrid model achieves significantly better performance than prior work. On the data collected from our field test, we demonstrated that our model successfully differentiated between areas of high and low snaring activity. These findings demonstrated that our model's predictions are selective and also that its superior laboratory performance extends to the real world. Based on these promising results, future work will focus on deploying these models as part of a software package to UWA to aid in planning future anti-poaching patrols.

References

Bishop, C. M. 2006. Pattern recognition. *Machine Learning*, **128**, 1–58.

Critchlow, R., Plumptre, A.J., Driciru, M., et al. 2015. Spatiotemporal trends of illegal activities from ranger-collected data in a Ugandan national park. *Conservation Biology*, **29**(5), 1458–1470.

Critchlow, R., Plumptre, A.J., Alidria, B., et al. 2016. Improving law-enforcement effectiveness and efficiency in protected areas using ranger-collected monitoring data. *Conservation Letters.*

Eck, J., Chainey, S., Cameron, J., and Wilson, R. 2005. Mapping crime: Understanding hotspots. National Institute of Justice, Washington DC.

Gholami, S., Wilder, B., Brown, M., et al. 2016. Divide to defend: collusive security games. Pages 272–293 in GameSec 2018 – Conference on Decision and Game Theory for Security. Springer.

Gholami, S., Ford, B., Fang, F., et al. 2017. Taking it for a test drive: a hybrid spatiotemporal model for wildlife poaching prediction evaluated through a controlled field test. Pages 292–304 in *Joint European Conference on Machine Learning and Knowledge Discovery in Databases.* Springer.

Great Elephant Census. 2016 (August). The Great Elephant Census – A Paul G. Allen Project. Press Release.

Kar, D., Ford, B., Gholami, S., et al. 2017. Cloudy with a chance of poaching: adversary behavior modeling and forecasting with real-world poaching data. Pages 159–167 in *Proceedings of the 16th Conference on Autonomous Agents and MultiAgent Systems.* International Foundation for Autonomous Agents and Multiagent Systems.

Lee, W.S., and Liu, B. 2003. Learning with positive and unlabeled examples using weighted logistic regression. Pages 448–455 in *ICML'03 Proceedings of the Twentieth International Conference on International Conference on Machine Learning*, vol. 3. AAAI Press.

Nguyen, T.H., Sinha, A., Gholami, S., et al. 2016. CAPTURE: a new predictive anti-poaching tool for wildlife protection. Pages 767–775 in *Proceedings of the 2016 International Conference on Autonomous Agents & Multiagent Systems.* International Foundation for Autonomous Agents and Multiagent Systems

O'Kelly, H. J. 2013. Monitoring conservation threats, interventions, and impacts on wildlife in a Cambodian tropical forest. Dissertation, Imperial College, London.

Convention on International Trade in Endangered Species of Wild Fauna and Flora. 2016 (March). African elephants still in decline due to high levels of poaching. Press Release.

Rashidi, P., Wang, T., Skidmore, A., et al. 2015. Spatial and spatiotemporal clustering methods for detecting elephant poaching hotspots. *Ecological Modelling*, **297**, 180–186.

Rashidi, P., Wang, T., Skidmore, A., et al. 2016. Elephant poaching risk assessed using spatial and non-spatial Bayesian models. *Ecological Modelling*, **338**, 60–68.

Seiffert, C., Khoshgoftaar, T.M., Van Hulse, J., and Napolitano, A. 2010. RUSBoost: a hybrid approach to alleviating class imbalance. *IEEE SMC-A: Systems and Humans*, **40**(1), 185–197.

Solberg, A.H.S., Taxt, T., and Jain, A.K. 1996. A Markov random field model for classification of multisource satellite imagery. *IEEE TGRS*, **34**(1), 100–113.

Yin, Z., and Collins, R. 2007. Belief propagation in a 3D spatio-temporal MRF for moving object detection. Pages 1–8 in *2007 IEEE Conference on Computer Vision and Pattern Recognition* IEEE.

4

Optimal Patrol Planning Against
Black-Box Attackers

Haifeng Xu, Benjamin Ford, Fei Fang, Bistra Dilkina,
Andrew J. Plumptre, Milind Tambe, Margaret Driciru, Fred Wanyama,
Aggrey Rwetsiba, Mustapha Nsubuga, and Joshua Mabonga

Introduction

Worldwide, wildlife conservation agencies have established protected areas to protect threatened species from dire levels of poaching. Unfortunately, even in many protected areas, species' populations are still in decline [Di Marco et al. 2014; Critchlow et al. 2016]. These areas are protected by park rangers who conduct patrols to protect wildlife and deter poaching. Given that these areas are vast, however, agencies do not have sufficient resources to ensure rangers can adequately protect the entire park.

At many protected areas, rangers collect observational data while on patrol, and these observations on animals and illegal human activities (e.g., poaching, trespassing) are commonly recorded into a park-wide database (e.g., SMART, Cybertracker). Once enough patrols have been conducted, a patrol manager will analyze the data and generate a new patrolling strategy to execute. However, given the vast area and limited financial budgets of conservation agencies, improving the efficiency of ranger patrols is an important goal in this domain.

Following the success of automated planning tools used in domains such as fare enforcement and seaport protection [Yin et al. 2012; Shieh et al. 2012], novel planning tools have also been proposed and applied to ranger patrol planning. Nguyen et al. (2016) developed a new game-theoretic model that optimized a proposed poacher behavior model to generate randomized patrol strategies. However, they did not account for spatial constraints (i.e., are two areas adjacent?) in their planning and thus cannot guarantee the implementability of their proposed strategies. Moreover, the planning in Nguyen et al. (2016) is specific to one poacher behavior model and cannot be applied to different predictive models. Critchlow et al. (2016) demonstrated the potential for automated planning tools in the real world via a successful field test. However, the planning process in Critchlow et al. (2016) is deterministic and thus is predictable to poachers.

In this chapter, we present OPERA (Optimal patrol Planning with Enhanced RAndomness), a general patrol planning framework with the following key features. First, OPERA optimally generates patrols against a black-box poaching prediction model. Unlike other approaches in this domain that can only optimize against their specified prediction model [Nguyen et al. 2016; Haas and Ferreira 2017], OPERA is capable of optimizing against a wide range of prediction models. Second, OPERA optimizes directly over the space of feasible patrol routes and guarantees implementability of any generated patrol strategy. Lastly, OPERA incorporates entropy maximization in its optimization process to ensure that the generated strategies are sufficiently randomized and robust to partial information leakage – a frequently observed phenomenon in practice whereby poachers try to infer the patroller's patrolling route by monitoring part of the patroller's movements [Nyirenda and Chomba 2012; Moreto 2013; Xu et al. 2018].

We evaluate OPERA on a real-world dataset from Uganda's Queen Elizabeth Protected Area (QEPA). Our experiments show that, compared to benchmark heuristic planning algorithms, OPERA results in significantly better defender utility and more efficient coverage of the area. Moreover, the experiments also show that the new entropy maximization procedure results in patrol routes that are much more unpredictable than those routes generated by classical techniques. This effectively mitigates the issue of partial information leakage. Finally, we integrate OPERA with a predictive model of a bagging ensemble of decision trees to generate patrolling routes for QEPA and compare these routes with the past routes used by rangers at QEPA. The experiments show that OPERA is able to detect all the attacks that are found by past ranger patrolling and also predicted by the predictive model. Moreover, OPERA results in better attack detection and more efficient coverage of the area than the ranger routes.

Related Work

Prior work in planning wildlife patrols has also generated patrol strategies based on a predictive model [Nguyen et al. 2016]. Nguyen et al. (2016) modeled poacher behavior via a two-layered graphical model, and a randomized patrolling strategy was planned in a Stackelberg Security Game (SSG) framework. Similarly, SSGs have been applied to the problem of interdicting rhino poachers. Haas and Ferreira (2017) generated optimal interdiction strategies for rangers by solving an SSG. However, patrol strategies generated by Nguyen et al. (2016) were not guaranteed to be implementable in the form of patrol routes that satisfy spatial constraints, while the approach of Haas and Ferreira (2017) optimized over a very small set of patrols specified a priori. In contrast, our scalable approach optimizes over the space of all feasible patrol routes and is guaranteed to generate executable routes. Additionally, both the patrol strategy generation approaches of Nguyen et al. (2016) and Haas and Ferreira (2017) were constrained to their own adversary behavior models, while our black-box approach can generate a patrol strategy for a wide range of adversary frameworks and corresponding behavior models.

Green Security Games (GSGs) [Yang et al. 2014; Fang et al. 2015] have been introduced to model the interaction in domains such as wildlife protection, fishery protection, and forest protection. Fang et al. (2015) proposed a multi-stage game to model the repeated interactions in these domains. In the case in which the defender's strategy in one stage can affect the attacker's behavior in future stages, look-ahead planning algorithms were proposed to compute a sequence of defender strategies against attackers that follow a specific behavior model [Fang et al. 2015]. OPERA can also handle multi-stage planning to generate a sequence of strategies to use, but OPERA additionally introduces a novel and scalable approach to handle black-box attackers.

Other work in this domain has resulted in the successful field testing of planned patrols [Critchlow et al. 2016; Fang et al. 2016]. Critchlow et al. (2016) generate a patrol strategy by reorganizing historical patrol efforts such that areas of highest predicted activity would receive the highest patrol effort. However, such reorganization leads to a deterministic patrol strategy that can be easily exploited by poachers. Fang et al. (2016) introduced a patrol planning tool that incorporated spatial constraints to plan detailed patrol routes. However, it relied on a specific type of attacker behavior model proposed by Nguyen et al. (2013), while OPERA can optimize against any black-box attacker model that can be approximated by a piece-wise linear function of the patrolling effort.

Green Security Games with Black-Box Attackers

In this section, we provide an overview of GSGs and how they can work with a black-box attacker model.

Green Security Games

GSGs are security games that specifically focus on the unique challenges present in conservation domains (e.g., protecting wildlife, fisheries); GSGs focus on protecting threatened natural resources, with limited defender capacity, from repeated outside attacks. Like most of the previous work in GSGs [Yang et al. 2014; Fang et al. 2015], we consider a discrete setting in which the conservation area is divided into N grid cells, each treated as a *target*. Let $[N]$ denote the set of all cells, among which one cell is designated as the *patrol post*. Any patrol route must originate from and return to the patrol post. Without loss of generality, we will treat cell 1 as the patrol post throughout the chapter. There is one patroller resource (e.g., ranger team) that patrols $[N]$ cells each day. Due to real-world spatial constraints, from one cell the patroller can only move to neighboring cells. We assume that traversing each cell requires one unit of time, and we let T denote the upper bound of the total units of time that the patroller can patrol each day. As a result, the patroller can traverse at most T cells each day. These spatial constraints can be captured by a time-unrolled graph G (e.g., Figure 4.1). Any node $v_{t,i}$ in G denotes the cell i at time t. The edges in G, only connecting two consecutive time steps, indicate feasible spatial traversals from one cell to another within a unit of time. Recall that cell 1 is the patrol post, so a feasible patrol route will be a path in G starting from $v_{1,1}$ and ending at $v_{T,1}$ (e.g., the dotted path in Figure 4.1).

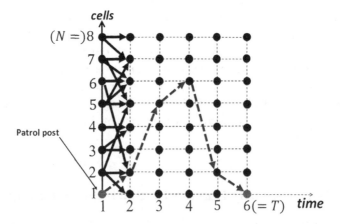

Figure 4.1 An example of the time-unrolled graph.

Black-Box Attackers

Unlike previous security game models which explicitly assume an attacker behavior model (rational or boundedly rational), we assume that for each cell i there is a black-box function g_i that takes as input a certain measure of the defender's patrolling effort l_i^1, l_i^0 at the current and previous period respectively, and outputs a prediction of attacks at cell i. Note that the dependence of the prediction on static features (e.g., animal density, distance, and terrain features) is integrated into the function form of g_i and thus will not be an explicit input into g_i. This is motivated by the recent surge of research efforts in using machine learning models to predict attacks in conservation areas [Yang et al. 2014; Haghtalab et al. 2016; Kar et al. 2017]. Each of these models can be treated as a black-box function that describes the attacker's behavior, though we note that the function g_i can also capture perfectly rational or other models of boundedly rational attackers. In this chapter, we assume that the function g_i outputs the predicted number of *detected attacks* at cell i (i.e., attacks that happen and are also detected by the patroller) since the real-world data and corresponding machine learning model we use fit this task. However, we remark that our framework and algorithms are *also applicable to other forms of g_i*.

We wish to optimize the design of patrol routes against such black-box attackers. Of course, one cannot hope to develop a general, efficient algorithm that works for an arbitrary function g_i. We thus make the following assumption: g_i depends *discretely* on the *patrolling effort* at cell i. More specifically, we assume that there are $m + 1$ levels of patrolling effort at any time period, ranging increasingly from 0 to m, and $g_i : \{0, 1, \ldots, m\}^2 \to \mathbb{R}$ takes level l_i^1, l_i^0 as input. We remark that this discretization is a natural choice since it can be viewed as a *piece-wise constant* approximation for the attacker behavior function. It's worth noting that some machine learning models in this domain indeed directly use discrete patrolling levels as input features [Kar et al. 2017]. The output of g_i can be any number (e.g., 0–1 for classifiers, a real number for regression).

Patrolling Effort and Its Implementation

Recall that each patrol route is an $s - d$ path in G for $s = v_{1,1}$ and $d = v_{T,1}$. Equivalently, a patrol route can also be viewed as a one-unit *integer flow* from s to d (e.g., the path in Figure 4.1 is also a one-unit s to d flow). In our patrol design, we allow the defender to *randomize* her choice of patrol routes, which is called a *defender mixed strategy* and corresponds to a *fractional s to d* flow.

Within any period, the patrolling effort x_i at each cell i is the expected total amount of time units spent at cell i during T time steps. For example, using the path in Figure 4.1, the effort x_2 equals 2 since the path visits cell 2 twice and the efforts $x_5 = 1, x_7 = 0$, etc. When a mixed strategy is used, the effort will be the expected time units. Let $\mathbf{x} = (x_1, \ldots, x_N)$ denote the patrolling effort vector, or effort vector for short. One important property of the patrolling effort quantity is that it is additive across different time steps. Such additivity allows us to characterize feasible effort vectors using a flow-based formulation. An effort vector is *implementable* if there exists a mixed strategy that results in the effort vector. The following is a precise characterization of implementable effort vectors:

Definition 4.1 *The effort vector* $(x_1, \ldots, x_N) \in \mathbb{R}_+^N$ *within any period is implementable if and only if there exists a flow* $f = \{f_e\}_{e \in E}$ *in G such that*

$$x_i = \sum_{t=1}^{T} \left[\sum_{e \in \sigma^+(v_{t,i})} f_e \right], \qquad for\ i = 1, \ldots, N$$
$$f\ is\ a\ feasible\ one\text{-}unit\ s\ to\ d\ flow\ in\ G$$

where $\sigma^+(v_{t,i})$ *is the set of all edges entering node* $v_{t,i}$.

Let $\alpha_0 < \alpha_1 \ldots < \alpha_m < \alpha_{m+1}$ be $m+2$ threshold constants which determine the patrol level of any patrolling effort. By default, we always set $\alpha_0 = 0$ and $\alpha_{m+1} = +\infty$. The patrolling effort x_i has level $l \in \{0, 1, \ldots, m\}$ if $x_i \in [\alpha_l, \alpha_{l+1})$. In most applications, these thresholds are usually given together with the function $g_i(l_i^1, l_i^0)$.

Patrol Design to Maximize Attack Detection

Recall that the black-box function g_i in our setting predicts the number of detected attacks at cell i. In this section, we look to design the optimal (possibly randomized) patrol route so that the induced patrol effort maximizes the *total number of detected attacks* $\sum_{i \in [N]} g_i(l_i^1, l_i^0)$. For simplicity, we first restrict our attention to the planning of the patrol routes at only *current* period without looking into the future periods. We illustrate at the end of this section how our techniques can be generalized to planning with look-ahead.

When designing the current patrol routes, the patrolling level l_i^0 at the previous period has already happened, thus is fixed. Therefore, only the input l_i^1 for g_i is under our control. To that end, for notational convenience we will simply view g_i as a function of l_i^1. In fact, we further omit the superscript "1" and use l_i as the variable of function g_i for simplicity. We start by illustrating the computational intractability of the problem. The following theorem implies that the problem of patrolling optimization to maximize attack detection (with inputs: a time-unrolled graph G with $N \times T$ nodes, $\{g_i(j)\}_{i \in [N], j \in [m]}$, $\{\alpha_l\}_{l \in [m]}$) is unlikely to have a provably efficient polynomial time algorithm.

Theorem 4.1 *It is NP-hard to compute the optimal patrolling strategy.*

The underlying intuition is that patrolling a cell at different levels results in different "values" (i.e., the number of detected attacks). Given a fixed budget of patrolling resources, we need to determine which cell has what patrolling level so that it maximizes the total "value." This turns out to encode the Knapsack problem, which is weakly NP-hard.

Next, we propose a novel mixed integer linear program (MILP) to solve the problem. We start by observing that the following abstractly described mathematical program (MP), with integer variables $\{l_i\}_{i=1}^N$ and real variables $\{x_i\}_{i=1}^N$, encodes the problem.

$$
\begin{aligned}
\text{maximize} \quad & \sum_{i=1}^N g_i(l_i) \\
\text{subject to} \quad & \alpha_{l_i} \le x_i \le \alpha_{l_i+1}, && \text{for } i \in [N] \\
& l_i \in \{0, 1, \ldots, m\}, && \text{for } i \in [N] \\
& (x_1, \ldots, x_N) \text{ is an implementable effort vector.}
\end{aligned}
$$

$$(4.1)$$

We remark that in equation (4.1), the constraint $\alpha_{l_i} \le x_i < \alpha_{l_i+1}$ is relaxed to $\alpha_{l_i} \le x_i \le \alpha_{l_i+1}$. This is without loss of generality since, in practice, if $x_i = \alpha_{l_i+1}$ for some cell i, we can decrease x_i by a negligible amount of effort and put it anywhere feasible. This will not violate the feasibility constraint but makes x_i strictly less than α_{l_i+1}.

Though equation 4.1 has complicated terms like $g_i(l_i)$ and α_{l_i} which are *nonlinear* in the variable l_i, we show that it can nevertheless be "linearized" to become a compactly represented MILP. The main challenge here is to eliminate these nonlinear terms. To do so, we introduce m new *binary* variables $\{z_i^j\}_{j=1}^m$, for each i, to encode the integer variable l_i and linearize the objective and constraints of equation 4.1 using the new variables. Specifically, we will set $z_i^j = 1$ if and only if $l_i \le j$. As a result, we have $l_i = \sum_{j=1}^m z_i^j$, $\alpha_{l_i} = \sum_{j=1}^m z_i^j(\alpha_i^j - \alpha_i^{j-1})$, etc., which can be represented as linear functions of z_i^j. By properly constraining the new variables $\{z_i^j\}_{i,j}$, we obtain the following novel MILP (equation 4.2), which we show is equivalent to equation 4.1. Equation 4.2 has binary variables $\{z_i^j\}_{i \in [N], j \in \{1, \ldots, m\}}$ (thus mN binary variables), continuous effort value variables $\{x_i\}_{i \in [N]}$ and flow variables $\{f_e\}_{e \in E}$. Note, however, $g_i(j)$ are constants given by the black-box attacker model.

By conventions, $\sigma^+(v)$ $(\sigma^-(v))$ denotes the set of edges that enter into (exit from) any node v.

maximize $\sum_{i=1}^{N}(g_i(0) + \sum_{j=1}^{m} z_i^j \times$
$[g_i(j) - g_i(j-1)])$

subject to $x_i \geq \sum_{j=1}^{m} z_i^j \cdot [\alpha_j - \alpha_{j-1}],$ for $i \in [N]$

$x_i \leq \alpha_1 + \sum_{j=1}^{m} z_i^j \cdot [\alpha_{j+1} - \alpha_j],$ for $i \in [N]$

$z_i^1 \geq z_i^2 \cdots \geq z_i^m,$ for $i \in [N]$

$z_i^j \in \{0,1\},$ for i,j (4.2)

$x_i = \sum_{t=1}^{T} \left[\sum_{e \in \sigma^+(v_{t,i})} f_e \right],$ for $i \in [N]$

$\sum_{e \in \sigma^+(v_{t,i})} f_e = \sum_{e \in \sigma^-(v_{t,i})} f_e,$ for $v_{t,i} \neq s, d$

$\sum_{e \in \sigma^+(v_{T,1})} f_e = 1$

$\sum_{e \in \sigma^-(v_{1,1})} f_e = 1$

$0 \leq x_i \leq 1, \quad 0 \leq f_e \leq 1,$ for i, e

Theorem 4.2 *Equation 4.2 is equivalent to the equation 4.1.*

Generalizations

These techniques can be easily generalized to handle more general tasks and models. First, it is applicable to any defender objective that is linear in g_i, not necessarily the particular one in equation 4.1. For example, if the attacks at different cells have different impacts, we can generalize the objective to be a weighted sum of g_i. Second, the assumption that g_i depends discretely on the patrol level is equivalent to assuming that g_i is a piece-wise *constant* function of x_i. This can be further generalized. Particularly, when g_i is a piece-wise *linear* function of x_i, we can still use a similar MILP to solve the problem with a slightly more involved formulation of the objective [e.g., Wolsey 1998]. Finally, when g_i is a Lipschitz continuous function in x_i, its piece-wise linear approximation usually serves as a good estimation of g_i.

Generalization to Route Design with Look-Ahead

We now illustrate how the previous techniques can be generalized to patrol design with look-ahead. The designer will plan for multiple periods and needs to take into account the effect of current patrolling on the next period's prediction. For simplicity, we focus on planning for two periods: the current period 1 and the next period 2. The approach presented here can be generalized to planning for any small number of periods. Moreover, in the real-world domain we focus on, there is usually no need for a long-term patrol plan because patrolling resources and environments are dynamic – new plans will need to be frequently designed. The optimal planning for two periods can be formulated as the following MP. Note that here we bring back the omitted superscripts for l_i to indicate different time periods. Moreover, we use g^1, g^2 to denote the prediction function at period 1 and 2 respectively. We note that equation 4.3 can be similarly reformulated as an MILP by employing the techniques above.

$$
\begin{aligned}
\text{maximize} \quad & \sum_{i=1}^{N} [g_i^2(l_i^2, l_i^1) + g_i^1(l_i^1, l_i^0)] \\
\text{subject to} \quad & \alpha_{l_i^2} \le x_i^2 \le \alpha_{l_i^2+1}, && \text{for } i \in [N] \\
& \alpha_{l_i^1} \le x_i^1 \le \alpha_{l_i^1+1}, && \text{for } i \in [N] \\
& l_i^2 \in \{0, 1, \ldots, m\}, && \text{for } i \in [N] \\
& l_i^1 \in \{0, 1, \ldots, m\}, && \text{for } i \in [N] \\
& \mathbf{x}^2, \mathbf{x}^1 \text{ are both implementable effort vectors.}
\end{aligned}
$$

$$(4.3)$$

Increasing Unpredictability via Entropy Maximization

The algorithms in the previous section output only a flow $\{f_e\}_{e \in E}$ together with the corresponding effort vector. To implement this effort vector in the real world, one needs to decompose the flow into an executable mixed strategy, i.e., a distribution over deterministic patrolling routes. The classical approach is to use a standard flow decomposition algorithm. Unfortunately, these algorithms often output a decomposition with a very small number of route choices. For example, in one real-world patrol post we tested, the optimal mixed strategy we obtained essentially randomizes over only two patrol routes, as depicted in Figure 4.2 (the dark black node in the middle is the patrol post).

Despite its optimality, such a mixed strategy is problematic due to its lack of randomness and unpredictability. First, since there are only two routes, the poacher can quickly learn these patrolling routes. Then, knowing these two routes, a poacher can easily figure out where the patroller will be at any time during the day by simply looking at whether their initial move is to the northeast or southwest, since this initial move uniquely indicates which route the patroller takes.

To overcome this issue, we turn to the notion of (Shannon) entropy, which is a measure of the average randomness of a random distribution. We thus seek to compute a mixed strategy that implements the (same) optimal effort vector but is the "most random" in the sense that it has the maximum possible (Shannon) entropy. The underlying intuition is that the increased randomness will make patrolling more unpredictable even when poachers can observe part

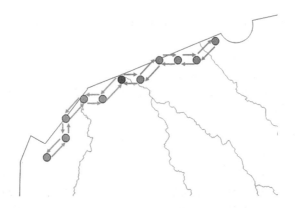

Figure 4.2 Two patrol routes from a post.

of the patroller's movement. A thorough experimental justification of the max-entropy approach is provided in a later section.

The max-entropy distribution is usually difficult to compute since the support of the distribution is very large – in particular, it is supported on the set of all s to d paths, which is exponentially large. Fortunately, in our setting the max-entropy distribution can be efficiently computed via a delicate algorithm combining convex analysis, combinatorial algorithm design, and duality. We refer the curious reader to Xu et al. (2017) for details.

Real-World Dataset

Our analysis focuses on a real-world wildlife crime dataset from Uganda's QEPA. QEPA spans approximately 2,520 km^2 and is patrolled by wildlife park rangers. While on patrol, they collect data on animal sightings and signs of illegal human activity (e.g., poaching, trespassing). In addition to this observational data, the dataset contains terrain information (e.g., slope, vegetation), distance data (e.g., nearest patrol post), animal density, and the kilometers walked by rangers in an area (i.e., effort).

We divide QEPA into 1 km^2 grid cells and compute several features based on the dataset's contents (e.g., observations, terrain, effort). Additionally, we group the observations and effort values (i.e., the values that change over time) into a series of month-long time steps. Finally, we compute two effort features, previous effort and current effort, that represent the amount of patrolling effort expended by rangers in the previous time step and current time step, respectively. Because effort is a continuous value (0 to ∞), we discretize the effort values into m effort groups (e.g., $m = 2$: high and low).

Predictive Model Analysis

In this section, we analyze an example attack prediction model that can predict poaching activity for the real-world dataset described in the previous section using an ensemble of decision trees [Gholami et al. 2017]. This model can serve as the black-box attack function $g_i(l_i)$ for OPERA and, indeed, will be used to evaluate OPERA in the next section.

The goal of the analysis is two-fold. First, we analyze the performance of the prediction model to verify that it is a realistic model that can provide $g_i(l_i)$. Second, we analyze how the model's predictions change as a function of ranger effort, which can provide intuition on why planning patrols using OPERA can help increase the efficiency of patrols.

Note that although the hybrid model proposed by Gholami et al. (2017) is currently the best-performing predictive model in this domain, conducting such an analysis on this model may be confounded by its complexity. For instance, the hybrid model's reaction to a change in effort may be due to the underlying bagging ensemble's reaction, or it may be due to a reaction in the Markov random field that boosts predictions under specific conditions. For scientific rigor, we instead focus on the analysis of a single model's reactivity – the bagging ensemble (which outperforms the previously most accurate model by Kar et al. (2017)).

Ensemble Model

Bagging (bootstrap aggregation technique) is an ensemble method (in this case applied to decision trees) in which each tree is trained on a bootstrap replicate of the whole dataset. The subsets are generated by randomly choosing, with replacement, M observations where M is the dataset size. Once all trees in the ensemble are trained, the ensemble's predictions are generated by averaging the predictions from each tree. We trained a bagging ensemble using the *fitcensemble* function in MATLAB. For this model, the best training period consists of five years of data (based on repeated analyses for different train/test splits). As described in the previous section, the 11 input features consist of terrain and geospatial features, and two patrol effort features (one for the previous time step's effort and one for current effort). Each data point's label corresponds to whether an attack was detected at that cell. For the training set, the label will be 1 if at any point in the training period an attack was detected (0 otherwise). For the test set, the label will be 1 if an attack was detected during the current time step.

We present results for a bagging ensemble on a three-month time scale where the ensemble is trained on five years of data (effort values are in

Table 4.1. *Model performances*

Model	F1	Precision	Recall	PR-AUC
TrainBaseline	0.4	0.25	0.96	-
RUSBoost	0.21	0.12	0.96	0.28
AdaBoost	0.49	0.35	0.82	0.50
Bagging	**0.65**	**0.52**	**0.86**	**0.79**

three-month chunks) and is used to predict detections for a test period of three months. The test set corresponds to September through November 2016, and the training set contains data for 2,129 patrolled cells from September 2012 to August 2016.

In Table 4.1, we present prediction performance results as verification that subsequent analyses are done on a realistic model. We also present baseline results from common boosting models – AdaBoost and RUSBoost [Seiffert et al. 2010]. Additionally, we present a baseline, TrainBaseline, where if an attack was detected at a cell in the training data, the baseline will predict a detected attack for the test data (for cells that were not patrolled in the training data, and thus there is no training sample for that cell, a uniform random binary prediction is made). Due to the large class imbalance present in the dataset (many more negative labels than positives), we compute the area under a precision–recall curve (PR-AUC[1]) instead of the standard ROC curve (which is not as informative for such a dataset) [Davis and Goadrich 2006]. We also present F1, precision, and recall scores.

As can be seen, the bagging model outperforms all other models in terms of F1, precision, and PR-AUC. While bagging does not always score the highest in recall, its precision score greatly outperforms that of the other models. In practical terms, this means that the bagging model will predict far fewer false positives and can thus better ensure that the patrol generation algorithm is not needlessly sending rangers to areas where they will not detect attacks.

Effort Function Analysis

The goal of the patrol generation algorithm is to allocate effort such that the total number of attack detections (poaching activity) is maximized. For the following analysis, we examine how the bagging ensemble's predictions change as a function of ranger effort. For example, if we increase effort in an

---

[1] Because TrainBaseline makes binary predictions and thus does not have continuous prediction values, PR-AUC is not computed for TrainBaseline.

Table 4.2. *Prediction changes as function of current effort*

Effort change	$- \rightarrow +$	$+ \rightarrow -$	$+ \rightarrow +$	$- \rightarrow -$
Low to high	119	30	172	1693
High to low	2	110	122	274

Table 4.3. *Prediction probability changes as function of current effort*

Effort change	Inc.	Mean inc.	Dec.	Mean dec.	$+ \rightarrow +$	$- \rightarrow -$
Low to high	1,546	0.16	423	0.09	4	41
High to low	142	0.09	358	0.22	0	8

area over a period of three months, will rangers detect an attack in that area in any of the three months?

For this analysis, we present the changes in (1) the model's detected attack predictions $g_i(l_i)$ and (2) the model's detected attack prediction probabilities when the effort in the current time step is changed. Both values are computed by MATLAB's *predict* function for our learned ensemble. We refer to effort group 0 as low and group 1 as high; an increase in allocated effort, for example, would result in l_i changing from low to high. Results for changes in predictions and prediction probabilities are shown in Tables 4.2 and 4.3 respectively. In the tables, "$-, +$" denote negative and positive predictions, respectively; "$+ \rightarrow +$" means both predictions are positive, thus there is no change (similar for "$- \rightarrow -$").

In Table 4.2, for each type of change in effort (low to high or high to low), there are three possible outcomes for a prediction change: a negative prediction (no detection) can change to a positive prediction (detected attack), referred to as **Neg to Pos**, positive can change to negative (**Pos to Neg**), and there can be no change in the prediction (for either the positive or negative prediction cases). Given these outcomes, we make the following observations. First, there are a substantial number of cells whose corresponding detection predictions do not change as a result of changes in effort. In the case of the unchanged positive predictions, these are predicted to be high-risk cells where rangers will find poaching activity even if they allocate relatively low effort. For unchanged negative predictions, these correspond to low-risk cells that are essentially predicted to not be attacked at all. Second, while there are substantially more instances of predicted detections increasing as a result of increasing effort, there are still some instances of predicted detections decreasing as a result of increasing effort. However, because there is not a rational explanation for this trend, these rare instances are likely due to noise in the model. Finally, we make the same observation regarding the case where detections mostly decrease as a result of decreasing effort while detections increase at only two cells.

For the prediction probability changes in Table 4.3, we examine changes in the prediction probability with increases and decreases, referred to as **Inc.** and **Dec.** respectively (i.e., any increase or decrease), the mean changes in prediction probability for the increase and decrease cases (referred to as **Mean inc.** and **Mean dec.** respectively), and also in the instances where there was no change in the probability for both the positive (i.e., probability ≥ 0.50) and negative (i.e., probability < 0.50) cases (referred to as $+ \rightarrow +$ and $- \rightarrow -$ respectively). First, when effort is increased, many more cells are predicted to have a substantial increased prediction probability (mean change of 16 percent). While a nontrivial number of cells have a decrease in their prediction probability, the mean decrease is approximately half that of the mean increase, with the difference being statistically significant ($\alpha < 0.01$), and is thus interpreted as noise. Second, when effort is decreased, there are many more cells with a decrease in prediction probability than increase. Additionally, the mean decrease in prediction probability is more than twice that of the mean increase (22 versus 9 percent) and is also statistically significant ($\alpha < 0.01$). Finally, as with the prediction changes in Table 4.2, a few cells are low-risk and increasing effort will not result in a corresponding increase in predicted detection probability. While changes in predicted probability do not necessarily correspond to changes in actual predictions (0/1), the shifts in probability do provide a concrete indication of the actual impacts that coverage has on the model's predictions.

Experimental Evaluations

Evaluation of the Patrol Optimization Algorithm

We start by experimentally testing OPERA using the aforementioned real-world data and bagging ensemble predictive model. The inputs to all the tested algorithms are specified as follows: graph G is constructed according to the real-world terrain in QEPA; the function g_i, together with the corresponding $\{\alpha_i\}_{i=1}^m$, are precisely the predictive model described in the previous section for the test period September through November 2016; we set the maximum patrol distance $T = 12$ as suggested by domain experts. Since we are not aware of any previous patrol generation algorithm that deals with attackers described by a black-box machine learning model,[2] we instead compare our patrol optimization algorithms with the following two heuristic planning algorithms. Note that we will also compare OPERA with its preliminary version without entropy maximization, i.e., the Optimal patrol Planning by flow Decomposition (OPD).

GREED: A heuristic patrol planning algorithm that, at any cell i, greedily picks the next cell j such that it is feasible to go from i to j and patrolling cell j at high is the most *beneficial* (results in more predicted attacks than patrolling j at low). If there are multiple such cells, pick one uniformly at random; if there are no such cells, then pick any neighbor cell uniformly at random. To guarantee that the patrol path starts and ends at the patrol post, this procedure continues until time $\lceil T/2 \rceil$ and then the patroller returns via its outgoing route.

RAND: A heuristic patrol planning algorithm that, at any cell i, chooses a feasible neighbor cell j to visit uniformly at random without considering the prediction model. The patroller returns via the same route at $\lceil T/2 \rceil$.

There are 39 patrol posts at QEPA. We test the algorithms on the real data/model at patrol posts 11, 19, and 24, which are the three posts with the most attacks in the three months of our testing. In our data, all posts have fewer than 100 cells/targets reachable from the post by a route of maximum duration $T = 12$ and all the algorithms scale very well to this size (the MILP takes at most two seconds in any tested instance). We thus focus on comparing these algorithms' ability in detecting attacks under multiple criteria, as follows:

- **#Detection**: total number of detected attacks under the prediction model. Since the prediction model we adopt is a 0–1 classification algorithm, in this case **#Detection** also equals the number of cells at which the corresponding patrolling levels result in detected attacks. However, here we exclude those cells for which high or low patrol effort results in the same prediction because patrolling levels at these cells do not make a difference to the criterion.
- **#Cover**: total number of cells that are patrolled with high. Note that due to limited resources, not every cell – in fact, only a small fraction of the cells – can be covered with high.
- **#Routes**: the number of different patrol routes in 90-day route samples (corresponding to a three-month patrolling period).
- **Entropy**: the entropy of the empirical distribution of the 90 samples.

---

[2] Most previous algorithms either require knowledge of the patroller's and poacher's payoffs [Fang et al. 2015; Haas and Ferreira 2017] which are not available in our setting, or generate patrolling strategies that are not guaranteed to be implementable [Nguyen et al. 2016].

Table 4.4. *Comparisons of different criteria for post 11*

	#Detection	#Cover	#Routes	Entropy
OPERA	15/19	20/47	61	4.0
OPD	15/19	20/47	10	2.0
GREED	5/19	4/47	84	4.4
RAND	4/19	6/47	89	4.5

Table 4.5. *Comparisons of different criteria for post 19*

	#Detection	#Cover	#Routes	Entropy
OPERA	6/6	24/72	22	2.6
OPD	6/6	24/72	6	1.3
GREED	2/6	2/72	1	0
RAND	2/6	6/72	90	4.5

Note that the last two criteria are used particularly to compare the unpredictability of these algorithms in an environment with partial observations by the attacker. A higher value of **#Routes** means that the patroller has more choices of patrol routes, therefore the patrolling strategy is less explorable by the poacher. **Entropy** is a natural measure to quantify uncertainty. The experimental results for patrol posts 11 and 19 are shown in Tables 4.4 and 4.5, respectively. The results for post 24 are similar to those for post 19, and are omitted here to avoid repetition. For the **#Detection** criterion, a/b means that out of the b cells for which low or high makes a prediction difference, a of them are "hit" correctly – i.e., patrolled at the right level that results in predicted attack detection – by the patrolling algorithm. For example, in Table 4.4, the "15/19" comes from the following: there are 19 cells at the post for which patrol level high or low makes a difference in attack detection; the patrol levels by OPERA result in positive attack detections in 15 out of these 19 cells. For the **#Cover** criterion, a/b means that out of b cells in total, a cells are patrolled with high. From the analysis in the previous section we know that compared to the low patrol level, the high patrol level is more likely to result in attack detections. Therefore, a larger **#Cover** value will be preferred in our comparisons.

As we can see from both tables, OPERA and OPD[3] result in significantly more detected attacks and cells with high coverage than the GREED and

---

[3] They always have the same **#Detection** and **#Cover** since they are both optimal.

RAND heuristics. GREED results in slightly more detected attacks than RAND, but RAND covers more cells with `high`. This is because GREED biases toward cells that need more patrolling, thus easily concentrates on these cells. For the **#Routes** and **Entropy** criteria, RAND is the most unpredictable (as expected). GREED is unstable. Particularly at patrol post 19, GREED always chooses the same path. This is because it reaches a cell for which `high` is better and always gets stuck at the same cell due to its greedy choice. This is a critical drawback of GREED. In fact, the same phenomenon is also observed at post 24. Clearly, OPERA exhibits more unpredictability than OPD, and is more stable than GREED. This shows that among these tested algorithms, OPERA provides the best balance among unpredictability, stability, and the ability to detect attacks and cover more cells.

Comparisons with the Past Patrol Routes

We now compare the patrol routes generated by OPERA with the past patrol routes used by rangers at QEPA. We adopt the measures in the previous subsection. Since there is no ground truth (for the past patrolling, we do not know what happened at those cells that are not patrolled), as an approximation we will treat the bagging ensemble predictive model as the ground truth. This is a reasonable choice since Gholami et al. (2017) recently showed that this model outperforms all previous poaching prediction models and provides relatively accurate predictions on the QEPA dataset.

The results are jointly presented in Table 4.6. As we can see, the patrol routes generated by OPERA clearly outperform past patrolling in terms of the **#Detections** and **#Cover** criteria. Particularly, the routes we generate can detect attacks on most (if not all) cells by properly choosing their patrolling levels, and also result in more cells covered with `high`. In terms of unpredictability, the past patrolling does not have stable performance. Particularly, it follows only a few routes at post 11 and 24 with low unpredictability

Table 4.6. *Comparisons of Different Criteria at different Patrol Posts*

Criteria	Post 11		Post 19		Post 24	
	OPERA	Past	OPERA	Past	OPERA	Past
#Detections	15/19	4/19	6/6	5/6	4/4	3/4
#Cover	20/47	6/47	24/72	11/72	20/59	14/59
#Routes	61	4	22	33	34	5
#Entropy	4.0	1.2	2.6	3	2.8	1.4

but takes many different routes at post 19 with high unpredictability. This is a consequence of various factors at different posts, such as patrollers' preferences, location of the patrol post (e.g., inside or at the boundary of the area), and terrain features. On the other hand, OPERA always comes with a good unpredictability guarantee. This shows the advantage of OPERA over the past patrolling.

Conclusion

In this chapter, we presented a general patrol planning framework OPERA. It can optimize against a wide range of prediction models and generate implementable patrol strategies. In addition, OPERA maximizes the randomness of generated strategies and increases robustness against partial information leakage (i.e., poachers may infer the patroller's patrolling route by monitoring part of the patroller's movements). Experimental results on a real-world dataset from Uganda's QEPA show that OPERA results in better defender strategies than heuristic planning algorithms and the past real patrol routes used by rangers at QEPA in terms of defender utility, coverage of the area, and unpredictability.

Acknowledgements

Part of this research was supported by NSF grant CCF-1522054. Fei Fang is partially supported by the Harvard Center for Research on Computation and Society fellowship.

References

Critchlow, R., Plumptre, A.J., Alidria, B., et al. 2016. Improving Law-Enforcement Effectiveness and Efficiency in Protected Areas Using Ranger-Collected Monitoring Data. *Conservation Letters*.

Davis, J., and Goadrich, M. 2006. The Relationship Between Precision-Recall and ROC Curves. In: *Proceedings of the 23rd International Conference on Machine Learning*. ICML.

Di Marco, M., Boitani, L., Mallon, D., et al. 2014. A retrospective evaluation of the global decline of carnivores and ungulates. *Conservation Biology*, **28**(4), 1109–1118.

Fang, F., Stone, P., and Tambe, M. 2015. When Security Games Go Green: Designing Defender Strategies to Prevent Poaching and Illegal Fishing. In: *Twenty-Fourth International Joint Conference on Artificial Intelligence.* AAAI Press.

Fang, F., Nguyen, T.H., Pickles, R., et al. 2016. Deploying PAWS: Field Optimization of the Protection Assistant for Wildlife Security. In: *Twenty-Eighth IAAI Conference.* AAAI Press.

Gholami, S., Ford, B., Fang, F., et al. 2017. Taking it for a Test Drive: A Hybrid Spatio-Temporal Model for Wildlife Poaching Prediction Evaluated Through a Controlled Field Test. In: *Proceedings of the European Conference on Machine Learning & Principles and Practice of Knowledge Discovery in Databases.* Springer.

Haas, T. C., and Ferreira, S.M. 2017. Optimal Patrol Routes: Interdicting and Pursuing Rhino Poachers. *Police Practice and Research,* **19**, 61–82.

Haghtalab, N., Fang, F., Nguyen, T.H., et al. 2016. Three Strategies to Success: Learning Adversary Models in Security Games. In: *Proceedings of the Twenty-Fifth International Joint Conference on Artificial Intelligence.* AAAI Press.

Kar, D., Ford, B., Gholami, S., et al. 2017. Cloudy with a Chance of Poaching: Adversary Behavior Modeling and Forecasting with Real-World Poaching Data. In: *Proceedings of the 16th Conference on Autonomous Agents and MultiAgent Systems.* International Foundation for Autonomous Agents and Multiagent Systems.

Moreto, W. 2013. *To conserve and protect: examining law enforcement ranger culture and operations in Queen Elizabeth National Park, Uganda.* Ph thesis, Rutgers University Graduate School Newark, Newark, NJ.

Nguyen, T.H., Yang, Rong, Azaria, Amos, Kraus, Sarit, and Tambe, Milind. 2013. Analyzing the Effectiveness of Adversary Modeling in Security Games. In: Proceedings of the Twenty-Seventh AAAI Conference on Artificial Intelligence. AAAI Press.

Nguyen, T.H., Sinha, A., Gholami, S., et al. 2016. CAPTURE: a new predictive anti-poaching tool for wildlife protection. In: *Proceedings of the 2016 International Conference on Autonomous Agents & Multiagent Systems.* International Foundation for Autonomous Agents and Multiagent Systems.

Nyirenda, V.R., and Chomba, C. 2012. Field Foot Patrol Effectiveness in Kafue National Park, Zambia. *Journal of Ecology and the Natural Environment,* **4**(6), 163–172.

Seiffert, C., Khoshgoftaar, T.M., Van Hulse, J., and Napolitano, A. 2010. RUSBoost: A Hybrid Approach to Alleviating Class Imbalance. *IEEE Transactions on Systems, Man, and Cybernetics-Part A: Systems and Humans,* **40**(1), 185–197.

Shieh, E., An, B., Yang, R., et al. 2012. Protect: A Deployed Game Theoretic System to Protect the Ports of the United States. Pages In: *Proceedings of the 11th International Conference on Autonomous Agents and Multiagent Systems, Volume 1.* International Foundation for Autonomous Agents and Multiagent Systems.

Wolsey, L.A. 1998. *Integer programming.* New York: Wiley-Interscience.

Xu, H., Ford, B., Fang, F., et al. 2017. Optimal Patrol Planning for Green Security Games with Black-Box Attackers. In: *International Conference on Decision and Game Theory for Security.* Springer.

Xu, H., Tambe, M., Dughmi, S., and Noronha, V.L. 2018. Mitigating the Curse of Correlation in Security Games by Entropy Maximization. In: *Proceedings of the 17th International Conference on Autonomous Agents and Multiagent Systems.* International Foundation for Autonomous Agents and Multiagent Systems.

Yang, R., Ford, B., Tambe, M., and Lemieux, A. 2014. Adaptive Resource Allocation for Wildlife Protection Against Illegal Poachers. In: *Proceedings of the 2014 International Conference on Autonomous Agents and Multi-agent Systems.* International Foundation for Autonomous Agents and Multiagent Systems.

Yin, Z., Jiang, A.X., Tambe, M., et al. 2012. TRUSTS: Scheduling Randomized Patrols for Fare Inspection in Transit Systems Using Game Theory. *AI Magazine*, **33**(4), 59.

5

Automatic Detection of Poachers
and Wildlife with UAVs

Elizabeth Bondi, Fei Fang, Mark Hamilton, Debarun Kar,
Donnabell Dmello, Venil Noronha, Jongmoo Choi, Robert Hannaford,
Arvind Iyer, Lucas Joppa, Milind Tambe, and Ram Nevatia

Introduction

Poaching has been on the rise recently, especially poaching of elephants
and rhinoceroses in Africa. The recent Great Elephant Census (2016) shows
the effect on elephants in particular. With elephant and rhinoceros numbers
dropping rapidly, it is imperative that we act swiftly before they are hunted
to extinction. Multiple strategies exist to combat poaching, including park
ranger patrols, and more recently, the use of unmanned aerial vehicles (UAVs
or drones), such as in the work of Ivošević et al. (2015). In particular,
UAVs equipped with long-wave thermal infrared (hereafter referred to as
thermal infrared) cameras can be used for nighttime surveillance to notify park
rangers of poaching activity, because there is increased poaching activity at
night, and because animals and humans are warm and emit thermal infrared
light. However, the video stream from these UAVs must be monitored at all
times in order to notify park rangers of poachers. Monitoring of streaming
footage is an arduous task requiring human supervision throughout the night,
and is also prone to systematic lapses in quality as human detection often
degrades with fatigue (Porikli et al. 2013). Furthermore, as more drones are
added to the system, more resources are required to monitor the additional
videos.

Whereas previous work in AI has focused on game theory for patrol planning, such as Xu et al. (2017) and Wang et al. (2017), and machine learning-
based poaching prediction, such as Gholami et al. (2017) and Critchlow et al.
(2015), to assist human patrollers in combating poaching, little effort has been
focused on decision aids to assist the UAV crew in detecting poachers and
animals automatically. Given the tedious work of monitoring UAV videos, such
a decision aid is in high demand to help reduce the burden on the personnel in
charge of monitoring, as well as reducing the probability of missing poachers.

It could notify the monitoring personnel or park rangers of a detection, which could then be confirmed. It could even be integrated with existing tools that predict poaching activity and guide human patrols. The integration would lead to a new generation of tools that use machine learning and game theory to guide the patrols of rangers and UAVs simultaneously.

In building this decision aid, there are several major challenges. First, automatic detection in thermal infrared videos captured using UAVs is extremely difficult, because (1) the varying altitude of the UAV can sometimes lead to extremely small images of humans and animals, possibly less than 10 pixels within the images; (2) the motion of the UAV makes stabilization, and consequently human and animal motion detection, difficult; and (3) the thermal infrared sensor itself leads to lower resolution, single-band images, which are very different to typical RGB images. Second, we must provide notification in near real time so the UAV can immediately start following humans in order to provide park rangers with current locations. Real-time detection is an especially difficult challenge due to the limited computing power and internet in the field.

In this chapter, we present SPOT (Systematic POacher deTector), a novel AI-based application that addresses these issues and augments conservation drones with the ability to automatically detect humans and animals in near real time. In particular, SPOT consists of (1) offline training and (2) online detection. During offline training, we treat each video frame as an image, and use a set of labeled training data collected for this application (Bondi et al. 2017) to fine-tune a model that has shown success in detecting objects of interest in images, Faster RCNN. During online detection, the trained model is used to automatically detect poachers and animals in new frames from a live video stream, *showing that modern computer vision techniques are capable of conquering difficulties that have not been addressed before*, namely detection in aerial thermal infrared videos.

We also use a series of efficient processing techniques to improve the online detection speed of SPOT in the field and provide detections in near real time. Online detection can be completed either in the Cloud or on a local computer. Therefore, we have experimented with several different architectures that trade off between local and remote computers, depending on network strength.

Finally, we evaluate SPOT based on both historical videos and a real-world test run by the end-users of a conservation program, AirShepherd (2017), in the field. The promising results from the test in the field have led to a plan for larger-scale deployment, and encourage its use in other surveillance domains.

Problem Domain and Current Practice

Conservation programs such as AirShepherd (2017) send crews to fly UAVs in national parks in Africa (Figure 5.1) in order to notify park rangers of poaching activity. Current parks where AirShepherd operates include Liwonde National Park in Malawi, Ezemvelo KZN Wildlife in South Africa, and Hwange National Park in Zimbabwe. Teams of people are required for UAV missions, including several UAV operators and personnel capable of repairing the UAVs should any damage occur. While flying in a national park, the team generally sets up a base station in a van with all of the necessary equipment, including the UAV, 3D printers for repairs, and laptop computers with some form of internet connection. The UAV of AirShepherd (2017) is a fixed-wing UAV with a range of 50 km that can fly for five hours on one battery charge. It carries an FLIR 640 Vue Pro thermal infrared camera. The UAV flight path is programmed based on typical poaching hotspots or tips. While flying at night, the UAV operators monitor the live video stream, transmitted via radio waves, for any signs of poachers. Should anyone be spotted, the team will manually take control to follow the suspects, notify nearby park rangers who are sometimes on patrol or in the van with the team, and guide them to the poachers. A diagram summarizing this practice is shown in Figure 5.2.

However, as we already mentioned, monitoring these videos all night is a difficult task. Several example frames from thermal infrared videos are also shown in Figure 5.1, with objects of interest highlighted in transparent white boxes on the right. Notice that these frames are grayscale, with few pixels on objects of interest and many objects that look similar to those of interest. It is often a difficult task for humans to recognize objects in these videos – not only is the work extremely tedious, but it is also error prone, especially overnight. As such, there is a great need for a tool that automatically detects poachers and animals, the main objects of interest in these videos for conservation purposes. This tool should be able to provide detections with as much accuracy

Figure 5.1 Example UAV and thermal frames from UAV, with white boxes surrounding poachers.

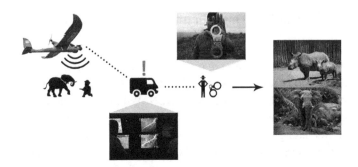

Figure 5.2 UAV team anti-poaching process. Our contribution is meant to help with monitoring at the base station.

as possible, at near real-time speeds on a laptop computer in the field with a potentially slow internet connection.

There has been some effort toward automatic detection. EyeSpy, developed by Hannaford (pers. comm.), the application that is used in current practice, detects moving objects based on edge detection. When in use, it first asks the monitoring personnel to provide parameters such as various edge detection thresholds and sizes of humans in pixels, and then detects these objects as the UAV flies, while taking as input the information from the UAV and camera, such as altitude and camera view angle. Three limitations restrict the use of this tool. First, it relies heavily on a well-trained expert who can manually fine-tune the parameters based on the UAV and camera information, but novices are often unable to find the correct settings for the particular video in the field. Second, the parameters (e.g., thresholds) need to be compatible with flight altitude and camera view angle. To make this tool usable, the UAV crew either needs to restrict the way the UAV flies by keeping the flight altitude and camera view angle almost the same throughout the mission, or have the expert monitoring personnel manually adjust the parameters from time to time as the settings change. Third, this tool cannot differentiate between wildlife and poachers, and thus cannot highlight the detection of poachers to the monitoring personnel or the patrol team. We will examine this tool further in the evaluation section.

Related Work and Design Choices

We arrive at the current framework of SPOT after several rounds of trial and error. As humans and animals are typically warmer than other objects in the

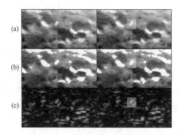

Figure 5.3 Traditional computer vision techniques. (a): original thermal infrared image, (b): thresholded, where white pixels are above the threshold, (c): stabilized frame difference. Original results (left), manually added transparent white boxes around true poachers (right). These figures illustrate the difficulty traditional techniques face in locating poachers automatically, given background noise.

scene, and consequently brighter, we first consider thresholding techniques such as those of Otsu (1979) to separate warmer and cooler objects in the scene. However, other objects such as vegetation often have similar digital counts and lead to many false positives (Figure 5.3(b)). Because humans and animals tend to move, while other objects do not, we also consider motion using algorithms such as Lucas and Kanade's (1981) optical flow, and general correlation-based tracking, such as that of Ma et al. (2015). However, many objects look similar to the objects we want to track, which often leads to tracking vegetation instead (Figure 5.1). Assuming a planar surface, small moving objects can also be detected between two consecutive frames after applying video stabilization, as in Pai et al. (2007). In particular, we used a pixel-wise difference between the stabilized frames. An example of this is shown in Figure 5.3(c), in which there are several "differences" (bright spots) near the humans and trees. As can be seen, motion is often incorrectly detected by this method if the surface is not planar because stabilization applies to a single plane. In the case of tall trees as in Figure 5.3(c), the trees are not in the plane of stabilization and exhibit parallax motion. More complex algorithms to track moving objects throughout videos, such as those of Kristan et al. (2015) and Milan et al. (2016), rely on high-resolution, visible-spectrum videos or videos taken from a fixed camera.

Given the limitations of these traditional computer vision techniques and the great strides in object detection using convolutional neural networks (CNNs), we turn to deep learning-based approaches. A CNN can be viewed as a complex function of the input image, parameterized by a set of weights. More specifically, a CNN is composed of a sequence of layers of nodes (or neurons), and directed edges connecting the nodes in consecutive layers. Each node's value is a function of the values of the nodes at the tail of the incoming edges, with function parameters (weights) to be determined through training. In our case, we treat each frame of the video as an image, and apply techniques to both localize and classify the objects of interest in the images. Faster RCNN by Ren et al. (2015) and YOLO by Redmon et al. (2016) are two state-of-the-art algorithms suitable for this purpose. They both propose regions automatically, and then classify the proposed regions. According to Redmon et al. (2016), Faster RCNN tends to have higher accuracy than YOLO, particularly for smaller objects, although YOLO tends to be faster. A newer version, YOLOv2 by Redmon and Farhadi (2016), has improved performance over YOLO and could be used as an alternative to Faster RCNN. In this work, we focus on using Faster RCNN for detection.

Other emerging techniques such as deep learning-based optical flow or tracking, for example by Zhu et al. (2017) and Fan and Ling (2017), may fail due to drastic UAV motion and low-resolution frames, and they do not classify the objects, only locate them. Tubelets, such as those introduced by Kang et al. (2017), propose bounding boxes over time, but are not performing well enough in real time, even on GPUs. Recently, there has also been some work on automatic wildlife detection and counting based on videos from UAVs using other traditional computer vision or machine learning techniques, but they either rely on RGB images in high resolution, such as Olivares-Mendez et al. (2015), or do not consider real-time detection, such as van Gemert et al. (2014). Due to the unique challenges of our problem, these techniques cannot be applied to detecting poachers during night flights.

SPOT

Overview

SPOT includes two main parts: (1) offline training and (2) online detection (Figure 5.4). In this section, we introduce both parts in detail, with an emphasis on labeling and the robust and faster processing techniques used to improve the online detection efficiency and provide detections in near real time.

Offline Training

In our problem, detection means to localize the objects of interest in the scene, and classify them as poachers or animals. We choose a state-of-the-art object detection algorithm, Faster RCNN, to serve this purpose. Faster RCNN both chooses regions of interest and classifies them. To do this, it is composed of

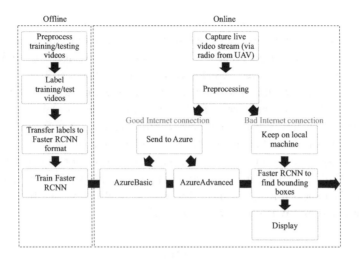

Figure 5.4 SPOT Overview.

a region proposal network (RPN) and the Fast Region-based Convolutional Network method (Fast RCNN) of Girshick (2015). In short, the RPN uses convolutional layers to provide low-level features, followed by additional layers to propose regions. Fast RCNN takes as input a region, and uses convolutional layers to provide low-level features followed by additional layers (pooling, ReLU, fully connected, and softmax layers) to provide classification results for the given region. Both share the convolutional layers of the CNN contained in Faster RCNN to accomplish these two tasks more quickly, with the RPN providing regions of interest for classification. The particular CNN architecture (e.g., number of layers, filters, etc.) that we use within Faster RCNN is VGG-16, which is introduced by Simonyan and Zisserman (2014). In brief, it is a deep CNN with 16 layers.

We must now ensure that Faster RCNN works for our data. In general, the first step in using CNN models is training them based on a set of images (or specific regions within them) and ground truth classification labels, which we call training data. During the training process, a CNN will start with random weights and use them to classify an image in the training set. If it is wrong, the weights will be altered throughout the CNN in order to classify it correctly in the future. After this is repeated for all of the training data, the trained model can then be used for prediction on images that were not in the training data. Faster RCNN is slightly more complex, but has already been trained in a similar way using an enormous database of photographs called ImageNet.

As such, this model can already be used for prediction in new images, often with reasonable performance off-the-shelf. It is called a pre-trained network when it has already been trained. However, our thermal images look different to the images in ImageNet, meaning we must update the Faster RCNN model. To do this, we first initialize the convolutional layers in Faster RCNN with the pre-trained weights from ImageNet. Because we begin with pre-trained weights and adjust them during new training iterations with our data, this process is known as fine-tuning. Note that the pre-trained version of Faster RCNN expects color images, since ImageNet contains color photographs, so we replicate the single-channel thermal infrared frames we have three times to fill the expected RGB channels. The annotated labels for each frame were collected using VIOLA by Bondi et al. (2017).

VIOLA

VIOLA, the application we developed for labeling UAV videos in wildlife security domains, includes an easy-to-use interface for labelers and a basic framework to enable efficient usage of the application, which involves one person labeling a video and a second person reviewing the first person's labels to ensure they are accurate.

User Interface of VIOLA

The user interface of VIOLA is written in Java and Javascript, and hosted on a Cloud computing service so it can be accessed using a URL from anywhere with an internet connection.

Before labeling, labelers are asked to log in to ensure data security (Figure 5.5(a)). The first menu that appears after logging in (Figure 5.5(b)) asks the labeler which mode they would like: whether they would like to label a new video or review a previous submission. Then, after choosing "Label," the second menu (Figure 5.5(c)) asks them to choose a video to label. Figure 5.6 is an example of the next screen used for labeling, also with sample bounding boxes that might be drawn at this stage. Along the top of the screen is an indication of the mode and the current video name, and along the bottom of the screen is a toolbar.

The toolbar contains the controls for the application. First, in the bottom-left corner, is a percentage measurement indicating progress through the video. Then, there are four buttons used to navigate through the video. The two arrows move backward or forward, the play button advances frames at a rate of one frame per second, and the square stop button returns to the first frame of the video. When a new frame is displayed, the bounding boxes on the previous

Log in to ec2-52-35-132-17.us-west-2.compute.amazon
aws.com:8080
Your password will be sent unencrypted.

User Name

Password

☐ Remember this password

                                        Cancel   Log In

(a)

Please select an action:
1. Label
2. Review

Enter your choice:

1

                                        Cancel   OK

(b)

Please select a video:
1. 0000000191_0000000043
2. 0000000301_0000000038
3. 0000000345_0000000000
4. 0000000209_0000000001
5. 0000000305_0000000001
6. 0000000360_0000000000

Enter your choice:

4

                                        Cancel   OK

(c)

Please select an entry to review:
1. Mon Jun 19 21:05:23 UTC 2017
2. Mon Jun 19 21:11:26 UTC 2017

Enter your choice:

1

                                        Cancel   OK

(d)

Figure 5.5 The menus to begin labeling.

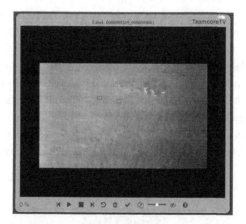

Figure 5.6 An example of a labeled frame in a video. This is the next screen
displayed after all of the menus; it allows the labeler to navigate through the video
and manipulate or draw bounding boxes throughout.

frame are either tracked or copied to the new frame. The navigation buttons
are followed by the undo button, which removes the bounding boxes just
drawn in the current frame, just in case they are too small to easily delete.
Also, to help with the nuisance of creating tiny boxes by accident, there is a

filter on bounding box size. The trashcan button deletes the labeler's progress and takes them back to the first menu after the log-in page (Figure 5.5(b)). Otherwise, work is automatically saved after each change and reloaded each time the browser is closed and reopened. The application asks for confirmation before deleting the labeler's progress and undoing bounding boxes to prevent accidental loss of work. The checkmark button is used to submit the labeler's work, and is only pressed when the whole video is finished. Again, there is a confirmation screen to avoid accidentally submitting half of a video. When selected, the paper button copies the bounding boxes from the current frame to the following frame. Otherwise, tracking is used based on the following slider, which corresponds to tracking search area size. The eye button allows the labeler to toggle the display of the bounding boxes on the frame, which is often helpful during review to check that labels are correct. Finally, the question-mark button provides a help menu with a similar summary of the controls of the application. Animal and poacher labels are differentiated by changing the color of the bounding box.

To draw bounding boxes within the application, the labeler can simply click and drag a box around the object of interest, then click the box until the color reflects the class. Deleting a bounding box is done by pressing SHIFT and clicking; selecting multiple bounding boxes is done by pressing CTRL and clicking, which allows the labeler to move multiple bounding boxes at once.

If "Review" is chosen in the first menu after log-in, the second menu also asks the labeler to choose a video to review, and then a third menu (Figure 5.5(d)) asks them to choose a labeling submission to review. It finally displays the video with the labels from that particular submission, and they may begin reviewing the submission. The two differences between the labeling and review modes in the application are (1) that the review mode displays an existing set of labels; and (2) labels are not moved to the next frame in review mode.

Use of VIOLA

Our goals in labeling the challenging videos in the wildlife security domain are first to keep the data secure, and second to collect more usable labels. In addition, we aim for exhaustive labels with high accuracy and consistency. We first prioritize security because poachers may be able to discern flight locations or patrolling patterns from videos. To achieve these goals, we securely distribute the work among a small group of labelers, assign labelers to either provide or review others' labels, and provide guidelines and training for the labelers.

To keep the data (historical videos from our collaborators) secure, instead of using a service such as Amazon Mechanical Turk, we recruit a small group of student labelers. Labelers are given a username and password to access the labeling interface, and the images on the labeling interface cannot be downloaded. Labeling and reviewing assignments are organized using shareable spreadsheets.

In order to achieve accuracy and consistency of labels, we provide guidelines and training for the labelers. During the training, we show the labelers several examples of the videos and point out the objects of interest. We provide them with general guidelines on how to start labeling a video, and special instructions for the videos in our domain. For example, animals tend to be in herds, obviously shaped like animals, and/or significantly brighter than the rest of the scene, and humans tend to be moving.

VIOLA Development

We were able to make improvements throughout the development of the application to achieve the current version discussed here. In the initial version of the application, we had five people label a single video, which was automatically checked for a majority consensus among these five sets of labels. We used the intersection over union (IoU) metric to check for overlap with a threshold of 0.5, as suggested by Everingham et al. (2010). If at least three out of five sets of labels overlapped, it was deemed to be consensus, and we took the bounding box coordinates of the first labeler. Our main motivation for having five opinions per video was to compensate for the difficulty of labeling thermal infrared data, though we also took into account the work of Nguyen et al. (2013) and Park et al. (2012). The interface of the initial version allowed the user to draw and manipulate bounding boxes, navigate through the video, save work automatically, and submit the completed video. Boxes were copied to the next frame and could be moved individually. To get where we are today, the changes were as listed in Table 5.1.

The most significant change made during the development process was the transition from five labelers labeling the same video and using majority voting to get the final labels (referred to as "MajVote") to having one labeler label the video followed by a reviewer reviewing the labels (referred to as "LabelReview"). We realized that having five people label a single video was very time consuming, and the quality of the labels was still not perfect because of the ambiguity of labeling thermal infrared data, which led to little consensus. Furthermore, when there was consensus, there were three to five different sets of coordinates to consider. Switching to LabelReview eliminated this problem, providing a cleaner and also time-saving solution.

Table 5.1. *Changes made throughout development*

Version	Change	Date	Brief Description
1	-	-	Draws and edits boxes, navigates video, copies boxes to next frame
2	Multiple box selection	March 23, 2017	Moves multiple boxes at once to increase labeling speed
3	Five majority to review	March 24, 2017	Requires only two people per video instead of five to improve overall efficiency
4	Labeling days	April 12, 2017	Has labelers assemble to discuss difficult videos
5	Tracking	June 17, 2017	Copies and automatically moves boxes to next frame

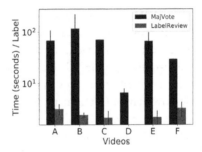

Figure 5.7 Overall efficiency with different labeling frameworks. For Video D, LabelReview is 0.63 seconds/label, with a standard error of 0.09.

Figure 5.7 shows a comparison of overall efficiency between MajVote and LabelReview. The total person-time per final label was lower on average when we used LabelReview, based on data collected in additional tests. We tested two versions of VIOLA using MajVote and three versions using LabelReview, which means the value of each bar is averaged over two or three samples. We exclude one sample for Video C where no consensus labels were achieved through MajVote. The LabelReview efficiency for Video D is 0.63, with a standard error of 0.09. Figure 5.8 shows that there were large discrepancies in the number of labels between individual labelers, which led to fewer consensus labels. Figure 5.9 shows that MajVote leads to fewer final labels than LabelReview in the additional tests as well. This indicates that using the LabelReview framework can get us closer to the goal of exhaustive labels when compared to MajVote.

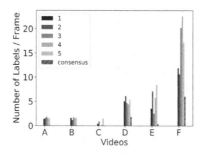

Figure 5.8 Number of labels per frame for individual labelers and for consensus.

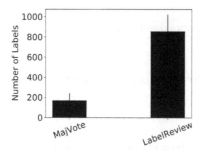

Figure 5.9 Number of final labels for MajVote and LabelReview in additional tests.

Another change, "Labeling Days," consisted of meeting together in one place for several hours per week so labelers were able to discuss ambiguities with us or their peers during labeling. Finally, the tracking algorithm (Algorithm 5.1) was added to automatically track the bounding boxes when the labeler moved to a new frame to improve labeling efficiency, as the labelers would be able to label a single frame, then check that the labels were correct. Given a bounding box in the previous frame, Algorithm 5.1 searches in the same region (plus a few pixels of buffer) in the next frame. The buffer size can be changed by the labeler based on the video. For example, if there is only one object and a significant amount of camera motion, a larger buffer is better. A threshold is used to select only bright pixels within the region in the next frame, and then the bounding box is placed at the center of the largest connected component of the bright pixels. If there is no connected component or the bounding box is too large, we simply copy the bounding box to the same position in the next frame. This is repeated for all bounding boxes in the previous frame.

Algorithm 5.1 Basic tracking algorithm

 1: *buffer* ← *userInput*
 2: **for all** *boxesPreviousFrame* **do**
 3:     **if** *boxSize* > *sizeThreshold* **then**
 4:         *newCoords* ← *coords*
 5:     **else**
 6:         *searchArea* ← *newFrame*[*coords* + *buffer*]
 7:         *threshIm* ← THRESHOLD(*searchArea*, *thresh*)
 8:         *components* ← CCA(*threshIm*)
 9:         **if** *numberComponents* > 0 **then**
10:             *newCoords* ← GETLARGEST(*components*)
11:         **else**
12:             *newCoords* ← *coords*
13:         **end if**
14:     **end if**
15:     COPYANDMOVEBOX(*newFrame*, *newCoords*)
16: **end for**

An example of the tracking process in use is shown in Figure 5.10. First, the labeler drew two bounding boxes around the animals (Figure 5.10(a)), then adjusted the search size for the tracking algorithm using the slider in the toolbar (Figure 5.10(b)). The tracking algorithm was applied to produce the new bounding box location (Figure 5.10(c)). In contrast, the copy feature, activated when the copy button was selected on the toolbar, only copied the boxes to the same location (Figure 5.10(d)). In this case, because there was movement, and the animals were large and far from one another, the tracking algorithm correctly identified the animals in consecutive frames. If several bright objects were in the search region, it could track incorrectly and copying could be better. One direction for future work is to improve the tracking algorithm by setting thresholds automatically and accounting for close objects.

Results of Using VIOLA and Fine-Tuning

Using VIOLA, all frames in approximately 70 videos containing animals and poachers were labeled. Because consecutive frames are often similar, we do not have enough heterogeneous data samples to train VGG-16 from scratch. We therefore start with pre-trained weights for VGG-16 and fine-tune it by treating each video frame as a separate image. Furthermore, we fine-tune different models for poacher and animal detection, so that depending on the mission type, whether monitoring a park for poachers or counting animals, for example, the user may choose a model to provide better detection results. For

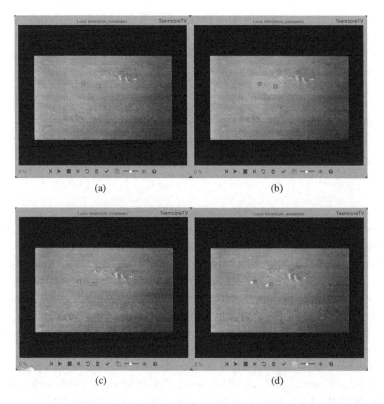

Figure 5.10 Sample labeling process. Animals are labeled (a), then tracking is adjusted (b) and used (c), and finally copying (d) is used instead of tracking.

the poacher-specific model, we fine-tuned using 4,183 frames (six videos), and for the animal-specific model, we fine-tuned using 18,480 frames (20 videos), as we have more animal videos.

Online Detection

Preprocessing

Thermal infrared images can be "black-hot" or "white-hot," meaning warm objects are darker or lighter, respectively. During the online detection, we first ask the user if the video is white-hot, and if the answer is no, we will invert every frame we receive from the UAV. In addition, there is occasionally a border or text on the videos, consisting of date, flight altitude, and other metadata. We ask the users to provide the area of interest at the beginning and display detections in this area of interest only throughout.

Run Faster RCNN

We treat each frame of the video stream as an image and feed it to the trained Faster RCNN as input. The trained model computes a set of regions and classes associated with each region.

User Interface

Figure 5.11 shows the user interface of SPOT for online detection. A file can be selected for detection, or a live stream video can be used. In Figure 5.11(a) we gather preprocessing information about the video, and then begin detection in Figure 5.11(b).

Architectures and Efficiency

According to Ren et al. (2015), Faster RCNN runs at approximately five frames per second (fps) on a K40 GPU. Given that the live video stream produces frames at approximately 25 fps, efficiency and computation speed are paramount for good performance in the field, where there may be limited computational power. We examine several different Microsoft Azure architectures for SPOT, and document several techniques to improve performance in the field and trade off between local and remote computation, particularly due to potential network delays.

The first, and simplest, Cloud architecture we investigate, which we will refer to as AzureBasic, is an NC-6 Series Virtual Machine (VM) with a Tesla K80 NVIDIA GPU hosted on Microsoft Azure 5.12 (Figure 5.12). In order to communicate with this machine, we simply transfer frames from the local laptop to the VM using Paramiko, a Python SFTP client. The remote machine then evaluates the fine-tuned Faster RCNN model to detect objects in the

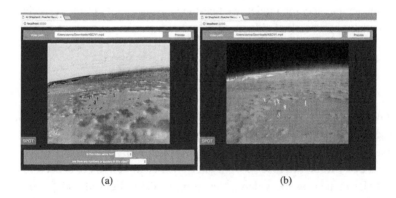

(a)   (b)

Figure 5.11 GUI created for SPOT for use in the field. (a) inquiries about video, (b) detection.

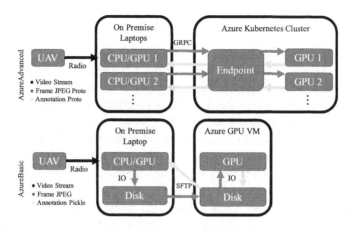

Figure 5.12 AzureBasic and AzureAdvanced overview.

frame. We then display the annotated frame locally using X forwarding. For the purposes of testing, we use Paramiko to transfer annotated frames instead of displaying. Speed could be improved by transferring annotations instead of annotated frames.

Although AzureBasic allows us to improve our throughput through Cloud GPU acceleration compared to a CPU laptop, it is limited to a single Azure GPU VM and a single local laptop linked together by SFTP. To scale up SPOT, we utilize Tensorflow Serving, a framework for efficiently operationalizing trained Tensorflow computation graphs. Tensorflow Serving provides a way to evaluate Faster RCNN without the overhead of file IO, for example. Furthermore, Tensorflow Serving communicates through protocol buffers, a flexible and efficient data representation language that significantly reduces size of large tensors. For serving scenarios with large requests and responses, such as video processing, this reduces network communication and improves performance on slow networks. Tensorflow Serving also supplies tools for creating multi-threaded clients. We use four threads for our tests. Like AzureBasic, we also process the images in batches to ensure that there is no downtime between uploading frames and downloading the results. Finally, we use Azure-Engine to create a cluster of NC-6 series GPU VMs managed with Kubernetes, a fault-tolerant load balancer for scalable Cloud-based services. This keeps the latency of SPOT low in potential computation-intensive, multi-UAV scenarios. We deploy on a GPU-enabled docker image with Tensorflow Serving, and add tools for convenient and automatic redeployment of models hosted on Azure Blob Storage. We refer to this architecture as AzureAdvanced.

Evaluation

To provide a working prototype system, SPOT needs to meet two major criteria: (1) detection accuracy and (2) efficiency. Detection accuracy is most important for poacher identification, particularly to make sure we have few false negatives and false positives. Efficiency is critical to being able to quickly notify monitoring personnel and the ranger team. In this section, we evaluate SPOT in the lab using six historical videos, consisting of 15,403 frames in total, as test video streams. We will first evaluate the performance of the object detection, and then the efficiency, particularly comparing the different methods discussed in earlier sections.

EyeSpy by Hannaford (pers. comm.), the application tool that is used in current practice, requires users to tune eight parameters to correctly identify objects of interest, plus six flight metadata parameters such as altitude and camera angle. Because there are so many parameters, it is often difficult to successfully tune all of them as a novice. On the other hand, our application does not require the user to fine-tune any parameters – it can be used as-is. We therefore consider EyeSpy as used by a novice (ESN). Of our six test videos, only the three animal videos have average flight metadata records (i.e., not flight metadata per frame). For analysis of EyeSpy as used by a novice, we use flight metadata parameters if present, and make educated guesses for altitude if not, in order to get the baseline performance only because inexact flight metadata parameters can severely degrade EyeSpy's performance. Otherwise, we utilize default values for all parameters. We also include results from EyeSpy as used by an expert (ESE). These parameters are adjusted by our collaborator at AirShepherd, Hannaford (pers. comm.), who created EyeSpy. We do not make educated guesses for flight metadata parameters for EyeSpy as used by an expert, again because a lack of exact parameters could drastically reduce performance of EyeSpy, which would not be a fair comparison for the expert level. We record the output from EyeSpy, which is a video with red outlines around objects of interest, and place bounding boxes around any red outlines obtained. We then use an IoU threshold of 0.5 as is typical in Ren et al. (2015). Finally, we choose a low confidence threshold because missing a poacher detection is extremely undesirable, and we report the precision and recall. Precision and recall are numbered between 0 and 1, with 1 being best. Recall is 1 when no positive instances (e.g., poachers) are missed. Precision is 1 when there are no mistakes in the positive classifications. For example, a mistake could be a bush accidentally classified as a poacher.

We compare the performance of SPOT and ESN on videos containing animals or poachers with labels of small, medium, or large average sizes in

Table 5.2. *Precision–recall for SPOT and EyeSpy Novice (ESN) for animals*

Video	Precision		Recall	
	SPOT	ESN	SPOT	ESN
SA	0.5729	0.1536	0.0025	0.0072
MA	0.5544	0.0032	0.0131	0.0058
LA	0.5584	0.0235	0.2293	0.0694

Table 5.3. *Precision–Recall for SPOT and EyeSpy Novice (ESN) for poachers*

Video	Precision		Recall	
	SPOT	ESN	SPOT	ESN
SP	0	0.00003	0	0.0007
MP	0.0995	0.0004	0.0073	0.0009
LP	0.3977	0.0052	0.0188	0.0159
Test	0.4235	0.0024	0.3697	0.0432

Table 5.4. *Precision–recall for SPOT and EyeSpy Expert (ESE) for animals*

Video	Precision		Recall	
	SPOT	ESE	SPOT	ESE
SA	0.5729	0.6667	0.0025	0.0062
MA	0.5544	0.0713	0.0131	0.0162
LA	0.5584	0.0433	0.2293	0.0832

Tables 5.2 and 5.3. We also compare the performance of SPOT and ESE in Table 5.4. We perform better than the novice in both precision and recall for medium- and large-sized poachers and animals. We also perform better than the expert for large-sized animals, and comparably for small- and medium-sized animals. Because we perform better than ESN and similarly to ESE, we thus reduce a significant burden. For small poachers, which is a challenging task for object detection in general, both tools perform poorly, with EyeSpy being able to identify a small number of poachers correctly. Small animals also prove to be a challenge for SPOT. To improve performance for small objects

Table 5.5. *Timing results for CPU, AzureAdvanced (AA),*
AzureBasic (AB), and GPU

	# GPUs	Network	s/img
CPU	0	-	10.4354
AB	1	Fast	0.5785
AB	1	Slow	2.2783
GPU	1	-	0.3870
AA	2	Fast	0.3484
AA	2	Slow	0.4858

in the future, we expect pooling the results of video frames and incorporating motion will be beneficial.

Next, we evaluate the efficiency by comparing CPU performance to the initial Azure system, to the improved Azure system, and finally to the single-GPU performance. The GPU laptop is a CUK MSI GE62 Apache Pro, with Intel Skylake i7-6700HQ, 32GB RAM, 512GB SSD and 2TB HDD, and an NVIDIA GTX 960M, with 2GB RAM, and is deployed in the field. The CPU laptop has an Intel i5-3230M CPU at 2.60GHz. In order to compare the Azure systems, we time how long it takes from the frame being sent to Azure, to the prediction, to the return to the local machine, and finally to reading the final image back into memory. We conducted these tests in two different networking environments: 533.20 Mbps upload and 812.14 Mbps download, which we call "fast," and 5.33 Mbps upload and 5.29 Mbps download, which we call "slow." We repeat the experiment for several images and show the final time per image in Table 5.5. The results show that both AzureAdvanced and the GPU laptop perform detection almost 100 times faster than the CPU laptop, and AzureAdvanced drastically improves over AzureBasic when a slower network is present. Therefore, we can achieve detection in near real time.

Implementation in the Field

In addition to testing in the lab, we also evaluate the in-field performance of SPOT. So far, these tests have been run by AirShepherd at a testing site in South Africa, where training exercises take place. Figure 5.13 shows a screenshot of the testing environment, in which there are seven figures in the scene that should be detected as poachers. During this particular test flight, SPOT was run for approximately half-hour with AzureBasic. Our collaborators at AirShepherd reported that SPOT performed poacher detection well during

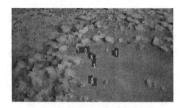

Figure 5.13 A screenshot of the field test environment with annotated figures.

this test flight, and was so promising that they want to move forward with further development and deployment. They also showed excitement because SPOT requires no tuning from the user. Although the network connection was poor for some of the flight and caused detection to occur slowly, especially because AzureBasic was used, the GPU laptop can now provide consistent detection speeds in its place when too slow, which our collaborators also found encouraging, and we also now have the additional option of using AzureAdvanced. With the promising results from the field test, wider deployment is being planned.

Lessons Learned and Conclusion

In conclusion, we developed a system, SPOT, to automatically detect poachers as well as animals in thermal infrared UAV videos taken at night in near real time, which shows that modern computer vision techniques are capable of conquering difficulties that have not been addressed before. This system works in various situations and does not require the user to adjust parameters. Thus, it is easily accessible to users without any training. Furthermore, the system can detect poachers in near real time with either good or bad network connectivity. The system has been tested in the field, and will be deployed in the near future in several national parks in Africa, including one in Botswana. SPOT opens the door for exciting new research questions in object detection in difficult videos, and for new anti-poaching strategies utilizing UAVs in the field.

Acknowledgments

This research was supported by UCAR N00173-16-2-C903, with the primary sponsor being the Naval Research Laboratory (Z17-19598). It was also partially supported by the Harvard Center for Research on Computation and

Society Fellowship and the Viterbi School of Engineering PhD Merit Top-Off Fellowship. Parts of this work were originally published in Bondi et al. (2017) and Bondi et al. (2018). ©2018 AAAI, reprinted with permission.

References

AirShepherd. 2017. *AirShepherd: The Lindbergh Foundation.* http://airshepherd.org. Accessed: November 9, 2011.

Bondi, E., Fang, F., Kar, D., et al. 2017. VIOLA: Video Labeling Application for Security Domains. Pages 377–396 of: *International Conference on Decision and Game Theory for Security.* Springer.

Bondi, E., Fang, F., Hamilton, M., et al. et al. 2018. SPOT Poachers in Action: Augmenting Conservation Drones with Automatic Detection in Near Real Time. In: *Proceedings of the 30th Annual Conference on Innovative Applications of Artificial Intelligence (IAAI-18).* AAAI Press.

Critchlow, R., Plumptre, A.J., Driciru, M., et al. 2015. Spatiotemporal Trends of Illegal Activities from Ranger-Collected Data in a Ugandan National Park. *Conservation Biology,* **29**(5), 1458–1470.

Everingham, M., Van Gool, L., Williams, C. K. I., Winn, J., and Zisserman, A. 2010. The Pascal Visual Object Classes (VOC) Challenge. *International Journal of Computer Vision,* **88**(2), 303–338.

Fan, H., and Ling, H. 2017. Parallel Tracking and Verifying: A Framework for Real-Time and High Accuracy Visual Tracking. *arXiv preprint arXiv:1708.00153.*

Gholami, S., Ford, B., Fang, F., et al. 2017. Taking It for a Test Drive: A Hybrid Spatio-temporal Model for Wildlife Poaching Prediction Evaluated Through a Controlled Field Test. In: *Proceedings of the European Conference on Machine Learning & Principles and Practice of Knowledge Discovery in Databases.* Springer.

Girshick, R. 2015. Fast R-CNN. Pages 1440–1448 of: *International Conference on Computer Vision Workshop.* IEEE.

Great Elephant Census. 2016 (August). The Great Elephant Census, A Paul G. Allen Project. Press Release.

Ivošević, B., Han, Y.G., Cho, Y., and Kwon, O. 2015. The Use of Conservation Drones in Ecology and Wildlife Research. *Ecology and Environment,* **38**(1), 113–188.

Kang, K., Li, H., Xiao, T., et al. 2017. Object Detection in Videos with Tubelet Proposal Networks. *arXiv preprint arXiv:1702.06355.*

Kristan, M., Matas, J., Leonardis, A., et al. 2015. The Visual Object Tracking VOT2015 Challenge Results. Pages 1–23 of: *International Conference on Computer Vision Workshop.* IEEE.

Lucas, B.D., and Kanade, T., 1981. An Iterative Image Registration Technique with an Application to Stereo Vision. *Proceedings of the 7th International Joint Conference on Artificial Intelligence.* Morgan Kaufmann Publishers.

Ma, C., Yang, X., Zhang, C., and Yang, M.H. 2015. Long-Term Correlation Tracking. Pages 5388–5396 of: *Conference on Computer Vision and Pattern Recognition.* IEEE

Milan, A., Leal-T., Laura, Reid, I., Roth, S., and Schindler, K. 2016. MOT16: A Benchmark for Multi-Object Tracking. *arXiv preprint arXiv:1603.00831.*

Nguyen, P., Kim, J., and Miller, R.C. 2013. Generating Annotations for How-to Videos Using Crowdsourcing. Pages 835–840 of: *CHI '13 Extended Abstracts on Human Factors in Computing Systems.* ACM.

Olivares-Mendez, M.A., Fu, C., Ludivig, P., et al. 2015. Towards an Autonomous Vision-Based Unmanned Aerial System Against Wildlife Poachers. *Sensors,* **15**(12), 31362–31391.

Otsu, N. 1979. A Threshold Selection Method from Gray-Level Histograms. *IEEE Transactions on Systems, Man, and Cybernetics,* **9**(1), 62–66.

Pai, C.H., Lin, Y.P., Medioni, G.G., and Hamza, R.R. 2007. Moving Object Detection on a Runway Prior to Landing Using an Onboard Infrared Camera. Pages 1–8 of: *Conference on Computer Vision and Pattern Recognition.* IEEE.

Park, S., Mohammadi, G., Artstein, R., and Morency, L.P. 2012. Crowdsourcing Micro-level Multimedia Annotations: The Challenges of Evaluation and Interface. Pages 29–34 of: *Crowdsourcing for Multimedia.* ACM.

Porikli, F., Bremond, F., Dockstader, S.L., et al. 2013. Video Surveillance: Past, Present, and Now the Future [DSP Forum]. *IEEE Signal Processing Magazine,* **30**(3), 190–198.

Redmon, J., and Farhadi, A. 2016. YOLO9000: Better, Faster, Stronger. *arXiv preprint arXiv:1612.08242.*

Redmon, J., Divvala, S., Girshick, R., and Farhadi, Ali. 2016. You Only Look Once: Unified, Real-Time Object Detection. Pages 779–788 of: *Conference on Computer Vision and Pattern Recognition.* IEEE.

Ren, S., He, K., Girshick, R., and Sun, J. 2015. Faster R-CNN: Towards Real-time Object Detection with Region Proposal Networks. Pages 91–99 of: *Advances in Neural Information Processing Systems.* Curran Associates Inc.

Simonyan, K., and Zisserman, A. 2014. Very Deep Convolutional Networks for Large-Scale Image Recognition. arXiv preprint arXiv:1409.1556..

van Gemert, J.C., Verschoor, C.R., Mettes, P., et al. 2014. Nature Conservation Drones for Automatic Localization and Counting of Animals. Pages 255–270 of: *European Conference on Computer Vision.* Springer.

Wang, B., Zhang, Y., and Zhong, S. 2017. On Repeated Stackelberg Security Game with the Cooperative Human Behavior Model for Wildlife Protection. In: *Proceedings of the 16th Conference on Autonomous Agents and MultiAgent Systems.* International Foundation for Autonomous Agents and Multiagent Systems.

Xu, H., Ford, B., Fang, F., et al. 2017. Optimal Patrol Planning for Green Security Games with Black-Box Attackers. In: *International Conference on Decision and Game Theory for Security.* Springer.

Zhu, Y., Lan, Z., Newsam, S., and Hauptmann, A.G. 2017. Guided Optical Flow Learning. *arXiv preprint arXiv:1702.02295.*

PART II

6

Protecting Coral Reef Ecosystems via Efficient Patrols

Yue Yin and Bo An

Coral reefs are valuable and fragile ecosystems that are under threat from human activities like coral mining. Many countries have built marine protected areas (MPAs) and protect their ecosystems through boat patrols. However, it remains a significant challenge to efficiently patrol the MPAs given the limited patrol resources of the protection agency and potential destructors' strategic actions. In this chapter, we view the problem of efficiently patrolling for protecting coral reef ecosystems from a game-theoretic perspective and propose (1) a new Stackelberg game model to formulate the problem of protecting MPAs, (2) two algorithms to compute the efficient protection agency's strategies: CLP, in which the protection agency's strategies are compactly represented as fractional flows in a network, and CDOG, which combines the techniques of compactly representing defender strategies and incrementally generating strategies. Experimental results show that our approach leads to significantly better solution quality than that of previous works.[1]

Introduction

Coral reefs are precious natural resources and form some of the world's most productive ecosystems, providing complex marine habitats that support a wide range of other organisms. However, some human activities, like coral mining, can severely damage coral reef ecosystems. Once coral reefs are destroyed, it may take tens of years for them to be restored. Therefore, many countries have built MPAs to restrict potentially damaging activities by patrolling the MPAs (Bellwood et al. 2004). It is a great challenge to efficiently protect MPAs

---

[1] A previous version of this work was published in the 25th International Joint Conference on Artificial Intelligence (Yin and An 2016).

through patrolling since protection agencies usually have to protect a large, open water area using very limited resources (e.g., the protection agency in the Yalongwan MPA in China protects an 85 km^2 area with three patrol boats). In addition, potential destructors can learn the protection agency's strategies through surveillance, then choose the most undetectable time and the most covert path in the open water to arrive at a specific area to perform illegal activities. We aim at developing efficient patrol strategies for protecting the coral reef ecosystems.

Though the crisis faced by coral reefs has been investigated by many researchers (Bellwood et al. 2004; Pandolfi et al. 2003), most previous works focus on conservation planning instead of detecting and deferring potential damage (Carwardine et al. 2009). Meanwhile, there has been significant progress on applying game theoretic approaches to security domains like protection of infrastructures (Tambe 2011; Shieh et al. 2012; An et al. 2013; Letchford and Conitzer 2013; Yin et al. 2014, 2015; Wang et al. 2016). In our scenario, the interaction between the protection agency (defender) and the potential destructor (attacker) can also be modeled as a game, but previous work cannot be directly used here due to two new challenges. First, the playfield is a large open water area, and both players' strategies are time-dependent paths, i.e., the defender patrols while the attacker chooses some time to sail to his target area. Second, unlike activities such as igniting a bomb, which can be done quickly, damaging activities at an MPA (e.g., coral mining) only succeed if they last for a relatively long time. Most previous works assume that at most one player takes paths (Basilico et al. 2009; Fang et al. 2015), or that time is irrelevant (Jain et al. 2013) and attack can be done immediately (Gan et al. 2015). For previous works that considered attack duration, they either consider time duration of attacks as external parameters but not part of the attacker's strategy (Alpern et al. 2011), or have different goals from us (Yin et al. 2012; Bosansk et al. 2015). The two new challenges make the strategy spaces of the players larger and more complicated, which leads to great challenges in computation.

This chapter makes four key contributions. First, we propose a defender–attacker Stackelberg game model to formulate the problem of protecting MPAs, in which both game players take time-dependent paths, and payoffs of players are affected by the time duration of the attack. Second, we propose a compact linear program to solve the game, in which we compactly represent defender strategies as fractional flows on graphs to reduce the number of variables in the game. To further scale up the algorithm, our third contribution is a compact-strategy double-oracle algorithm on graphs (CDOG) which combines the techniques of compactly representing defender strategies and incrementally generating strategies. Finally, extensive experimental results show that our algorithms lead to significantly better solution quality than that of other algorithms in the literature, and CDOG scales up well.

Motivating Scenario

Figure 6.1(a) shows the landscape of the Great Barrier Reef Marine Park in Australia. There is an authority (defender) responsible for the protection of the park, with offices located on the coast, shown as stars in Figure 6.1(a). The defender can divide the MPA into several zones to design patrol strategies. Figure 6.1(b) shows an example division. The defender can stay at a zone or take a path among zones. Each zone is a potential attack target. The effect of damaging different zones can be different and is time-dependent. The attacker enters the park at some time, takes a path to his target zone and determines how long to perform activities at this zone. Both agents may be limited to start and finish the path at certain zones, e.g., office locations, peripheral zones in the park (all zones except zone 6 in Figure 6.1(b)). Strategic attackers can observe the defender's patrol strategies, then act considering both defender's strategies and attractiveness of zones. Since performing activities at a zone needs time-consuming preparation (e.g., equipment setup), we assume that the attacker targets a single zone. We did not consider how the attacker escapes after attacking since the coral reefs are damaged anyway after the attack. In addition, before the attacker finishes the attack, he needs to look for a location and operate the equipment, which can make him suspicious; after the attack, he can easily camouflage himself and flee quickly, which makes it difficult to catch him.

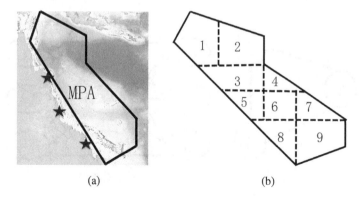

(a)   (b)

Figure 6.1 The Great Barrier Reef Marine Park: (a) landscape and offices; (b) example division.

Model

We model the problem as a Stackelberg game (Tambe 2011) in which the defender commits to a randomized strategy first, then the attacker conducts surveillance and chooses the optimal strategy to respond to the defender's strategy. We first construct a transition graph with a timeline. We denote an MPA as a collection of n zones $Z = \{1, 2, \ldots, n\}$. We evenly discretize a day as a sequence of τ time points $\mathbf{t} = \langle t_1, \ldots, t_\tau \rangle$ with interval δ. Assume that the time needed to travel between two adjacent zones is a multiplier of δ (this assumption holds as long as δ is small enough). Assume that the defender and the attacker travel at the same speed and they only move at time points $t_k \in \mathbf{t}$. Let $D = \langle d_{ij} \in \{1, 2, \ldots\} \rangle$ with d_{ij} representing that the time needed to move from zone i to adjacent zone j is $d_{ij} \cdot \delta$. To represent players' strategies, we construct a directed transition graph $G = \langle V, E \rangle$ where a vertex $v = \langle i, t_k \rangle$ corresponds to zone i and time t_k. There is an edge $e = \langle v = \langle i, t_k \rangle, v' = \langle j, t_{k'} \rangle \rangle$ if one of the following two conditions holds:

1. $j = i, k' = k + 1$. We call such edges *stay edges*.
2. i and j are adjacent zones and $k' = k + d_{ij}$. We call such edges *moving edges*.

Consider a simple MPA graph in Figure 6.2(a) which includes three zones. Let $\mathbf{t} = \langle t_1, t_2, t_3 \rangle$ and $d_{ij} = 1, \forall i, j \in \{1, 2, 3\}, i \neq j$. We can get the transition graph in Figure 6.2(b). The edge between $\langle 1, t_1 \rangle$ and $\langle 1, t_2 \rangle$ indicates that the defender can patrol in zone 1 and the attacker can perform activities in zone 1 during (t_1, t_2). An edge connecting $\langle 1, t_1 \rangle$ and $\langle 2, t_2 \rangle$ indicates that if a player moves from zone 1 at time t_1, he will arrive at zone 2 at time t_2.

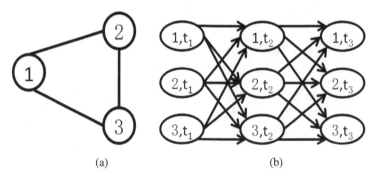

(a)   (b)

Figure 6.2 MPA graph and transition graph: (a) divided MPA; (b) transition graph.

Defender Strategies

Assume that the defender has m resources, i.e., m patrol boats, and each resource can keep patrolling for time duration $\theta\delta$. Let $Z^d \subset Z$ be zones that the defender can start and end her patrol.[2] Since the patrol can start at any time before $t_{\tau-\theta}$, we add a collection of virtual source vertices to the transition graph, i.e., $S = \langle S_1, S_2, \ldots, S_{\tau-\theta} \rangle$. For $S_k \in S$, we add an edge from S_k to vertex $\langle i, t_k \rangle (\forall i \in Z^d)$. Similarly, we add a collection of virtual terminal vertices $T = \langle T_1, T_2, \ldots, T_{\tau-\theta} \rangle$ such that $\forall T_k \in T$, there is an edge from vertex $\langle i, t_{k+\theta} \rangle (\forall i \in Z^d)$ to T_k. Therefore, a patrol strategy P_r of a resource r is a flow from S_k to T_k. A pure strategy of the defender is a set of m "patrol strategy flows," i.e., $P = \{P_r : r \in \{1, \ldots, m\}\}$. A mixed strategy of the defender is a distribution over pure strategies, i.e., $\mathbf{x} = \langle x_P \rangle$ where x_P represents the probability of P being used.

Consider the example in Figure 6.2(b). Assume that $Z^d = \{1, 3\}$ and $\theta = 1$, thus the source vertices and terminal vertices can be added, as is shown in Figure 6.3(a), i.e., S_1 is connected to $\langle 1, t_1 \rangle$ and $\langle 3, t_1 \rangle$, meaning that the defender can start the patrol from zone 1 or 3 at time t_1, while T_1 is connected to $\langle 1, t_2 \rangle$ and $\langle 3, t_2 \rangle$, meaning that patrols starting from S_1 should end in zone 1 or 3 at time t_2. Any flow from S_k to T_k is a feasible patrol strategy, e.g., $S_2 \rightarrow \langle 1, t_2 \rangle \rightarrow \langle 3, t_2 \rangle \rightarrow T_2$ represents that the defender patrols on the way from zone 1 to zone 3.

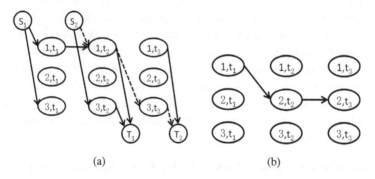

(a)   (b)

Figure 6.3 Strategies as paths in the transition graph: (a) defender strategies; (b) attacker strategies.

---

[2] Our model can be easily expanded to handle cases in which the defender starts from and finishes at different sets of zones.

Attacker Strategies

Assume that the attacker can also start at a subset of the zones $Z^a \subset Z$. An attacker's strategy includes two parts: a path in the transition graph to go to his target zone, and how long he attacks at the target zone. We assume that the attack duration is a multiplier of δ (this holds when δ is small enough) and denote an attacker's strategy as $Y = \langle H_Y, A_Y \rangle$, where H_Y is a path leading to his target vertex $\langle i, t_k \rangle$ and A_Y is a path consisting of l adjacent stay edges, representing that the attacker performs activity at zone i from time t_k to time t_{k+l}. Consider the previous three-zone example. Assume that $Z^a = \{1\}$. Figure 6.3(b) shows a feasible attacker strategy where the attacker enters the MPA from zone 1 at t_1, arrives at his target zone 2 at t_2, then attacks zone 2 till t_3. As previous in work in security games, we restrict attacker strategies to pure strategies (Kiekintveld et al. 2009).

Utilities and Equilibrium

We assume that each stay edge $e = \langle \langle i, t_k \rangle, \langle i, t_{k+1} \rangle \rangle$ in the transition graph has a value of V_e, representing the attacker's payoff of successfully performing activities in zone i during time (t_k, t_{k+1}). If an attacker successfully plays strategy $Y = \langle H_Y, A_Y \rangle$, he gains a utility of $U(Y) = \sum_{e \in A_Y} V_e$, while the defender gets a utility of $-U(Y)$. If the attacker is detected by the defender, he fails and both agents get a utility of 0. The attacker may be detected by the defender if their strategies share the same edges. Specifically, if their paths share a stay edge, the attacker may be detected when he is staying at some zone; if their paths share a moving edge, the attacker may be detected when he is moving from one zone to another. Naturally, the defender may not be able to perform detection every time she meets a boat which could be a potential attacker. To describe the probability that the defender detects a boat, we make the following two assumptions, which are realistic enough to describe most real-world scenarios.

Assumption 6.1 If the defender and the attacker first meet on edge e, the probability that the defender detects the attacker, i.e., the detecting factor of edge e, is $f_e \in [0, 1]$.

The next assumption is about the probability that the defender detects the attacker after they meet for the first time. Since patrol areas are usually somewhere prone to being maliciously damaged but not popular travel sites, a boat appearing in such areas frequently is very suspicious. Therefore, if the defender has met a boat many times on her way before she arrives at edge e, then the boat seems more suspicious than a boat that is seen for the first time on edge e, and thus should be detected with a higher probability than f_e.

Assumption 6.2 Assume that the defender and the attacker have been on the same edges $e_1, e_2, \ldots, e_{k-1}$[3] and the attacker has not been detected. If they meet on edge e_k, the probability that the defender detects the attacker is $\min\{1, \frac{f_{e_k}}{1 - \sum_{i=1}^{k-1} f_{e_i}}\}$.

The probability shown in Assumption 6.2 ranges in $[f_{e_k}, 1]$, which satisfies the intuition that a more suspicious boat should be detected with a higher probability. Based on Assumption 6.2, if the defender's strategy and the attacker's strategy share the same edges $e_1, e_2, \ldots, e_{k-1}, e_k$, let F_{k-1} represent the probability that the attacker is detected on any edge in $e_1, \ldots, e_{k-1}$, then the total probability that the attacker is detected given the defender strategy is $F_{k-1} + (1 - F_{k-1}) \min\{1, \frac{f_{e_k}}{1 - \sum_{i=1}^{k-1} f_{e_i}}\}$. Note that when $k = 2$, $F_1 = f_{e_1}$. Simple recursion results in that, given a patrol strategy P_r of a resource r and an attacker strategy Y, assume that the overlapping edges of P_r and Y are $P_r \cap Y = \langle e_1, e_2, \ldots, e_k \rangle$, then the probability that the attacker is detected by this resource is $\min\{1, \sum_{i=1}^{k} f_{e_k}\}$.

We also assume that when several security resources and the attacker are at the same edge, the security resources can cooperate with each other to come up with a detection probability which is the sum of their respective detection probability capped by 1.[4] Therefore, given a pure strategy of the defender $P = \{P_r\}$ and a pure strategy of the attacker Y, the overall detection probability for the attacker is:

$$dp(P, Y) = \min \left\{ 1, \sum_{r=1}^{m} \sum_{e \in P_r \cap Y} f_e \right\}. \tag{6.1}$$

Based on equation 6.1, given a pair of strategies $\langle P, Y \rangle$, the expected utility of the attacker is $U^a(P, Y) = (1 - dp(P, Y))U(Y)$. Given a mixed strategy $\mathbf{x} = \langle x_P \rangle$ of the defender and a pure strategy Y of the attacker, the attacker's expected utility is $U^a(\mathbf{x}, Y) = \sum_P x_P U^a(P, Y)$, while the expected utility of the defender is $U^d(\mathbf{x}, Y) = -U^a(\mathbf{x}, Y)$.

Our goal is to compute the Stackelberg equilibrium of the game, hence the optimal strategy for the defender. Given the zero-sum assumption, the Stackelberg equilibrium is equivalent to maximizing the defender's utility when the attacker responds the best. Technically, let $\mathbf{X}, \mathbf{Y}$ be the defender's

---

[3] The subscripts are indexes of edges in the players' paths.
[4] If the security resources work independently, the overall detection probability will be higher than is computed by equation 6.1. In this case, the defender strategies computed based on equation 6.1 will lead to a utility which is a lower bound of the defender.

and attacker's strategy space respectively. Let the attacker's optimal response function be $f(\mathbf{x}) = \{Y \in \mathbf{Y}\}$. A pair of strategies $(\mathbf{x}, Y)$ form an equilibrium if they satisfy the following:

$$U^a(\mathbf{x}, f(\mathbf{x})) \geq U^a(\mathbf{x}, Y'), \forall Y' \in \mathbf{Y},$$
$$U^d(\mathbf{x}, f(\mathbf{x})) \geq U^d(\mathbf{x}', f(\mathbf{x}')), \forall \mathbf{x}' \in \mathbf{X}.$$

CLP Based on Compact Representation

The number of the defender's pure strategies increases exponentially as the game size increases. To address this challenge, we compactly represent mixed patrol strategies by marginal coverage c_e on edges e in the transition graph G, i.e., the expected number of patrollers that will be on the edges. Given a mixed strategy $\mathbf{x}$, we have

$$c_e = \sum_P x_P P(e), \forall e \in G, \tag{6.2}$$

where $P(e)$ represents the number of patrols in pure strategy P which go through edge e. Therefore, based on equation 6.2, given a mixed strategy $\mathbf{x}$ and its corresponding coverage vector $\mathbf{c} = \langle c_e : e \in E \rangle$, and given a pure strategy Y of the attacker, the expected attacker utility can be represented as

$$U^a(\mathbf{c}, Y) = (1 - \min\left\{1, \sum_{e \in Y} c_e f_e\right\}) U(Y). \tag{6.3}$$

Our problem now lies in computing the marginal coverage which corresponds to the optimal mixed strategy of the defender. First, we need to construct marginal coverages corresponding to feasible mixed strategies. One challenge of the construction lies in that a mixed defender strategy consists of pure strategies starting from different time points. Yin et al. (2012) have proven that the problem can be solved by constructing an extended version EG of the transition graph G, and considering the marginal coverage as the sum of several flows on EG. Technically, EG is composed of multiple restricted copies of G (i.e., subgraphs of G), corresponding to different possible starting time points for the defender. For the copy corresponding to starting time points t_k, we only keep the subgraph G_k on vertices $\langle S_k, T_k, v = \langle i, t_{k'} \rangle : i \in Z, k' \in \{k, \ldots, k + \theta\}\rangle$. Therefore, any defender patrol strategy starting at t_k can be represented as an $S_k - T_k$ flow in subgraph G_k. Let $z_k(e)$ represent the expected number of patrollers on edge e which come from patrol strategies starting at time point t_k ($z_k(e) \geq 0$). Let $\Gamma(e)$ represent the set of subgraphs which include edge e. Let $c_e = \sum_{k:G_k \in \Gamma(e)} z_k(e)$. Yin et al. (2012) show that if $z_k(e)$ satisfies conservation of flow, a defender mixed strategy which leads to the same utility

---

Algorithm 6.1. CDOG

---

1 Initialize with a subgraph G' of G and a subset $\mathbf{Y}' \subset \mathbf{Y}$;
2 **repeat**
3 | $(\mathbf{c}, \mathbf{y}) \leftarrow \text{CLP}(G', \mathbf{Y}')$;
4 | $P \leftarrow \text{DO}(\mathbf{y}), Y \leftarrow \text{AO}(\mathbf{c})$;
5 | $G' \leftarrow G' \cup \{P\}, \mathbf{Y}' \leftarrow \mathbf{Y}' \cup \{Y\}$;
6 **until** G' *and* $\mathbf{Y}'$ *are not expanded*;
7 return $(\mathbf{c}, \mathbf{y})$

---

as corresponding $\mathbf{c} = \langle c_e : e \in G \rangle$ can be constructed in polynomial time. We present a compact linear program CLP to compute the optimal marginal coverage (the details are in Yin and An 2016).

CDOG Algorithm

The number of constraints in CLP, being the same as the number of attacker strategies, increases exponentially with the game size. This leads to the poor scalability of the LP formulation. To deal with the scalability issue, we propose CDOG, a *compact-strategy double-oracle algorithm on graphs*. CDOG is based on the widely used *double oracle* framework (e.g., Jain et al. 2011). The main idea is to find an equivalent small-size sub-game to avoid solving the original exponentially large game. Specifically, the framework starts from solving a sub-game involving only a very small subset of each player's pure strategy set. The solution obtained, being an equilibrium of the sub-game, is not necessarily an equilibrium of the original game since the players may have incentive to deviate by choosing strategies not in the current strategy subsets. Thus the framework expands the players' strategy sets based on the current equilibrium and gets a larger sub-game. The process is repeated until no player can benefit from expanding their strategy sets. It usually ends with a sub-game with reasonable (instead of exponential) size, and the final solution is provably also an equilibrium to the original game (McMahan et al. 2003).

A traditional double oracle framework can take a long time to converge for large games, since the sub-game is expanded slowly, while once it gets large, solving a sub-game is also very time-consuming. For example, Jain et al.'s algorithm (Jain et al. 2013) solves games with around 200 vertices, corresponding to 10 zones and 20 time points in our model, in around nine hours. To scale it up, CDOG exploits the graph structure of our problem, uses a subgraph of the transition graph (instead of a pure strategy set) to characterize the defender's strategy space, and solves each sub-game through compactly representing defender strategies as coverage on edges in the subgraph. The main structure of CDOG is depicted in Algorithm 6.1. Here, line 1 initializes the sub-game with a random subgraph G' of G and a random subset $\mathbf{Y}'$ of the attacker's pure strategies. Using the LP formulation, line 3 computes the equilibrium of the sub-game, where defender patrols on G' and attacker plays with strategies in $\mathbf{Y}'$. Notably, $\mathbf{c} = \langle c_e \rangle$ is the solution to LP, while $\mathbf{y}$ is an attacker mixed strategy over pure strategies in $\mathbf{Y}'$. Then through lines 4–6, CDOG implements the core of double oracle framework by calling two oracles – *defender oracle* (DO) and *attacker oracle* (AO) – to obtain the players' best responses for expanding the sub-game. The details about how these two oracles are implemented can be found in Yin and An (2016).

Experimental Evaluation

We evaluate the proposed algorithms in terms of (1) solution quality, (2) scalability, and (3) robustness. The CLP is solved by Knitro 9.0.0. Each point in the figures is the average value over 30 sample games. We test the algorithms on graphs based on the geology of the Great Barrier Reef Marine Park as shown in Figure 6.1. Given that the MPA can be divided differently due to different purposes (Watts et al. 2009), in each game in the experiments, we generate an MPA graph based on a random division of the park. We randomly generate the time needed to move between adjacent zones, i.e., d_{ij}, in $[1, \frac{|\mathbf{t}|}{2}]$, where $|\mathbf{t}|$ is the number of time points in the game. Transition graphs are then constructed based on the MPA graphs and d_{ij}s, in which each zone has $|\mathbf{t}|$ copies. We randomly choose the value of each stay edge in (0, 100].

Solution Quality

Solution quality of algorithms is measured by attacker utility. Given the zero-sum assumption, higher attacker utility indicates lower defender utility. We compare our algorithms with two baseline algorithms, ANP and AND. ANP assumes that the attacker does not take paths, but directly attacks anywhere at any time instantaneously, which is similar to Fang et al. (2013). AND assumes that the attacker can take paths in the graph to arrive at a target, but still attacks instantaneously, which is similar to Yin et al. (2012). The baseline algorithms are under extra assumptions since no previous algorithms can exactly solve our problems. We assume three patrollers and nine zones, and divide the timeline into 12 points unless otherwise specified.

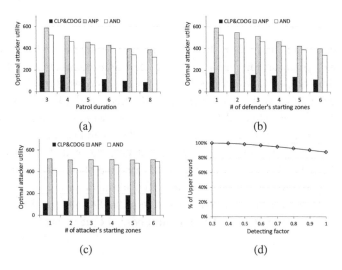

Figure 6.4 Solution quality: (a) increase patrol duration; (b) increase defender's starters; (c) increase attacker's starters; (d) percentage of upper bound.

In Figures 6.4(a)–(c), the y-axis indicates the attacker's utility, while the x-axis indicates the patrol duration of a defender's resource (i.e., the value of θ), the number of starting zones for the defender, and the number of starting zones for the attacker respectively. Since CLP and CDOG lead to the same attacker utility, their results are represented by a single bar. The solution quality of CLP and CDOG is significantly better than that of ANP and AND despite the value of the three parameters. It is unsurprising that as the patrol duration increases (Figure 6.4(a)) or the number of the defender's starting zones increases (Figure 6.4(b)), the attacker utilities computed by all algorithms decrease. As the number of the attacker's starting zones increases (Figure 6.4(c)), ANP's performance is not affected since it does not consider the attacker's paths, while other algorithms show an increasing trend in attacker utilities.

Figure 6.4(d) depicts the percentage of the true optimal defender utility versus the theoretical upper bound returned by CLP and CDOG. The x-axis indicates the maximum value of the detecting factor f_e, i.e., 0.3 indicates that f_e is randomly chosen in $(0, 0.3]$. Equation 6.1 indicates that with smaller f_e, CLP and CDOG are less likely to overestimate the detection probability. Figure 6.4(d) shows a decreasing trend in the percentage of the true defender utility versus CLP and CDOG's results. Fortunately, even when $f_e = 1$, the percentage is still around 90 percent, indicating that the upper bound computed by CLP and CDOG is very close to the true utilities.

Scalability

In Figures 6.5(a) and 6.5(b), the y-axis indicates runtime while the x-axes respectively indicate the number of zones and time points. In both figures, the runtime of CLP shows a much more obvious increasing trend. Actually, CLP cannot solve games with more than 20 targets and 20 time points due to the RAM limit, while CDOG can solve games with 40 targets in around six minutes and games with 50 time points in less than two minutes. We also evaluate the runtime of the defender oracle, attacker oracle, and CLP in CDOG in detail. Table 6.1 shows an example of the runtime of the three parts in the CDOG algorithm, which solves a game after ten iterations. The runtime of the CLP shows an increasing trend. The size of the DO and the AO is barely affected by the iteration, thus their runtime does not change much.

Table 6.1. *Runtime (ms) of CLP and oracles in CDOG*

	Iteration									
	1	2	3	4	5	6	7	8	9	10
CLP	4,301	5,172	5,637	6,131	6,151	6,231	6,332	6,300	6,449	6,547
DO	1,626	1,620	1,650	1,652	1,648	1,715	1,639	1,620	1,640	1,634
AO	328	352	322	323	326	319	320	334	318	320

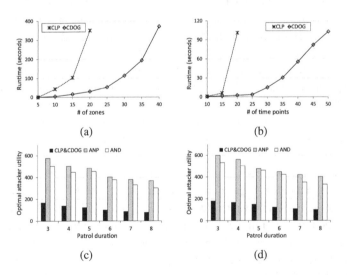

(a)   (b)

(c)   (d)

Figure 6.5 Scalability and robustness: (a) increase targets; (b) increase time points; (c) observation noise; (d) payoff noise.

Robustness

We first consider observation noise of the attacker. We add zero-mean Gaussian noise with standard deviations chosen randomly from $U[0, 0.5]$ to the coverage on each edge observed by the attacker. Figure 6.5(c) shows the attacker utilities considering observation noise for the same class of games considered in Figure 6.4(a). Compared with Figure 6.4(a), all algorithms lead to lower attacker utilities in Figure 6.5(c) since the observation noise prevents the attacker from responding the best. CLP and CDOG still significantly outperform ANP and AND. We also consider payoff noise of the defender. For each stay edge in the transition graph, we add the same Gaussian noise as the previous setting to the defender's knowledge on the value of the edge. Figure 6.5(d) considers the class of games in Figure 6.4(a) with payoff uncertainties. Compared with Figure 6.4(a), all algorithms lead to higher attacker utilities in Figure 6.5(d) since the payoff noise affects the defender's judgement on the attacker's action. The advantage of CLP and CDOG over ANP and AND is still significant.

Conclusion

This chapter models the problem of patrolling MPAs to protect coral reef ecosystems as a defender–attacker Stackelberg game, in which both players' strategies are time-dependent paths, and the payoffs are affected by the duration of the attack. We propose a linear program (CLP) to solve the game, in which defender strategies are compactly represented as flows on graphs. We also propose a more scalable algorithm, CDOG, which combines techniques of compactly representing defender strategies and incrementally generating strategies. Experimental results show that our algorithms lead to significantly better solution quality than that of baseline algorithms, and the CDOG algorithm can scale up.

References

Alpern, S., Morton, A., and Papadaki, K. 2011. Patrolling games. *Operations Research*, **59**(5), 1246–1257.

An, B., Brown, M., Vorobeychik, Y., and Tambe, M. 2013. Security games with surveillance cost and optimal timing of attack execution. Pages 223–230 of: *Proceedings of the 12th International Conference on Autonomous Agents and Multiagent Systems (AAMAS)*. ACM Press.

Basilico, N., Gatti, N., and Amigoni, F. 2009. Leader–follower strategies for robotic patrolling in environments with arbitrary topologies. Pages 57–64 of: *Proceedings of the 8th International Conference on Autonomous Agents and Multiagent Systems (AAMAS)*. ACM Press.

Bellwood, D.R., Hughes, T.P., Folke, C., and Nyström, M. 2004. Confronting the coral reef crisis. *Nature*, **429**(6994), 827–833.

Bosansk, B., Jiang, A.X., Tambe, M., and Kiekintveld, C. 2015. Combining compact representation and incremental generation in large games with sequential strategies. Pages 812–818 of: *Proceedings of the 29th Conference on Artificial Intelligence*. AAAI Press.

Carwardine, J., Klein, C.J., Wilson, K.A., Pressey, R.L., and Possingham, H.P. 2009. Hitting the target and missing the point: target-based conservation planning in context. *Conservation Letters*, **2**(1), 4–11.

Fang, F., Jiang, A.X., and Tambe, M. 2013. Optimal patrol strategy for protecting moving targets with multiple mobile resources. Pages 957–964 of: *Proceedings of the 12th International Conference on Autonomous Agents and Multiagent Systems (AAMAS)*. ACM Press.

Fang, F., Stone, P., and Tambe, M. 2015. When security games go green: designing defender strategies to prevent poaching and illegal fishing. Pages 2589–2595 of: *Proceedings of the 24th International Joint Conference on Artificial Intelligence (IJCAI)*. AAAI Press.

Gan, J., An, B., and Vorobeychik, Y. 2015. Security games with protection externality. Pages 914–920 of: *Proceedings of the 29th Conference on Artificial Intelligence*. AAAI Press.

Jain, M., Korzhyk, D., Vanek, O., et al. 2011. A double oracle algorithm for zero-sum security games on graphs. Pages 327–334 of: *Proceedings of the 10th International Conference on Autonomous Agents and Multiagent Systems (AAMAS)*. ACM Press.

Jain, M., Conitzer, V., and Tambe, M. 2013. Security scheduling for real-world networks. Pages 215–222 of: *Proceedings of the 12th International Conference on Autonomous Agents and Multiagent Systems (AAMAS)*. ACM Press.

Kiekintveld, C., Jain, M., Tsai, J., et al. 2009. Computing optimal randomized resource allocations for massive security games. Pages 689–696 of: *Proceedings of the 8th International Conference on Autonomous Agents and Multiagent Systems (AAMAS)*. ACM Press.

Letchford, J., and Conitzer, V. 2013. Solving security games on graphs via marginal probabilities. Pages 591–597 of: *Proceedings of the 27th AAAI Conference on Artificial Intelligence (AAAI)*. AAAI Press.

McMahan, H.B., Gordon, G.J., and Blum, A. 2003. Planning in the Presence of Cost Functions Controlled by an Adversary. Pages 536–543 of: *Proceedings of the 20th International Conference on Machine Learning (ICML)*. ACM Press.

Pandolfi, J.M., Bradbury, R.H., Sala, E., et al. 2003. Global trajectories of the long-term decline of coral reef ecosystems. *Science*, **301**(5635), 955–958.

Shieh, E.A., An, B., Yang, R., et al. 2012. PROTECT: an application of computational game theory for the security of the ports of the United States. Pages 2173–2179 of: *Proceedings of the 27th AAAI Conference on Artificial Intelligence (AAAI)*. AAAI Press.

Tambe, M. 2011. *Security and Game Theory: Algorithms, Deployed Systems, Lessons Learned*. Cambridge: Cambridge University Press.

Wang, Z., Yin, Y., and An, B. 2016. Computing optimal monitoring strategy for detecting terrorist plots. In: *Proceedings of the 30th Conference on Artificial Intelligence (AAAI)*. AAAI Press.

Watts, M.E., Ball, I.R., Stewart, R.S., et al. 2009. Marxan with zones: software for optimal conservation based land- and sea-use zoning. *Environmental Modelling & Software*, **24**(12), 1513–1521.

Yin, Y., and An, B. 2016. Efficient resource allocation for protecting coral reef ecosystems. Pages 531–537 of: *Proceedings of the 25th International Joint Conference on Artificial Intelligence (IJCAI)*. AAAI Press.

Yin, Y., An, B., and Jain, M. 2014. Game-theoretic resource allocation for protecting large public events. Pages 826–834 of: *Proceedings of the 28th Conference on Artificial Intelligence (AAAI)*. AAAI Press.

Yin, Y., Xu, H., Gan, J., An, B., and Jiang, A.X. 2015. Computing optimal mixed strategies for security games with dynamic payoffs. Pages 681–687 of: *Proceedings of the 24th International Joint Conference on Artificial Intelligence (IJCAI)*. AAAI Press.

Yin, Z., Jiang, A.X., Johnson, M.P., and Tambe, M. 2012. TRUSTS: scheduling randomized patrols for fare inspection in transit systems. *AI Magazine*, **33**(4), 59–72.

7

Simultaneous Optimization of Strategic and Tactical Planning for Environmental Sustainability and Security

Sara M. McCarthy, Milind Tambe, Christopher Kiekintveld, Meredith L. Gore, and Alex Killion

Green security – protection of forests, fish, and wildlife – is a critical problem in environmental sustainability. We focus on the problem of optimizing the defense of forests against illegal logging, where often we are faced with the challenge of teaming many different groups, from national police to forest guards to non-governmental organizations (NGOs), each with differing capabilities and costs. This chapter introduces a new, yet fundamental problem: Simultaneous Optimization of Resource Teams and Tactics (SORT). SORT contrasts with most previous game-theoretic research for green security – in particular based on security games – that has solely focused on optimizing patrolling tactics, without consideration of team formation or coordination. We develop new models and scalable algorithms to apply SORT toward illegal logging in large forest areas. We evaluate our methods on a variety of synthetic examples, as well as a real-world case study using data from our ongoing collaboration in Madagascar.

Introduction

Illegal logging is a major problem for many developing countries. The economic and environmental impacts are severe, costing up to US$30 billion annually and threatening ancient forests and critical habitats for wildlife [WWF 2015]. As a result, improving the protection of forests is of great concern for many countries [Dhital et al. 2015, Allnutt et al. 2013]. Unfortunately in developing countries, budgets for protecting forests are often very limited, making it crucial to allocate these resources efficiently. We focus on deploying resources to interdict the traversal of illegal loggers on the network of roads and rivers around the forest area. However, we must first choose the right security team for interdiction; there are many different organizations that may be involved – from local volunteers, to police, to NGO personnel – each differing in their interdiction effectiveness (individual or jointly with others), and with varying costs of deployment. This results in a very large number of resource teams and allocation strategies per team with varying effectiveness that could be deployed within a given budget. Our challenge is to simultaneously select the best team of security resources and the best allocation of these resources.

Over the past decade, game-theoretic approaches, in particular *security games*, have become a major computational paradigm for security resource allocation [Tambe 2011, Korzhyk et al. 2010]. The sub-area of security games relevant to this chapter is at the intersection of *green security* (i.e., protection of forests, fish, and wildlife) [Fang et al. 2015, Johnson et al. 2012, Nguyen et al. 2015], and *network security games* (NSGs) (i.e., interdiction of adversaries on transportation networks) [Jain et al. 2011]. However, previous work in these areas suffers from two limitations relevant to our problem. First, they only consider the *tactical* allocation of a given team of resources, without considering the more *strategic* question of how to choose the right team. Indeed, the fact that the tactical question is already computationally challenging emphasizes the difficulty of our problem, which requires evaluating the effectiveness of *many* teams to select the right one. Second, previous work has mostly failed to consider heterogeneous teams, with varying individual and joint effectiveness.

To address these challenges we make the following key contributions. First, we introduce SORT as a new fundamental research problem in security games that combines *strategic* and *tactical* decision-making and provide a formal model of a SORT problem in an NSG. Second, at the strategic level, we introduce FORTIFY (Forming Optimal Response Teams for Forest safetY), a scalable algorithm for solving this problem. FORTIFY uses a hierarchical approach to abstract NSGs at varying levels of detail, providing bounds on the value of different teams of resources to speed up the search for the optimal team. Third, at the tactical level, we generalize previous methods for optimizing tactical resource allocation in NSGs to account for heterogenous teams with varying capabilities. Lastly, we present experimental results on synthetic problems, as well as *problem instances obtained from joint work with NGOs engaged in forest protection in Madagascar.*

Motivating Domain and Game Model

Forests in Madagascar are under great threat, with valuable hardwood trees such as rosewood and ebony being illegally harvested at an alarming rate

Figure 7.1 Illegal logging in progress in an at-risk area of Madagascar; images
provided by our partnering NGOs working in the area.

(Figure 7.1). There is broad interest in improving forest protection via
patrolling from different groups, e.g., NGOs, Madagascar National Parks,
local police, and community volunteers. These groups are working to combat
the problem of illegal logging in Madagascar by deploying teams of rangers,
police, and local volunteers to patrol the protected areas where these valuable
trees are located. However, there is very limited coordination among these
groups. As a result, there is limited attention paid at the *strategic level* to
optimize the selection of the right team of resources from among these groups,
and at the *tactical* level to optimally allocate the resulting team's resources.
Our formal model is designed to capture both the problem of determining the
best team of resources to deploy given a limited budget, as well as the problem
of optimizing the patrolling policies for specific teams.

Model

We now describe our model for the SORT problem. At the tactical level, the
decision of how to optimally allocate a team is an NSG problem. In these
NSGs, the defender's goal is to prevent an adversary from reaching his target
by defending edges. While this general model has multiple applications (e.g.,
interdiction of drug smuggling [Dell 2015], urban security [Jain et al. 2011]),
it is also well suited to modeling the strategic interaction between patrollers
and loggers in these forest areas, as movement is restricted to the underlying
road, river, and ridge line network of the forest.

   We model the physical space using a graph $G = (N,E)$, consisting of source
nodes $s \in S \subset N$, target nodes $t \in T \subset N$, and intermediate nodes. The attacker
(illegal loggers) acts by traversing a path from a source s_i to a target node t_i.

Table 7.1. *Notation and game description*

G(N,E)	Graph representing security domain
G^c	Compact graph representing security domain
$\tau(t_i)$	Payoff of the ith target t_i
K	Number of defender resource types
L_k	Number of edges covered by the kth resource type
b_k	Cost of the kth resource type
P_k	Detection probability of resource type k
B	Total budget for the team
m_k	Number of defender resources of type k
$\mathbf{X} = \{X_i\}$	Set of defender pure strategies
$\mathbf{x} = \{x_i\}$	Defender's mixed strategy over X
$\mathbf{A} = \{A_j\}$	Set of attacker pure strategies
$\mathbf{a} = \{a_j\}$	Attacker's mixed strategy over A
$U_d(X_i, \mathbf{a})$	Defender utility playing X_i against $\mathbf{a}$
$U_a(\mathbf{x}, A_j)$	Attacker utility playing A_j against $\mathbf{x}$

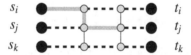

Figure 7.2 Pure strategies for the defender (bold line) and attacker (dashed line going from s to t).

For illegal logging, the s_i may be the attacker's originating villages and t_i may be areas containing valuable trees. Each target node t_i has a payoff value that is domain-dependent. Based on the research of collaborating domain experts in Madagascar, these depend on the density of valuable trees in a particular area, and the distance to the coast (for export) and local villages. See Table 7.1 for a full list of the notation.

Previously, models in NSGs have assumed a defender limited to homogeneous resources with no probability of failure, no joint effectiveness, and the ability to only cover a single edge [Jain et al. 2013, Okamoto et al. 2012]. This is insufficient to capture the complexities present in the illegal logging domain, and so we present a new model of the defender for green NSGs.

The defender conducts patrols in the network to interdict the attacker by placing resources on edges of the graph, as shown in Figure 7.2. The defender has K types of resources, each of which can conduct a patrol along L_k connected edges. Multiple environmental factors can cause a resource to fail in detecting an attacker, such as limited visibility or collusion with adversaries. We model this using an interdiction probability P_k for each resource type.

The defender has a total budget B; each resource type has a cost b_k, and a team consists of m_k resources of type k for $k = 1 \ldots K$. Multiple resources placed on a single edge results in a higher probability of detecting the attacker, which models coordination among resources.

A defender pure strategy X_i is an allocation of all resources in a given team to a set of edges of the graph, satisfying the connectedness and length constraints for each resource. An attacker pure strategy A_j is any path starting at a source node s_j and ending at a target node t_j. Figure 7.2 shows three attacker pure strategies. Although these strategies take the shortest path from source to target, it is not a requirement in the game. The allocation of one resource of size $L_k = 2$ is shown, which intersects paths i and j. The attacker and defender can play mixed strategies **a** and **x**, i.e., probability distributions over pure strategies. The probability of detecting an attacker on edge e if the defender follows a pure strategy X_i, allocating $m_{k,e}$ number of resources of type k to edge e is given in equation 7.1:

$$P(e, X_i) = 1 - \prod_1^K (1 - P_k)^{m_{k,e}} \tag{7.1}$$

The total probability that a defender pure strategy X_i protects against an attacker pure strategy A_j is given by the probability intersection function in equation 7.2, where we take the product over all the edges in the attack path:

$$P(X_i, A_j) = 1 - \prod_{e \in A_j} (1 - P(e, X_i)) \tag{7.2}$$

The attacker obtains a payoff of $\tau(t_i)$ if he is successful in reaching a target, and a payoff of zero if he is caught. We assume a zero-sum model, so the defender receives a penalty opposite of the attacker's payoff. For this zero-sum game, the optimal defender mixed strategy is the well-known minimax strategy. The game value is denoted $F(\lambda)$, and is a function of a team of resources λ selected from some set of resources R. The strategic aspect of the SORT problem can be formulated as the optimization problem in equation 7.3, where the utility $F(\lambda)$ is maximized subject to budgetary constraints:

$$\max_{\lambda \subset R} \left\{ F(\lambda) : \sum_{k \in \lambda} b_k \leq B \right\} \tag{7.3}$$

It can be shown that the SORT problem is NP-hard even if we can evaluate $F(\lambda)$ in constant time (using a reduction to knapsack). In the next section we present our solution approach to this problem, which uses varying levels of approximation of $F(\lambda)$ to determine the optimal team and deployment.

FORTIFY: The Hierarchical Search

In NSGs $F(\lambda)$ is computationally difficult to calculate, because it requires finding the optimal tactical allocation to assess the utility of a given team λ. Since there are exponentially many possible teams, the sequential approach of evaluating $F(\lambda)$ exactly for every team and picking the best one is impractical. Instead, in our approach to SORT, we integrate the analysis of the strategic and tactical aspects of the problem to search the space of teams much more efficiently. We use fast methods to quickly evaluate upper bounds on the utilities for specific teams. Using these bounds, we select the most promising team to evaluate in more detail, iteratively tightening the bounds as the search progresses until the optimal team is identified.

FORTIFY uses a three-layer hierarchical representation NSG to evaluate the performance of teams at different levels of detail. Starting from the full representation of the game, each layer abstracts away additional details to approximate the game value $F(\lambda)$. We call the bottom layer without any abstraction the optimal layer, the reduced layer is in the middle, and the compact layer is the most abstract.

FORTIFY is described in Algorithm 7.1 and Figure 7.3. Initially (line 1), we enumerate all teams Λ, that maximally saturate the cost budget B (so that no additional resources can be added to the team). Each team $\lambda \in \Lambda$ proceeds through the layers of the hierarchy by being promoted to the next layer; the first team to make it through all layers is the optimal team. When a team is promoted to a new layer, it is evaluated to compute a tighter upper bound on the value based on the abstraction specified for that layer.

At the start of the algorithm we have no information on the team values, so each team is evaluated and ordered based on the compact layer (lines 2–3). Next, the team with the highest bound is promoted to the reduced layer (line 9).

Algorithm 7.1 FORTIFY(B,R)

1:    $\Lambda \leftarrow$ getTeams(B,R), $\Lambda^c = \emptyset$, $\Lambda^r = \emptyset$, $\Lambda* = \emptyset$
2:    **for each** $\lambda \in \Lambda$:
3:      λ.value $\leftarrow$ Compact Layer(λ)
4:      $\Lambda^c \leftarrow \Lambda^c \cup \{\lambda\}$
5:    **repeat:**
6:      $\lambda_{max} \leftarrow \text{argmax}_{\lambda.\text{value}}(\Lambda^c, \Lambda^r, \Lambda*)$
7:      if $(\lambda_{max} \in \Lambda*)$ **return** λ_{max}
8:      else: λ.value $\leftarrow$ NextLayer(λ_{max})
9:        $\Lambda^{NextLayer} \leftarrow \Lambda^{NextLayer} \cup \{\lambda_{max}\}$

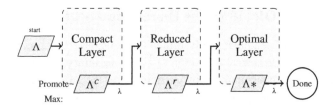

Figure 7.3 Flowchart for FORTIFY. Λ is the initial set of teams. Λ^c, Λ^r, and $\Lambda*$ are the sets of teams that have passed through the compact, reduced, and optimal layers. After all teams pass through the compact layer, one team (with max value) is promoted at each step.

This team can then be again promoted to the optimal layer or another team can be promoted to the reduced layer. The next team to be promoted is always the one with the highest current upper bound on the value, regardless of which layer it is in. When a team is evaluated in the optimal layer we know the true value of the team, so if this value is higher than the upper bounds on all remaining teams this team must be optimal (line 8), and the algorithm terminates.

Optimal Layer

We first introduce the optimal layer of FORTIFY in order to explain how the full NSG is solved. This step is computationally expensive as there are an exponential number of attacker and defender strategies and explicitly enumerating them all in computer memory is infeasible. Incremental strategy generation addresses the first challenge, allowing us to obtain the optimal defender mixed strategy without enumerating all pure strategies [McMahan et al. 2003]. This approach decomposes the problem into (1) master MiniMax linear program (LP); and (2) oracles for the defender and attacker which incrementally generate pure strategies to add to the current strategy space via a separate optimization problem. The master LP computes a solution restricted to the set of pure strategies generated by the oracles. The steps are shown in Algorithm 7.2. The formulation for the MiniMax LP is standard, but we provide new formulations for both oracles. The key novelty in our work is that the model complexities imply that we have a nonlinear optimization problem to solve in both oracles; we address this by constraining the variables to be binary valued, and we take advantage of efficient constraint programming methods in commercial tools like CPLEX.

Algorithm 7.2 Optimal layer(λ)

 1:    Initialize **X, A**

 2:    **do:**

 3:       $(U_d^*, \mathbf{x}, \mathbf{a}) \leftarrow$ MiniMax(**X, A**)

 4:       X $\leftarrow$ DefenderOracle(**a**)

 5:       **X** $\leftarrow$ **X** $\cup$ { X }

 6:       $A_j \leftarrow$ LinearAttackerOracle(**x**)

 7:       if $U_a(\mathbf{x}, A_j) - U_a(\mathbf{x}, \mathbf{a}) \le \epsilon$ then

 8:          $A_j \leftarrow$ AttackerOracle(x)

 9:       **A** $\leftarrow$ **A** $\cup$ { A_j }

10:    **until** convergence then **return** $(U_d^*, \mathbf{x})$

Minimax

The game value is computed (line 3) by solving for the minimax strategy using an LP formulation (equation 7.4). The inputs are the current set of attacker and defender pure strategies, **A** and **X**, and the outputs are the game utility U_d^*, and mixed strategies, **x** and **a**. $U_d(\mathbf{x}, A_j)$ is the defender utility playing **x** against the pure strategy A_j:

$$\max_{U_d^*, \mathbf{x}} \quad U_d^* \quad \text{s.t.} \quad U_d^* \le U_d(\mathbf{x}, A_j) \quad \forall j = 1 \ldots |A| \tag{7.4}$$

Defender Oracle

The defender oracle returns the best response strategy X_i to add to the MiniMax LP. The objective is to maximize the utility expressed in equation 7.5, given an input distribution **a** over the current attacker strategies **A**, where a_j is the probability of the attacker taking path A_j:

$$U_d(X_i, \mathbf{a}) = -\sum_j a_j (1 - P(X_i, A_j)) \tau(t_j) \tag{7.5}$$

A pure strategy implies a single allocation of the given team's resources. Resources are allocated by setting the binary decision variables $\lambda_{m,e}^k \in \{0, 1\}$, which corresponds to the mth resource of type k being allocated to edge e. Our contributions formalize the constraints needed to accommodate arbitrary path coverage as well as failure probability. Path constraints are enforced with $\sum_e \lambda_{m,e}^k = L_k$ in equations 7.6 and 7.7. Equation 7.6 ensures every allocated edge is connected to at least one other edge. Since the number of nodes in any path of length L_k should be $L_k + 1$, equation 7.7 counts the number of nodes that are either a source or target of allocated edges, making sure not to double-count nodes that belong to multiple edges. $\lambda_{n,m}^k \in \{0,1\}$ and equals 1 if a node n is the source or target of any allocated edge $\lambda_{e,m}^k = 1$:

$$\lambda_{m,e}^k \leq \sum_{e1 \in in(n_s)} \lambda_{m,e1}^k + \sum_{e2 \in out(n_t)} \lambda_{m,e2}^k \quad \begin{matrix} n_s \leftarrow \text{source(e)} \\ n_t \leftarrow \text{target(e)} \end{matrix} \quad \text{if } L_k \geq 1 \tag{7.6}$$

$$\lambda_{m,e}^k \leq \lambda_{m,n}^k \quad \text{s.t. } n \leftarrow \begin{matrix} \text{source(e)} \\ \vee \text{ target(e)} \end{matrix} \quad \sum_n \lambda_{m,n}^k = L_k + 1 \tag{7.7}$$

Attacker Oracle

The attacker oracle computes a best response strategy A_j which maximizes his utility (equation 7.8), playing against the defender mixed strategy $\mathbf{x}$. An optimization problem in the form of equations 7.8 and 7.9 is solved for each target t_j; the best path for each target is computed and the target with the highest utility is chosen. The decision variables $\gamma_e \in \{0,1\}$ are binary and correspond to edges $e \in A_j$:

$$U_a(\mathbf{x}, A_j) = \sum_i x_i (1 - P(X_i, A_j)) \tau(t_j) \tag{7.8}$$

$$\sum_{e \in out(s)} \gamma_e = 1; \quad \sum_{e \in in(t*)} \gamma_e = 1; \quad \sum_{e \in in(n)} \gamma_e = \sum_{e \in out(n)} \gamma_e \quad \begin{matrix} n \neq \text{source} \\ n \neq \text{target} \end{matrix} \tag{7.9}$$

Exactly solving the Attacker Oracle is computationally expensive. Therefore, in line 6, we introduce a new **Linear Attacker Oracle** approximation to quickly generate an approximate best response. Here, the probability intersection function is approximated with an additive linear function, $P(X_i, A_j) = \sum_{e \in A_j} P(e, X_i)$ so we can write the oracle as an LP. (In the attacker oracle, the value of $P(e, X_i)$ does not need to be approximated, as it does not depend on the attacker's decision variables, but rather on the defender's variables and thus is calculated outside the attacker oracle.) In the event that the approximation steps fail to generate a strategy that increases the oracle's expected utility (line 7), the oracle computes the optimal solution as a final step (line 8) to ensure that the algorithm converges to the true game value.

Compact Layer

The compact layer uses an *abstract representation* of the game model that reduces the problem in two ways: (1) the attacker is restricted to using *only a*

Algorithm 7.3 CompactGraph(G(N,E))

1:　for each $s_i \in N$, $t_j \in N$:
2:　　$\{E_j\} \leftarrow$ mincut(s_i,t_j)
3:　　for each $e \in E_j$:
4:　　　$A^c \leftarrow$ ShortestPath(s_i, e, t_j)
5:　　　$\mathbf{A^c} \leftarrow \mathbf{A^c} \cup \{A^c\}$
6:　　　$N^c \leftarrow N^c \cup$ newNode(A^c)
7:　for each $A_i^c \in \mathbf{A^c}, A_j^c \in \mathbf{A^c}$:
8:　　$w_{i,j} \leftarrow D(i,j)$
9:　　$G^c \leftarrow$ newEdge$(i,j,w_{i,j})$
10:　return G^c

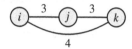

Figure 7.4 Compact graph.

subset of possible paths; (2) the defender chooses to allocate resources *directly to attacker paths* rather than edges in the graph.

Formally, the compact layer constructs a new graph $G^c(N^c, E^c)$ in Algorithm 7.3, where the attacker paths are represented by nodes N^c of the graph. We describe this using an example, transforming part of the graph from Figure 7.2 into its compact representation in Figure 7.4. To choose the subset of attacker paths, for each source–target pair of nodes we (1) calculate the min-cut for each target, and (2) find the shortest possible paths from source to target that go through each of the min-cut edges (lines 1–6). The three attacker paths A_i, A_j, and A_k in Figure 7.2 are among several calculated from the min-cut of the graph. These three paths become nodes i, j, and k respectively in part of the new compact graph. In order for a resource to cover paths i and j, its path coverage L_k must be at least as large as the minimum separation distance between the paths, plus any edges required to intersect the paths. We define this as $D(i,j)$, which is 3 for the example in Figure 7.2. Edges are added between any nodes i and j with weight $D(i,j)$, equal to the L_k required to cover both corresponding paths. These distances are calculated using Dijkstra's algorithm, and no edges are added between two nodes if the distance is greater than the largest path coverage of any defender resource.

The defender can choose to cover any subset of nodes in G^c with a resource of type k as long as the induced subgraph has the property that (1) the subgraph

---

Algorithm 7.4 Compact Layer

1:    $G^c \leftarrow$ CompactGraph(G(N,E))
2:    Initialize mixed strategy $\mathbf{a} \leftarrow$ Uniform(A^c)
3:    **do:**
4:      $X_i^c \leftarrow$ CompactDefenderOracle($\mathbf{a}$)
5:      $\mathbf{X^c} \leftarrow \mathbf{X^c} \cup \{X_i^c\}$
6:      $(\mathbf{x}, \mathbf{a}) \leftarrow$ MiniMax($\mathbf{X^c}, \mathbf{A^c}$)
7:    **until** convergence $U_d(X_i^c, \mathbf{a})$ - $U_d(\mathbf{x}, \mathbf{a}) \leq \epsilon$
8:    **return** $U_d(\mathbf{x}, \mathbf{a})$

---

is fully connected and (2) all edges have weight less than L_k. For example, the three paths in Figure 7.4 (i–j–k) can all be covered by a resource of size 4. If the defender has a resource of size 3, she can only cover paths (i–j) or (j–k).

The compact layer solves this abstract representation of the game for a single team. The problem is decomposed into master MiniMax and a single Defender Oracle. There is no oracle for the attacker, as the attacker's strategy space is enumerated using the compact graph and fixed at the start of the algorithm. The game value is calculated using Algorithm 7.4. The compact graph and subset of attacker paths are first generated (line 1). The attacker's mixed strategy is initialized with a uniform distribution (line 2). The compact defender oracle continuously adds strategies to the master LP until the defender's value cannot be improved. Convergence occurs when the oracle can no longer find a strategy to add that will improve the defender's utility (line 7).

Compact Defender Oracle

The same objective function (equation 7.5) is maximized; however, the constraints are modified to reflect the compact game representation. $P(X_i, A_j)$ is linearly approximated by equation 7.10 and is capped at 1. Here, we want to conservatively over-estimate the defender's interdiction probability to ensure that the compact layer returns an upper bound. Therefore, when a defender resource covers a node in G^c, we assume that the corresponding attacker path is interdicted by the entire entire patrol of length L^k of that resource. The probability of catching the attacker on the compact graph is set to $(1 - (1 - P_k)^{L_k})$. The defender chooses to allocate the mth resource of type k to a node n_j corresponding to attacker path A_j by setting the decision variables $\eta_{j,m}^k \in \{0,1\}$:

$$P(X_i, A_j) = \sum P_k^c \eta_{j,m}^k \qquad D(i,j)\eta_{i,m}^k \eta_{j,m}^k \leq L_k \qquad (7.10)$$

Algorithm 7.5 Reduced Layer

2:   Initialize mixed strategy $\mathbf{a} \leftarrow$ CompactLayer(A^c)
3:   **do:**
4:       $X_i^c \leftarrow$ DefenderOracle(a)
5:       $\mathbf{X^c} \leftarrow \mathbf{X^c} \cup \{X_i^c\}$
6:       $(\mathbf{x}, \mathbf{a}) \leftarrow$ MiniMax($\mathbf{X^c}, \mathbf{A^c}$)
7:   **until** convergence $U_d(X_i^c, \mathbf{a}) - U_d(\mathbf{x}, \mathbf{a}) \leq \epsilon$
8:   **return** $U_d(\mathbf{x}, \mathbf{a})$

For any fixed attacker strategy, the Compact Defender Oracle strategy space is a relaxation of the Optimal Defender Oracle's strategy space. This means that strategy feasible in the Optimal Oracle strategy space is also feasible for the Compact Oracle, and thus the optimal strategy is feasible for both oracles. The compact oracle will never return a strategy with lower utility than the true optimal strategy, because this strategy is always feasible, meaning that the game value of the compact layer will always upper bound the true game value.

Reduced Layer

The reduced layer uses the same restricted strategy space for the attacker as the compact layer. However, the defender uses the original, unrestricted strategy space to allocate resources. While the reduced layer is more difficult to solve than the compact layer, it allows us to iteratively tighten the upper bounds and avoid more computation in the optimal layer. The evaluation of teams in this layer follows Algorithm 7.5. We additionally reduce the computation effort spent in this layer by warm-starting the attacker's mixed strategy with the solution from the compact layer.

Evaluation

We present four sets of experimental results: (1) We evaluate the scalability and runtime performance of FORTIFY on several classes of random graphs. We benchmark with a sequential search which sequentially evaluates enumerated teams with cost saturating the budget. (2) We also evaluate the impact of the initial compact layer on the runtime by comparing the runtimes of FORTIFY with and without the compact layer. (3) We investigate the benefit of optimizing team composition as well as the diversity of optimal teams.

(4) We demonstrate that FORTIFY can scale up to the real world by testing performance on a case study of Madagascar using real graph data. All values are averaged over 20 trials. The experiments were run on a Linux cluster with HP-SL250, 2.4 GHz, dual-processor machines. We use the following graphs:

(1) Grid graphs labeled $G_{w,h,s,t}$ consist of a grid with width w, height h, sources s, targets t, and nearest neighbor connections between nodes. We define start and end points for the attacker, with sources located at one end and targets at another.

(2) Geometric graphs provide a good approximation of real road networks [Eppstein and Goodrich 2008], allowing us to model the networks of villages and rivers in forest regions. n nodes are distributed randomly in a plane and are connected based on their distance, which determines the density d of the graph. We label them $R_{n,s,t,d}$.

Scalability

We first evaluate the performance of FORTIFY using two sets of resource types, and target values of 50. Each set contains four resource types, with varying costs of $b = \{5, 6, 7, 8\}$. The first set of resource types Λ^1 have varied path coverages $L^1 = \{1, 2, 3, 4\}$ and constant detection probability $P^1 = \{1, 1, 1, 1\}$ while the second set Λ^2 has constant path coverage $L^2 = \{2, 2, 2, 2\}$ and varied detection probabilities $P^2 = \{0.5, 0.6, 0.7, 0.8\}$. Experiments that did not terminate in three hours were cutoff and are shown as missing bars. Figure 7.5 show the runtimes for our algorithms run on both graph types for both Λ^1 and Λ^2 teams. The budget varies on the x-axis and the runtime is shown on the y-axis in log scale. FORTIFY consistently outperforms the sequential method on both the grid and geometric graphs. FORTIFY performs particularly well on the grid graphs, and scaling past budgets of 25 while all instances of the sequential search were cutoff. We observe a peak in the runtime for teams with perfect detection probability in Figure 7.5(a) and (c) around a budget of 20–25, which is due to the deployment versus saturation phenomenon which occurs in these types of network models [Jain et al. 2012].

Removing the compact layer

We also compare the performance of FORTIFY with and without the compact layer in Figure 7.5. It is apparent that this layer is crucial to the performance of the algorithm, particularly for the grid graphs in parts (a) and (b) as FORTIFY without the compact layer performs almost as poorly as the sequential method. In fact, removing the compact layer can cause FORTIFY to perform worse

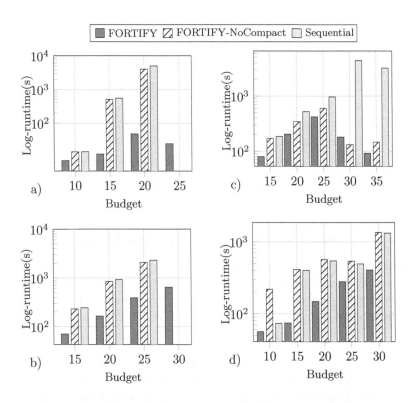

Figure 7.5   Runtime scalability comparing FORTIFY against sequential and no-compact method. (a) Λ^1 teams on a $G_{5,20,5,5}$ graph. (b) Λ^2 teams on a $G_{4,4,4,4}$ graph. (c) Λ^1 teams on a $R_{70,5,5,0.1}$ graph. (d) Λ^2 teams on a $R_{25,4,4,0.1}$ graph.

than the sequential method for small budgets due to the overhead required for the approximation.

Team Composition

We demonstrate the value of optimizing over team composition by looking at the loss in game value incurred by playing a uniform random team which saturates the budget. Games are played on $G_{4,4,4,4}$ and $R_{25,4,4,0.1}$ graphs with target values of 50. The results are shown in Figure 7.6 with budget on the x-axis and game value on the y-axis. As expected, the game value decreases with budget as we form larger teams; however, the relative benefit increases as well, with almost a 300 percent loss in solution quality at budgets of 25 without our team optimization algorithm. This is due to the increase in the space of possible teams which can be formed, making it more likely to form a suboptimal team.

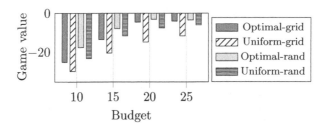

Figure 7.6 Team optimization comparison. Teams have six resource types, and vary both edge coverage $L = \{2, 2, 5, 3, 3, 6\}$, and detection probability $P = \{0.7, 0.9, 0.7, 0.6, 0.6, 0.6\}$, with costs $b = \{5, 8, 10, 5, 8, 10\}$.

Real World: Madagascar Protected Forests

We demonstrate the ability of FORTIFY to scale up to real-world domains, evaluating the performance on a network constructed from GIS data of at-risk forest areas in Madagascar. We present the following model which was built working closely with domain experts from NGOs.

Graph

Figure 7.1 shows the road and river networks used by the patrolling officers, as well as the known routes taken by groups of illegal loggers. We used this to build the nodes and edges of our network. Edges correspond to distances of 7–10 km. Ten target locations were chosen by clustering prominent forest areas. Eleven villages in the surrounding area were chosen as sources. Several domain experts identified the risk level and level of attractiveness for logging, based on the size of the forest, the ease of access, and the value of the trees. Using this information we assigned values ranging from 100 to 300 to each of the targets.

Resources

Communal policemen and local volunteers conduct patrols in the forest. A typical patrol covers 20 km in a day and a patroller can conduct two types of patrols, a short patrol covering two edges and a long patrol covering three edges. Based on expert input, we assign the detection probability for communal police as 0.9 for short patrols and 0.8 for long patrols; and for volunteers, 0.7 for short patrols and 0.6 for long patrols. The lower probabilities for volunteers are because they must call backup for interdiction, which may allow the adversary to escape. Thus, in total we have four resource types available

Table 7.2. *Runtime on Madagascar Graph*

B	Runtime(s)	GV
10	203	−266
15	388	−256
20	653	−239
25	1,308	−230
30	1,742	−220
35	2,504	−216
40	3,675	−204

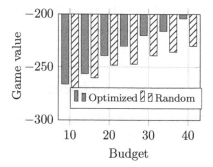

Figure 7.7 Team optimization on Madagascar graph.

$L = \{2, 3, 2, 3\}$, $P = \{0.7, 0.6, 0.9, 0.8\}$. The costs are proportional to the salaries patrollers receive for a day of patrolling $b = \{5, 5, 8, 8\}$.

Experiment

The runtime experiments are shown in Table 7.2 for increasing budgets. Data are averaged over 20 runs. FORTIFY can scale up to real-world networks, able to handle both the large graph size and number of source and target nodes, even for large budgets. The value of performing this optimization is shown in Figure 7.7 with the solution quality (game value) on the y-axis and budget on the x-axis, where we compare the optimal game value to the average value achieved by randomly generated teams.

Conclusion and Related Work

We study a fundamentally new problem in SORT. This new problem addresses the environmental protection challenge of optimal investment and deployment of security resource teams. We use the rising threat of illegal logging in Madagascar as a motivating domain where we must work with a limited budget to coordinate and deploy such teams. To address this problem, we develop FORTIFY, a scalable solution addressing both aspects of the SORT problem, with the ability to both model and solve real-world problem instances. FORTIFY provides a valuable tool for environmental protection agencies.

We have already discussed the shortcomings of related work in security games. In addition, there is significant research in team formation in multiagent systems, e.g., in network configuration [Gaston and des Jardins 2005], board gameplay [Obata et al. 2011] fantasy football [Matthews et al. 2012], and multi-objective coalition [Cho et al. 2013]). However, that work fails for security resource allocation at the tactical level.

Acknowledgments

We would like to thank Dr. Jonah Ratsimbazafy. This research was supported by MURI Grant W911NF-11-1-0332.

References

Cho, J.-H., Chen, I.-R., Wang, Y., Chan, K.S., and Swami, A. 2013. *Multi-Objective Optimization for Trustworthy Tactical Networks: A Survey and Insights*. Technical Report. Defense Technical Information Center.

Dell, M. 2015. Trafficking networks and the Mexican drug war. *American Economic Review*, **105**(6), 1738–1779.

Dhital, N., Vololomboahangy, R.R., and Khasa, D.P. 2015. Issues and challenges of forest governance in Madagascar. *Canadian Journal of Development Studies/Revue canadienne d'études du développement*, **36**(1), 38–56.

Eppstein, D., and Goodrich, M.T. 2008. Studying (non-planar) road networks through an algorithmic lens. Page 16 of: *Proceedings of the 16th ACM SIGSPATIAL International Conference on Advances in Geographic Information Systems*. ACM Press.

Fang, F., Stone, P., and Tambe, M. 2015. When security games go green: designing defender strategies to prevent poaching and illegal fishing. In: *International Joint Conference on Artificial Intelligence (IJCAI)*. AAAI Press.

Gaston, M.E., and des Jardins, M. 2005. Agent-organized networks for dynamic team formation. Pages 230–237 of: *Proceedings of the Fourth International Joint Conference on Autonomous Agents and Multiagent Systems*. ACM Press.

Jain, M., Korzhyk, D., Vaněk, O., et al. 2011. A double oracle algorithm for zero-sum security games on graphs. Pages 327–334 of: *Proceedings of the Tenth*

International Joint Conference on Autonomous Agents and Multiagent Systems. ACM Press.

Jain, M., Leyton-Brown, K., and Tambe, M. 2012. The deployment-to-saturation ratio in security games. In: *Conference on Artificial Intelligence.* AAAI Press.

Jain, M., Conitzer, V., and Tambe, M. 2013. Security scheduling for real-world networks. Pages 215–222 of: *Proceedings of the 2013 International Joint Conference on Autonomous Agents and Multiagent Systems.* ACM Press.

Johnson, M.P., Fang, F., and Tambe, M. 2012. Patrol strategies to maximize pristine forest area. In: *Conference on Artificial Intelligence.* AAAI Press.

Korzhyk, D., Conitzer, V., and Parr, R. 2010. Complexity of computing optimal stackelberg strategies in security resource allocation games. In: *Twenty-Fourth AAAI Conference on Artificial Intelligence.* AAAI Press.

Matthews, T., Ramchurn, S.D., and Chalkiadakis, G. 2012. Competing with humans at fantasy football: team formation in large partially-observable domains. Pages 1394–1400 of: *Proceedings of the 26th Conference of the Associations for the Advancement for Artificial Intelligence.* AAAI Press.

McMahan, H.B., Gordon, G.J., and Blum, A. 2003. Planning in the presence of cost functions controlled by an adversary. In: *Proceedings of the Twentieth International Conference on Machine Learning.* AAAI Press.

Nguyen, T.H., Fave, F.M. Delle, K., et al. 2015. Making the most of our regrets: regret-based solutions to handle payoff uncertainty and elicitation in green security games. In: *Conference on Decision and Game Theory for Security.* Springer.

Obata, T., Sugiyama, T., Hoki, K., and Ito, T. 2011. Consultation algorithm for computer Shogi: move decisions by majority. Pages 156–165 of: *Computer and Games'10.* Springer.

Okamoto, S., Hazon, N., and Sycara, K. 2012. Solving non-zero sum multiagent network flow security games with attack costs. Pages 879–888 of: *Proceedings of the 2012 International Joint Conference on Autonomous Agents and Multiagent Systems.* ACM Press.

Tambe, M. 2011. *Security and Game Theory: Algorithms, Deployed Systems, Lessons Learned.* Cambridge: Cambridge University Press.

Allnutt, T.F., Asner, G.P., Golden, C.D., and Powell, V.N. 2013. Mapping recent deforestation and forest disturbance in northeastern Madagascar. *Tropical Conservation Science,* **6**(1), 1–15.

WWF. 2015. Illegal logging. http://wwf.panda.org/about_our_earth/deforestation/deforestation_causes/illegal_logging.

8

NECTAR

Enforcing Environmental Compliance through Strategically
Randomized Factory Inspections

Benjamin Ford, Matthew Brown, Amulya Yadav, Amandeep Singh,
Arunesh Sinha, Biplav Srivastava, Christopher Kiekintveld, and
Milind Tambe

Introduction

The leather industry is a multi-billion dollar industry (Mwinyihija, 2011), and in many developing countries such as India and Bangladesh the tanning industry is a large source of revenue. Unfortunately, the chemical byproducts of the tanning process are highly toxic, and the wastewater produced by tanneries is sent to nearby rivers and waterways. As a result, the Ganga River (along with many others) has become extremely contaminated, leading to substantial health problems for the large populations that rely on its water for basic needs (e.g., drinking, bathing, crops, livestock) (Blacksmith Institute, 2011). Tanneries are required by law to run wastewater through sewage treatment plants (STPs) prior to discharge into the Ganga. In many cases, however, the tanneries either do not own or run this equipment, and it is up to regulatory bodies to enforce compliance. However, inspection agencies have a severe lack of resources; the combination of tanneries' unchecked pollution and inspection agencies' failure to conduct inspections forced India's national environment monitoring agency to ban the operation of 98 tanneries near Kanpur, India while threatening the closure of approximately 600 tanneries (Jainani, 2015). It is our goal to provide agencies with randomized inspection plans so tanneries reduce harmful effluents and an important facet of India's economy can operate.

In this chapter, we introduce a new game-theoretic application, NECTAR (Nirikshana for Enforcing Compliance for Toxic wastewater Abatement and Reduction),[1] that incorporates new models and algorithms to support India's

---

[1] Nirikshana, the Hindi word for inspect. As many mythological stories and even popular Bollywood songs attest, Ganga water is supposed to be NECTAR (or Amrit, the Hindi antonym of poison), which has inspired our project. The project name is intentionally chosen to fit this international and intercultural theme.

inspection agencies by intelligently randomizing inspection schedules. We build on previously deployed solutions based on Stackelberg security games (SSGs) for counter-terrorism (Tambe, 2011) and traffic enforcement (Brown et al., 2014). Our SSG models are also the first to focus on the problem of pollution prevention by modeling the interaction between an inspection agency (the leader) and leather tanneries (many followers) – an interaction that poses a unique set of challenges. (1) Because there is a large disparity between the number of inspection teams and the number of tanneries, inspection plans must be efficient. (2) We cannot assume that inspectors can catch 100 percent of violations. (3) Inspectors must travel to the tanneries via a road network, so solutions must be robust to delays (e.g., traffic). Finally, current fine policies may not be sufficient to induce compliance, so (4) it is important to investigate alternative fine structures.

NECTAR addresses these new challenges of tannery inspections. Our SSG model captures the inspection process and accounts for two types of inspections: thorough inspections and simple (i.e., quick) inspections. While thorough inspections take longer to conduct (and thus fewer of them can be conducted), they are more likely to detect violations than simple, surface-level inspections, which may only be able to check for obvious violations. To model the imperfect nature of these inspections, we introduce two failure rates: one for thorough inspections and one for simple inspections, with simple inspections failing at a higher rate. We also address the uncertainty involved with road networks by using a Markov decision process (MDP) that will represent and ultimately generate the game solution. Finally, we also investigate how tannery compliance is affected by two fine structures: fixed fines and variable fines, where the latter will result in larger tanneries receiving larger fines. For the evaluation of our model, we apply NECTAR to a real-world network of tanneries in Kanpur, India, evaluate the quality of NECTAR's generated solutions, and demonstrate how NECTAR's solutions can be visualized via a Google Earth overlay.

Related Work

Several theoretical papers have used game theory to model the impact of environmental policies. *Environmental games* (Tapiero, 2005) use Stackelberg games to model interactions between a regulator and a polluting firm, while Dong et al. (2010) used game theory to study the effect of environmental policies in the Chinese electroplating industry. *Inspection games* consider the general problem of scheduling inspections, and have been extensively studied in the literature. For example, Filar et al. (1985) model cases in which an inspector must travel to multiple sites and determine violations as a stochastic game. A general theory of inspection games for problems such as arms control and environmental policy enforcement has been studied by Avenhaus et al. (2002), including analysis of whether inspectors can benefit from acting first. Von Stengel (2014) also considered inspection games with sequential inspections, including compact recursive descriptions of these games. However, most of these works do not focus on concrete applications and thus, unlike our work, do not provide executable inspection schedules to inspectors.

Other areas of research have considered various models of patrolling strategies and scheduling constraints. These include patrolling games (Alpern et al., 2011; Bošanský et al., 2011; Basilico et al., 2012) and security games with varying forms of scheduling constraints on resources (Yin et al., 2012; Jain et al., 2013; Brown et al., 2014). There has also been recent work on utilizing MDPs to represent strategies in security games (Shieh et al., 2014; Bošanský et al., 2015). However, none of these efforts have focused on environmental inspections and have not investigated topics important in this domain, such as the impact of fine structures on adversary behavior (i.e., compliance).

Finally, decision support for water-related challenges is an emerging area with global relevance. Using Flint, Michigan as an example, Ellis et al. (2018) introduce a chatbot that assists users in making water quality decisions based on complex data sources.

Motivating Domain

The pollution of India's rivers is a major concern. The waters of India's largest river, the Ganga (or Ganges) River, are used by over 400 million people – roughly one-third of India's population and more than the entire population of the United States. Unfortunately, the Ganga is ranked the fifth dirtiest river in the world. Generated from various sources such as sewage and industrial effluents, the pollution inflicts serious health conditions on all life that depends on the river. In Kanpur, villagers suffer from health conditions (e.g., cholera, miscarriages), and livestock yield less milk and die suddenly (Gupta et al., 2007).

Situated around the city of Kanpur, the various leather tanneries are a major source of pollution in the Ganga River (Gupta et al., 2007). While there are a few STPs in Kanpur, they can neither treat the full volume nor the full range of produced pollutants (Planning Commission of India, 2013). In particular, treating heavy metals like chromium, mercury, arsenic, and nickel is costly and needs specialized personnel (in addition to the personnel required to operate the STPs). The government has put in place regulations requiring the tanneries to own and operate effluent plants to remove the pollutants before they discharge their sewage. However, the tanneries have not been willing to undertake the additional cost of installing and operating the treatment units. Even when tanneries have installed the units, they avoid operating them whenever possible.

To address non-compliance issues, the government sends inspection teams to visit the tanneries. Inspecting the tanneries is a time-consuming, quasi-legal activity where the "as-is" situation is carefully recorded and samples are collected that can later be subjected to judicial scrutiny. It is also costly because, apart from the inspectors themselves, help from local police is requisitioned for safety, lab work is done for sample testing, and movement logistics are carefully planned; a full inspection is costly to conduct. Due to these costs, the number of inspectors that can be sent on a patrol is very limited. Our application seeks to help by (1) generating randomized inspection patrols that maximize the effectiveness of available inspectors, and (2) introducing limited inspection teams that conduct simple inspections – a low-cost alternative to full inspection teams that conduct thorough inspections. While limited inspection teams cannot replace the needed capabilities of a full inspection team, they can still inspect tanneries and issue fines for obvious violations (e.g., the site not owning an STP). We will refer to full inspection teams and limited inspection teams as thorough inspection resources and simple inspection resources, respectively.

Model

In this section, we model this pollution prevention problem as a defender–attacker SSG. The task of the defender is to send resources to different tannery sites (i.e., the multiple adversaries) on a road network. The defender must devise a patrol strategy to maximize compliance among a number of sites (each site denoted by l), where each site has a number of factories f_l and each site's compliance cost increases with the number of factories. In addition, the defender must take into account the time it takes to travel to and inspect each site. We model the road network as a graph, where the nodes represent sites and the edges represent the roads connecting each site. Each edge also has a cost, e_{ab}, associated with it that represents the travel time from a site a to another site b. Using publicly available data regarding tannery locations in Kanpur, we constructed a graph consisting of 50 sites.

The defender has two types of resources: r_1 number of thorough inspection resources and r_2 simple inspection resources. For thorough inspection resources, the inspector conducts a detailed inspection that takes i time units. We model imperfect inspections such that even if a violation exists, the inspectors will fail to detect it with a low probability γ_1. For simple inspection resources, the inspector will conduct a superficial inspection that takes d time units. Since the inspection is not detailed, simple inspection resources will not detect anything but obvious violations. Thus, such resources have a higher probability of failure γ_2. Each of the defender's resources (thorough and simple) have a maximum time budget, t_1 and t_2 respectively, to conduct inspections and travel to sites.

In the SSG framework, the defender will commit to a randomized patrol strategy (a mixed strategy), which is a probability distribution over the executable daily inspection patrols (the pure strategies for all resources). The adversaries (the sites) can fully observe the defender's mixed strategy and know the probability of being inspected by a thorough inspection team or a simple inspection team on a given day. Formulating the mixed strategy requires enumerating all feasible pure strategies for the defender. However, this approach is impractical for two main reasons: (1) for any realistically sized patrolling problem, the defender's pure strategy space is so large that it cannot fit into memory. For example, with our Kanpur graph of 50 tanneries, only one defender resource, and a time horizon of ten hours, the pure strategy space size would be too large to enumerate (approximately 50 choose 10). Therefore, we adopt a compact representation (a transition graph) that will allow our approach to scale to large problem sizes. (2) Inspectors must travel to sites via a road network (with potential delays), and the corresponding uncertainty cannot be handled by a standard SSG formulation. Rather than reasoning about mixed strategies, we instead use the compact representation to reason about spatio-temporal flow through a transition graph. To account for stochasticity and uncertainty in the outcome of actions, we use an MDP to represent the defender's inspection patrolling problem. We can solve the corresponding linear program (LP) to compute the optimal inspection strategy, i.e., the optimal MDP policy.

Compact Game Representation: Transition Graph

Brown et al. also faced the challenge of large state spaces for a traffic enforcement domain (Brown et al., 2014). Since their game also takes place on a road network, there are sufficient similarities between our approach and theirs to apply their techniques, based on transition graphs, to improve the scalability of our model.

Instead of enumerating an exponential number of pure strategies, we need only enumerate a polynomial number of states and edges in the transition graph. We then compute the optimal probability flow (as seen in the next section), also called a marginal coverage vector, and sample from the vector to create inspection schedules. Because the defender resource types (thorough and simple) have different time constraints, each has its own transition graph.

We discretize time into a granularity of h hours. In the thorough inspection resource transition graph, a vertex is added for each site l every h hours until the resource time budget t_1 has been expended. Similarly for the simple resource's transition graph, vertices are added until the time budget t_2 has been expended.

MDP Formulation

We present an MDP $\langle S, A, T, R \rangle$ to incorporate uncertainty into the transition graph. An example MDP is shown in Figure 8.1 to illustrate these definitions.

- S: finite set of states. Each state $s \in S$ is a tuple (l, τ), where l is the site that the resource is located, and τ is the current time step. For example, an inspector at site A at hour 1 is represented as $s_{A,1}$. Each vertex in the transition graph corresponds to a state s.
- A: finite set of actions. $A(s)$ corresponds to the set of actions available from state s (i.e., the set of sites reachable from l) that the resource can travel to and inspect. For example, at site A at hour 1, the only available action is to move to site B (i.e., the solid arrow from A to B in Figure 8.1).
- $T_1(s, a, s')$: probability of an inspector ending up in state s' after performing action a while in state s. Travel time and inspection time are both represented here. As a simple example, there could be probability 0.7 for transition $T_1(s_{A,1}, a_B, s_{B,2})$: a transition from site A at hour 1 to move to and

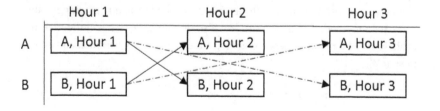

Figure 8.1 Illustrative MDP example.

inspect site B will, with a probability of 0.7, finish at hour 2 (a travel + inspection time of one hour). The dashed lines in Figure 8.1 represent the remaining probability (0.3) that the same action will instead finish at hour 3 (due to a delay). Note that the two resource types have separate transition functions due to the difference in action times (i for thorough inspection resources and d for simple inspection resources).

- $R(s, a, s')$: the reward function for ending in state s' after performing action a while in state s. As we are interested in the game-theoretic reward, we define the reward in the LP and define R = 0 $\forall s, a, s'$.

Inspection Patrol Generation

We provide an to compute the optimal flow through the MDP (i.e., the transition graph with uncertainty). By normalizing the outgoing flow from each state in the MDP, we obtain the optimal MDP policy from which we can sample to generate dynamic patrol schedules. In the following LP formulation, we make use of the following notation. A site l has a number of factories f_l, and if a site is caught violating during an inspection, they receive a fine, α_l. On the other hand, if a site wants to remain in compliance, they will need to pay a compliance cost β for each factory (total cost = βf_l). We represent the expected cost for each site l as v_l. As defined in the following LP, the expected cost corresponds to the lowest of either the site's expected fine or the site's full cost of compliance; we assume that these adversaries (i.e., the leather tannery sites) are rational and that they will choose to pay the lowest of those two values (expected fine or cost of compliance). Finally, we denote as S_l the set of all states that correspond to site l (i.e., all time steps associated with site l).

As discussed in the transition graph definition, the optimal flow through the graph corresponds to the optimal defender strategy, and that flow is represented by a marginal coverage vector. We denote the marginal probability of a resource type i (either thorough or simple inspection team) reaching state s and executing action a as $w_i(s, a)$. We also denote, as $x_i(s, a, s')$, the marginal probability of a resource type i reaching state s, executing action a, and ending in state s'.

$$\max_{w,x} \sum_l v_l \tag{8.1}$$

$$s.t. x_i(s, a, s') = w_i(s, a) T_i(s, a, s'), \forall s, a, s', i \tag{8.2}$$

$$\sum_{s',a',i} x_i(s',a',s) = \sum_{a,i} w_i(s,a), \forall s, i \qquad (8.3)$$

$$\sum_{a,i} w_i(s_i^+, a) = r_i \qquad (8.4)$$

$$\sum_{s,a,i} x_i(s,a,s_i^-) = r_i \qquad (8.5)$$

$$w_i(s,a) \geq 0 \qquad (8.6)$$

$$v_l \leq \alpha_l(p_{l1} + p_{l2}) \qquad (8.7)$$

$$p_{l1} = (1 - \gamma_1) \sum_{s \in S_l, a} w_1(s,a) \qquad (8.8)$$

$$p_{l2} = (1 - \gamma_2) \sum_{s \in S_l, a} w_2(s,a) \qquad (8.9)$$

$$p_{l1} + p_{l2} \leq 1 \qquad (8.10)$$

$$0 \leq v_l \leq \beta f_l \qquad (8.11)$$

The objective function in equation 8.1 maximizes the total expected cost over all sites. Constraints 8.2–8.5 detail the transition graph flow constraints (for thorough inspections and simple inspections). Constraint 8.2 defines that x is equal to the probability of reaching a state s and performing action a multiplied by the probability of successfully transitioning to state s'. Constraint 8.5 ensures that the flow into a state s is equal to the flow out of the state. Constraints 8.4 and 8.5 enforce that the total flow in the transition graph, corresponding to the number of defender resources r_i, is held constant for both the flow out of the dummy source nodes s_i^+ and into the dummy sink nodes s_i^-.

Constraint 8.7 constrains the expected cost for site l. Constraints 8.8 and 8.9 define the probability of successfully inspecting a given site l and is the summation of probabilities of reaching any of l's corresponding states (thus triggering an inspection) and taking any action a. Note that the failure probability γ means that even if a violating site is inspected, there may not be a fine issued. Constraint 8.10 limits the overall probability of a site being inspected. If a site is visited by both thorough and simple inspection resources, the site will only have to pay a fine, at most, once. Constraint 8.11 defines the bounds for the adversary's expected cost; if the adversary's expected cost is at the upper bound ($v_l = \beta f_l$), we assume that the adversary would prefer to have a positive public perception and choose to comply rather than pay an equivalent amount in expected fines.

Evaluation

In order to explore the strategic tradeoffs that exist in our model of the tannery domain, we ran a series of experiments on our Kanpur tannery graph. For each experiment, we generated three distinct patrolling strategy types. (1) NECTAR's strategy, (2) the uniform random (UR) strategy in which at each time step every site has an equal probability of being chosen, and (3) an ad-hoc (AH) strategy: a deterministic strategy in which sites are visited in numerical order (by ID number).

In order to analyze how different resource types affect performance, for each experiment we generated six defender strategies: the first three (NEC-TAR, UR, AH) correspond to when the defender had twice as many simple inspection resources as thorough inspection resources, and the last three (again NECTAR, UR, AH) correspond to when the defender had no simple inspection resources.

In addition to running experiments in which each site l has the same fine (α), we ran a set of experiments in which each site's fine α_l was: $\alpha_l = \alpha f_l$ or, in other words, the fine amount is a constant α multiplied by the number of factories f_l at that site – sites with more factories will be penalized for violations more harshly than sites with fewer factories. As this type of analysis requires heterogeneous sites, we randomize the number of factories at each site.

Ultimately, we are interested in inducing compliance in sites, and for our performance metric we compute the number of sites that would be in full compliance given the defender strategy (i.e., how many sites' cost $v_l = \beta f_l$). The maximum number of sites in compliance for each experiment is 50 (i.e., the number of sites on our graph). The default parameter values for each experiment (unless otherwise specified) are listed in Table 8.1.

Fixed Fine Amount

In Figure 8.2, we analyze the effects of the fixed fine amount α on the number of complying sites. The x-axis shows the fixed fine amount, and the y-axis shows the number of sites that are complying (i.e., $v_l = \beta f_l$).

From the figure, we observe the following trends: (1) The NECTAR strategy does not achieve any compliance until the fine amount is 350, with all sites in compliance at 400. This is due to the objective function attempting to maximize expected cost over all sites simultaneously with a homogeneous fine. (2) While the UR and AH strategies achieve compliance from some of the sites for smaller fine amounts, they do not achieve compliance for all of the sites

Table 8.1. *Default experiment values*

Variable	Value
Compliance cost β	10
Fixed fine amount α	100
Number of factories at each site f_l	2-5
Number of simple inspections r_2	2
Number of sites	50
Number of thorough inspections r_1	1
Patrol duration (hours) t_1, t_2	6
Simple inspection failure rate γ_2	0.6
Thorough inspection failure rate γ_1	0.1
Time granularity (hours) h	1
Time steps to complete simple inspection	1
Time steps to complete thorough inspection	2
Variable fine amount α_l	30

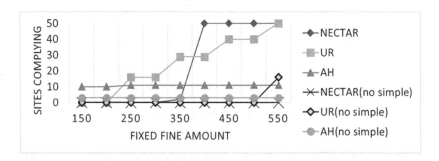

Figure 8.2 Fixed fine: number of sites in compliance.

as quickly as the NECTAR strategy. (3) The inclusion of simple inspection resources improves performance for every strategy, as expected.

Variable Fine Amount

In Figure 8.3, we analyze the effects of the variable fine amount α_l on the number of complying sites. The x-axis shows the variable fine amount, and the y-axis shows the number of sites in compliance (i.e., $v_l = \beta f_l$).

From the figure, we observe the following trends: (1) both the NECTAR and UR strategies achieve compliance from all sites for the same variable fine amount; (2) as the fines are not homogeneous for all sites, it is beneficial for NECTAR to try to maximize expected cost in sites with many factories first (unlike with the fixed fine, there is no "water filling" effect) as the NECTAR

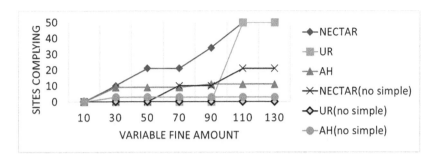

Figure 8.3 Variable fine: number of sites in compliance.

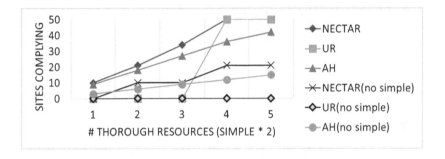

Figure 8.4 Number of resources, variable fine: number of sites in compliance.

approach achieves faster compliance from larger sites; and (3) NECTAR achieves compliance from the most sites at every point.

Number of Resources: Variable Fine

In Figure 8.4, we analyze the effect of the number of resources when there is a variable fine amount α_l on the number of complying sites. The x-axis shows the number of thorough inspection resources, r_1 (for the strategies with simple inspection resources, the number of simple inspection resources is $r_2 = 2 \times r_1$), and the y-axis shows the number of sites that are complying (i.e., $v_l = \beta f_l$).

From the figure, we observe the following trends: (1) the NECTAR and AH strategies achieve compliance from some sites even with few thorough inspection resources, but NECTAR achieves compliance from the most sites at every point; (2) both the NECTAR and UR strategies achieve compliance from all sites for the same number of thorough inspection resources; and (3) even when there are many resources, the AH strategy does not achieve compliance from all sites.

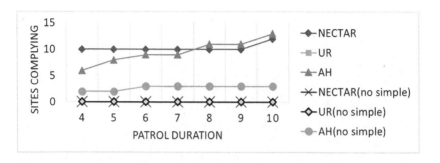

Figure 8.5 Patrol duration, variable fine: number of sites in compliance.

Patrol Duration: Variable Fine

In Figure 8.5, we analyze the effects of the patrol duration when there is a variable fine amount α_l on the number of complying sites. The x-axis shows the patrol duration, and the y-axis shows the number of sites that are complying (i.e., $v_l = \beta f_l$).

From the figure, we observe the following trends: (1) while the NECTAR strategy performs the best for lower values of patrol duration, it is eventually outpaced by the AH strategy; (2) regardless of the strategy, there is not much change in the number of sites in compliance as a function of patrol duration – For this experiment, the default values for the other parameters result in a low compliance rate regardless of the value of the variable of interest – and (3) having simple inspection resources is helpful for the NECTAR and AH strategies, but it is not very helpful for the UR strategy (zero sites complying in either case).

Discussion and Results Visualization

Based on these simulations, we make the following conclusions. (1) When the number of resources or variable fine amount is the experiment variable, NECTAR makes the most efficient use of its resources, regardless of whether it is using only thorough inspections or a combination of simple and thorough inspections. (2) Having more resources (more workers) is more useful than increasing the duration of patrols (longer work hours). This is intuitive when considering that each resource must spend time traveling to each site; two resources can each cover a separate subsection of the graph whereas one resource will be forced to spend more time traveling. Finally, (3) using a variable fine (in which sites are fined according to their number of factories)

Figure 8.6 Visualization example. Google Earth data: Google, DigitalGlobe.

leads to better compliance rates. This observation makes sense when put in the context of our LP's objective function: maximize the sum of the expected costs v_l over all sites.

Since our goal is to assist inspection agencies with patrol planning, it is useful to visualize the proposed inspection patrols. In Figure 8.6, we show a simple graph and strategy visualization in Google Earth (a visualization for the Kanpur area is shown in Figure 8.7). The lines represent edges on the graph (i.e., straight line connections between sites). Each line also has a time step and a coverage probability associated with it, where the probability represents the value of the MDP's transition function, $T(s, a, s')$. In other words, this information answers the question: If the defender resource starts at site l at time step t (i.e., state s), what is the probability that the resource will take action a and arrive at site l' at time step t' (i.e., state s')? By clicking on an edge, the user can call up the aforementioned defender strategy information (shown in Figure 8.6).

NECTAR has been proposed to decision-makers in governments, pollution control boards, and funding agencies that cover cleaning of large river basins. NECTAR could be delivered as a mobile application or a digital assistant to guide inspectors. While field inspectors have not used randomized inspection schemes in the past, they have given positive feedback on this approach. These proposals are still in a preliminary state, and experience from the literature suggests that the success of such initiatives, potentially lasting years, will

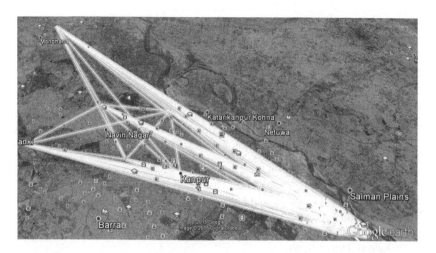

Figure 8.7 A Kanpur inspection patrol plan. Google Earth data: Google, Digital-Globe.

greatly depend on the collaboration of multiple stakeholders so that the tannery industry and economy can continue to grow while the urgent need to protect the environment is also satisfied.

Acknowledgments

This research was supported by MURI Grant W911NF-11-1-0332.

References

Alpern, S., Morton, A., and Papadaki, K. 2011. Patrolling games. *Operations Research*, **59**(5), 1246–1257.

Avenhaus, R., von Stengel, B., and Zamir, S. 2002. Inspection games. Pages 1947–1987 of: *Handbook of Game Theory with Economic Applications*, vol. 3. Amsterdam: Elsevier.

Basilico, N., Gatti, N., and Amigoni, F. 2012. Patrolling security games: definition and algorithms for solving large instances with single patroller and single intruder. *Artificial Intelligence Journal*, **184–185**, 78–123.

Blacksmith. Institute 2011. *Top Ten Toxic Pollution Problems: Tannery Operations*. Report.

Bošanský, B., Lisý, V., Jakob, M., and Pěchouček, M. 2011. Computing time-dependent policies for patrolling games with mobile targets. Pages 989–996 of: *The 10th International Conference on Autonomous Agents and Multiagent Systems*. International Foundation for Autonomous Agents and Multiagent Systems.

Bošanskỳ, B., Jiang, A., Tambe, M., and Kiekintveld, C. 2015. Combining compact representation and incremental generation in large games with sequential strategies. In: *Twenty-Ninth AAAI Conference on Artificial Intelligence*. AAAI Press.

Brown, M., Saisubramanian, S., Varakantham, P.R., and Tambe, M. 2014. STREETS: game-theoretic traffic patrolling with exploration and exploitation. In: *Proceedings of the Twenty-Eighth AAAI Conference on Artificial Intelligence*. AAAI Press.

Dong, X., Li, C., Li, J., Wang, J., and Huang, W. 2010. A game-theoretic analysis of implementation of cleaner production policies in the Chinese electroplating industry. *Resources, Conservation and Recycling*, **54**(12), 1442–1448.

Ellis, J., Srivastava, B., Bellamy, R.K.E., and Aaron, A. 2018. Water advisor: a data-driven, multi-modal, contextual assistant to help with water usage decisions. AAAI.

Filar, J. 1985. Player aggregation in the traveling inspector model. *IEEE Transactions on Automatic Control*, **30**(8), 723–729.

Gupta, S., Gupta, R., and Tamra, R. 2007. Challenges Faced by Leather Industry in Kanpur. Project report.

Jain, M., Conitzer, V., and Tambe, M. 2013. Security scheduling for real-world networks. In: *Proceedings of the 2013 International Conference on Autonomous Agents and Multi-agent Systems*. International Foundation for Autonomous Agents and Multiagent Systems.

Jainani, D. 2015. Kanpur leather industry in danger as NGT cracks whip on pollution. *Financial Express*, February 7.

Mwinyihija, M. 2011. Emerging world leather trends and continental shifts on leather and leathergoods production. In: *World leather Congress Proceedings*.

Planning Commission of India. 2013. *Evaluation Study on the Function of State Pollution Control Boards*. New Delhi: Planning Commission of India.

Shieh, E., Jiang, A.X., Yadav, A., et al. 2014. Unleashing Dec-MDPs in security games: enabling effective defender teamwork. In: *21st European Conference on Artificial Intelligence*. IOS Press.

Tambe, M. 2011. *Security and Game Theory: Algorithms, Deployed Systems, Lessons Learned*. New York: Cambridge University Press.

Tapiero, Charles S. 2005. Environmental quality control and environmental games. *Environmental Modeling & Assessment*, **9**(4), 201–206.

von Stengel, Bernhard. 2014. Recursive inspection games. *arXiv preprint arXiv: 1412.0129*.

Yin, Z., Jiang, A., Johnson, M., et al. 2012. TRUSTS: scheduling randomized patrols for fare inspection in transit systems. In: *Proceedings of the 24th Conference on Innovative Applications of Artificial Intelligence*. AAAI Press.

9

Connecting Conservation Research and Implementation

Building a Wildfire Assistant

Sean McGregor, Rachel M. Houtman, Ronald Metoyer, and Thomas G. Dietterich

Introduction

Nearly 1.6 billion people depend on forests for their livelihood. In many cases their economic activities place them in direct conflict with the best interests of 80 percent of all terrestrial animals, plants, and insects (United Nations, 2017). A common approach to balancing forest economic value with the inherent value of natural ecology is to publicly manage forests according to stakeholder objectives. Defining objectives serving all stakeholders is a challenging political process. For example, a period in the 1990s is referred to as the "Timber Wars" in the US Pacific Northwest because of the troubling and occasionally violent (Egan, 2005) conflicts that arose between stakeholder groups over forest management policies during that period. This is typical of many ecosystem management problems – the complexity of ecosystem dynamics and the broad array of interested parties makes it difficult to identify politically feasible policies.

A particularly challenging and controversial area of forest management is forest wildfire suppression decisions. Wildland fires pose immediate risks to wildlife, fire fighters, timber values, air quality, and recreation, but fires also produce long-term rewards in the form of biodiversity, reduced future fire risk, increased timber harvest, and more accessible forests. Despite a consensus in the forestry community on the necessity of allowing some wildfires to burn (Forest History Society, 2017), forest managers still suppress the vast majority of wildfires (Tephens and Ruth, 2005; United States Department of Agriculture, 2015).

The institutional constraints preventing forest managers from allowing more wildfires to burn is evident in their decision-support tools. Forest managers are required to use decision-support processes to *guide* and *document* wildfire management decisions (National Interagency Fire Center, 2009).

The Wildland Fire Decision Support System (WFDSS) fulfills this requirement with a web-based platform that includes components for situational assessment, hazard and risk analysis, and documentation of decision rationale. The WFDSS does not include a component estimating the future benefits of wildfires.

To help forest managers incorporate the future benefits of wildfires into their decision-making, we developed the WildFireAssistant system as a visual analytic environment for reward specification and policy optimization. Forest managers can modify the rewards realized over century time spans to represent different stakeholders, optimize a policy, and explore the results in a visualization. Forest managers can also document their decisions by saving the WildFireAssistant visualizations.

Developing WildFireAssistant posed several algorithmic challenges that are the focus of this work. The high-fidelity ecology, weather, and fire components of our Oregon Centennial Wildfire Simulator (OCWS) (Houtman et al., 2013) are extremely expensive computationally. Without a fast simulator, the forest manager cannot adequately explore the space of reward and policy functions. To address this problem we develop a method for pre-computing state transitions and avoid simulation when the forest manager interacts with WildFireAssistant. Further, we perform policy optimization on top of the pre-computed state transitions with a Bayesian policy search method. These two components reduce optimization time from hundreds of hours (fully parallelized) to less than a minute (without parallelization).

This work proceeds in four parts. First, we formally introduce the forest wildfire management problem. Second, we introduce the system architecture for WildFireAssistant as shown in Figure 9.1. The third part addresses the computational challenges associated with supporting interactive visualization and optimization of policies. Finally, we quantitatively evaluate the quality of WildFireAssistant visualization and optimization.

Wildfire Suppression Decisions in Context

Endert et al. (2014) recommend shifting from "human in the loop" design to "human *is* the loop" design. The difference between the two viewpoints is one in which humans assist the computational process (i.e., humans are *in* the loop) to one in which the computing process supports the human. For the cultural and practical considerations of forestry decisions, "human *is* the loop" is the proper design philosophy. The official training course for "Advanced Incident Management with WFDSS" (The National Wildfire Coordinating Group, 2009) states,

Figure 9.1 A complete view of the WildFireAssistant process. We begin by loading high-fidelity simulations into a state transition database. Next the user enters the optimization and exploration loop by specifying the reward function and requesting an optimized policy. Then the black box optimization algorithm SMAC produces a newly optimized policy by repeatedly calling a model-free Monte Carlo with independencies (MFMCi) surrogate model. After optimizing the policy, the MFMCi surrogate returns one more batches of trajectories for visualization. After exploring the trajectories with visualization, the user may then request an optimized policy for a different reward function.

Decision-making is not a science but an art. It requires judgment not calculation. There is no unit of measure which can weigh the substantive consequences of a decision against the political consequences, or judge the precise portions of public opinion and congressional pressure, or balance short-range against long-range, or private against public considerations.

This advice reveals the wider culture of forest policy research, which typically performs case study policy optimizations that either minimize market costs (like suppression expenses; Houtman et al., 2013), or maximize a non-market benefit (like species abundance; Ager et al., 2007). If the study includes a non-market reward with another reward component, then the specification of their relative importance requires extensive post-optimization analysis and justification. Despite the potential for controversy, there are considerable advantages to jointly optimizing multi-objective reward functions. For instance, Dilkina et al. (2016) showed considerable efficiency gains in jointly optimizing wildlife reserve land acquisition for multiple species.

In the wildfire simulations of the OCWS, we can optimize policies for any combination of biodiversity, fire suppression expenses, air quality, recreation, and timber. The OCWS defines a finite horizon discounted Markov decision process (MDP) with a designated start state distribution (Bellman, 1957; Puterman, 1994) $\mathcal{M} = \langle S, A, P, R, \gamma, P_0, h \rangle$. S is a finite set of states of the world; A is a finite set of possible actions that can be taken in each state; $P : S \times A \times S \mapsto [0, 1]$ is the conditional probability of entering state s' when action a is executed in state s; $R(s, a)$ is the reward received after performing action a in state s; $\gamma \in (0, 1)$ is the discount factor, P_0 is the distribution over starting states, and h is the horizon. The optimization goal is to find a policy, π, that selects actions maximizing the expected discounted sum of rewards of the MDP.

Figure 9.2 shows a snapshot of the landscape as simulated by the OCWS. The landscape is composed of approximately one million pixels, each with

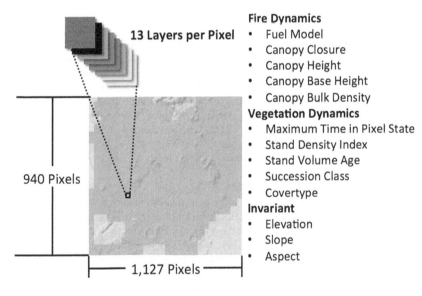

Figure 9.2 The landscape totals approximately one million pixels, each of which has 13 state variables that influence the spread of wildfire on the landscape (map is copyright of OpenStreetMap contributors).

13 layers summarizing the invariant properties of the location (i.e., elevation, slope, aspect) and the dynamic vegetation attributes (i.e., tree properties and density). When a fire is ignited by lightning, the policy must choose between two actions: *Suppress* (fight the fire) and *Let Burn* (do nothing). Hence, $|A| = 2$.

The simulator spreads wildfires with the FARSITE fire model (Finney, 1998) according to the surrounding pixel variables (X) and the hourly weather. Weather variables include *hourly wind speed, hourly wind direction, hourly cloud cover, daily maximum/minimum temperature, daily maximum/minimum humidity, daily hour of maximum/minimum temperature, daily precipitation,* and *daily precipitation duration.* These are generated by resampling from 25 years of observed weather (Western Regional Climate Center, 2011).

After computing the extent of the wildfire on the landscape, the simulator applies a cached version of the Forest Vegetation Simulator (Dixon, 2002) to update the vegetation of the individual pixels. Finally, a harvest scheduler selects pixels to harvest for timber value.

Simulating the spread of fire is computationally expensive. Generating a single 100-year trajectory of wildfire simulations takes up to seven hours to complete, which makes it very difficult to explore the policy space for many different reward functions. With fast simulations, we can support interactively changing the reward function and re-optimizing the results. We describe a method for quickly simulating wildfires after introducing WildFireAssistant.

WildFireAssistant for Forest Managers

Visual analytics combines automated analysis techniques with interactive visualizations for understanding, reasoning, and decision-making (Keim et al., 2008). WildFireAssistant is a visual analytics system that meets the following requirements:

1. **Modifiability**: users should be able to modify the reward function to represent the interests of various stakeholders.
2. **Automatic optimization**: users should be able to optimize policies for the updated reward functions without the involvement of a machine learning researcher.
3. **Visualization**: users should be able to visualize the system so that it is easy for users to explore the behavior of the system when it is controlled by the optimized policies.
4. **Interactivity**: users should be able to modify reward functions, optimize policies, and visualize the results many times within a single user session.

These requirements support a visual analytics knowledge generation model (Sacha et al., 2014) through a parameter space analysis (PSA) process (Sedlmair et al., 2014). PSA is defined as a set of techniques for understanding the relationship between input parameters and outputs by systematically varying model input parameters, generating outputs for each combination of parameters, and investigating the relation between parameter settings and corresponding outputs. In the case of MDPs, the policy, transition, and reward functions can all be parameterized and subjected to PSA.

Throughout the design and development process, we worked closely with forestry economics collaborators to design WildFireAssistant as a version of the MDPvis visualization system shown in Figure 9.3. MDPvis includes parameter control areas and three visualization panels. The parameter controls allow the forest manager to change reward parameters and request a newly optimized policy, as shown in Figure 9.1. The reward parameters and the policies they produce are saved in an exploration history for subsequent reference and generation of decision documentation.

The first two visualization areas show sets of trajectories and provide ways for applying filters to the current trajectory set. This supports a global-to-local (Sedlmair et al., 2014) exploration process in which the user starts with an overview of all trajectories before drilling down into specific trajectories.

To render distributions of time series, we represent state variables as fan charts, giving the deciles of each variable across trajectory time steps. To produce the fan chart, we first plot a lightly colored area whose top and bottom represent the largest and smallest value of the variable in each time step. On top of this lightest color, we plot a series of colors increasing in darkness with nearness to the trajectory set's median value for the time step.

Fan charts show both the diversity of outcomes and the probability of particular ranges of values. For instance, when a forest manager is examining the risk of a catastrophic fire, they can view the fan chart displaying the distribution of fire sizes through time. The worst-case scenarios will be shown by the maximum extent of the fan chart in each time step.

After generating trajectories for multiple parameter sets, the user can place the visualization into "comparison mode," which displays the difference between two trajectory sets in the visualization areas. When in comparison mode, the fan chart color extents are plotted by subtracting a color's maximum (minimum) extent from the corresponding maximum (minimum) extent of the other fan chart. By rendering the shift in decile boundaries, the user can see how different policies shape the probability of different outcomes through time. When the policies are optimized for different reward functions, it is possible to examine how the outcomes predicted for different stakeholder groups differ when executing their optimized policies.

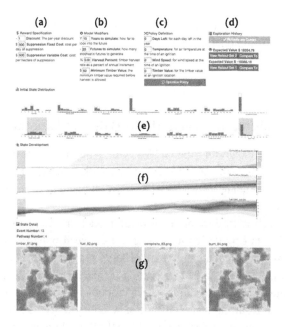

Figure 9.3 A high-level overview of the MDP visualization, MDPvis. The top row has the three parameter controls for (a) the reward specification, (b) the model modifiers, and (c) the policy definition. A fourth panel gives the history of Monte Carlo trajectory sets generated under the parameters of panels (a) through (c). Changes to the parameters enable the optimization button found under the policy definition and the Monte Carlo trajectories button found under the Exploration History section. The visualization has two buttons in the History panel for each set of Monte Carlo trajectories, one for visualizing the associated Monte Carlo trajectories and another for comparing two sets of trajectories. Below the control panels are visualization areas for (e) histograms of the initial state distribution, (f) fan charts for the distribution of variables over time, and (g) a series of individual states rendered by the simulator as images. For a readable version of the visualization we invite users to load the visualization in their browser by visiting *MDPvis.github.io*.

The final visualization area gives a "state detail" view, which is an extensible two-dimensional array of images or videos shown at the bottom of MDPvis. By supporting extensibility, it is possible to introduce ecology-specific visualizations like GIS maps.

To prototype the visualization, we interacted with an idealized fast wildfire simulator that supported **automatic optimization** and **Interactivity** (McGregor et al., 2015, 2016). Despite it being a simplistic wildfire domain, we discovered bugs in the fire spread implementation, harvest planner, random number generator, optimizer, and other components. Even after fixing these bugs the prototyping simulator is not sufficient for real-world policy. In the next section we integrate the OCWS and restore *interactive* visualization through additional modeling effort.

Adding Interactivity to WildFireAssistant

We now turn to integrating the OCWS with WildFireAssistant. Our starting point is running the simulator for every new policy query, which takes up to seven hours to simulate. How can we support interactivity when the simulator is so expensive?

Our approach is to develop a surrogate model that can substitute for the simulator. We start by designing a small set of "seed policies" and invoking the slow simulator to generate several 100-year trajectories for each policy. This gives us a database of state transitions of the form (s_t, a_t, r_t, s_{t+1}), where s_t is the state at time t, a_t is the selected action, r_t is the resulting reward, and s_{t+1} is the resulting state. Given a new policy π to visualize, we apply the method of model-free Monte Carlo (MFMC) (Fonteneau et al., 2013) to simulate trajectories for π by stitching together state transitions according to a specified distance metric Δ. Given a current state s and desired action $a = \pi(s)$, MFMC searches the database to find a tuple $(\tilde{s}, \tilde{a}, r, s')$ that minimizes the distance $\Delta((s, a), (\tilde{s}, \tilde{a}))$. It then uses s' as the resulting state and r as the corresponding one-step reward. We call this operation "stitching" (s, a) to $(\tilde{s}, \tilde{a})$. MFMC is guaranteed to give reasonable simulated trajectories under assumptions about the smoothness of the transition dynamics and reward function and provided that each matched tuple is removed from the database when it is used. Algorithm 9.1 provides the pseudocode for MFMC generating a single trajectory.

We selected the MFMC surrogate in lieu of two other approaches for quickly generating trajectories. First, we could write our own simulator for fire spread, timber harvest, weather, and vegetative growth that computes the state transitions more efficiently. For instance, Arca et al. (2013) use a custom-built model running on GPUs to calculate fire-risk maps and mitigation strategies. However, developing a new simulator requires additional work to design, implement, and (especially) validate the simulator. This cost can easily overwhelm the resulting time savings when deploying to new conservation domains. Further, forest managers trust the models incorporated into the OCWS simulator. It is critically important that the WildFireAssistant employ highly accurate state-of-the-art simulators in order to be trusted by decision-makers.

Algorithm 9.1. MFMC for a single trajectory. When generating multiple trajectories for a single trajectory set, the state transitions from D must not be reused (Fonteneau et al., 2010).

Input Parameters: Policy π, horizon h, starting state s_0, distance metric $\Delta(.,.)$, database D;

Returns: $(s, a, r)_1, ..., (s', a', r')_h$;

$t \leftarrow \emptyset$;

$s \leftarrow s_0$;

while *length(t)*$< h$ **do**

$\quad$ $a \leftarrow \pi(s)$;

$\quad$ $X \leftarrow \underset{(\tilde{s}, \tilde{a}, r, s') \in D}{\mathrm{argmin}} \; \Delta((s, a), (\tilde{s}, \tilde{a}))$;

$\quad$ $r \leftarrow X^r$;

$\quad$ append($t, (s, a, r)$);

$\quad$ $s \leftarrow X^{s'}$;

$\quad$ $D \leftarrow D \setminus X$;

end

return(t);

A second approach would be to learn a parametric surrogate model from data generated by the slow simulator. For instance, Abbeel et al. (2005) learn helicopter dynamics by updating the parameters of a function designed specifically for helicopter flight. Designing a suitable parametric model that can capture weather, vegetation, fire spread, and the effect of fire suppression would require a major modeling effort.

The advantage of MFMC surrogates over these techniques is the ability to build the transition database from state transitions of simulators trusted in the forestry community. Further, it is possible to build on standard database technologies that are guaranteed to be fast. Despite these advantages, MFMC has never been applied to high-dimensional MDPS. In high-dimensional spaces (i.e., where the states and actions are described by many features), MFMC breaks because of two related problems. First, distances become less informative in high-dimensional spaces. Second, the required number of seed-policy trajectories grows exponentially in the dimensionality of the space. Our main technical contribution is to introduce a modified algorithm, MFMCi, that reduces the dimensionality of the distance-matching process by factoring out certain exogenous state variables and removing the features describing the action. In many applications, this can very substantially reduce the dimensionality of the matching process to the point that MFMC is again practical.

We now describe how we can factor the state variables of an MDP in order to reduce the dimensionality of the MFMC stitching computation. State variables can be divided into Markovian and time-independent random variables. A time-independent random variable x_t is exchangeable over time t and does not depend on any other random variable (including its own previous values). A (first-order) Markovian random variable x_{t+1} depends on its value x_t at the previous time step. In particular, the state variable s_{t+1} depends on s_t and the chosen action a_t. Variables can also be classified as endogenous and exogenous. The variable x_t is exogenous if its distribution is independent of $a_{t'}$ and $s_{t'} \setminus \{x'_t\}$ for all $t' \leq t$. Non-exogenous variables are endogenous. In conservation problems, Markovian variables are typically the state of the landscape from one time step to another.

Let us factor the MDP state s into two vectors of random variables: w, which contains the time-independent, exogenous state variables and x, which contains all of the other state variables (see Figure 9.4). Time independent exogenous random variables can include wildfire ignitions, the introduction of an invasive species, macroeconomic conditions, weather, and government budgets. In our wildfire suppression domain, the state of the forest from one time step to another is Markovian, but our policy decisions also depend on exogenous weather events such as rain, wind, and lightning.

We can formalize this factorization as follows.

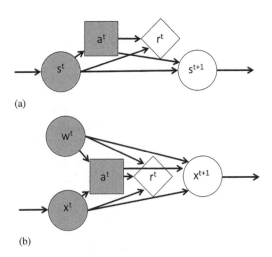

Figure 9.4 MDP probabilistic graphical models: (a) the standard MDP transition; (b) MDP transition with *exogenous* (w) and *Markovian* variables (x).

Definition 9.1   A factored exogenous MDP is an MDP such that the state (x, w) and next state (x', w') are related according to

$$Pr(x', w' | x, w, a) = Pr(w')Pr(x' | x, w, a).   \qquad (9.1)$$

This factorization allows us to avoid computing similarity in the complete state space s. Instead we only need to compute the similarity of the Markov state x. Without the factorization, MFMC stitches (s, a) to the $(\tilde{s}, \tilde{a})$ in the database D that minimizes a distance metric Δ, where Δ has the form $\Delta((s, a), (\tilde{s}, \tilde{a})) \mapsto \mathbb{R}^+$. Our new algorithm, MFMCi, makes its stitching decisions using only the Markov state. It stitches the current state x by finding the tuple $(\tilde{x}, \tilde{w}, a, r, x')$ that minimizes the lower-dimensional distance metric $\Delta_i(x, \tilde{x})$. MFMCi then adopts $(\tilde{x}, \tilde{w})$ as the current state, computes the policy action $\tilde{a} = \pi(\tilde{x}, \tilde{w})$, and then makes a transition to x' with reward r. The rationale for replacing x by $\tilde{x}$ is the same as in MFMC, namely that it is the nearest state from the database D. The rationale for replacing w by $\tilde{w}$ is that both w and $\tilde{w}$ are exchangeable draws from the exogenous time-independent distribution $P(w)$, so they can be swapped without changing the distribution of simulated paths.

There is one subtlety that can introduce bias into the simulated trajectories. What happens when the action $\tilde{a} = \pi(\tilde{x}, \tilde{w})$ is not equal to the action a in the database tuple $(\tilde{x}, \tilde{w}, a, r, x', w')$? One approach would be to require that $a = \tilde{a}$ and keep rejecting candidate tuples until we find one that satisfies this constraint; however, this method introduces a bias. Consider again the graphical model in Figure 9.4. When we use the value of a to decide whether to accept $\tilde{w}$, this couples $\tilde{w}$ and $\tilde{x}$ so that they are no longer independent.

We can remove this bias by changing how we generate the database D to ensure that for every state $(\tilde{x}, \tilde{w})$, there is always a tuple $(\tilde{x}, \tilde{w}, a, r, x', w')$ for every possible action a. To do this, as we execute a trajectory-following policy π, we simulate the result state (x', w') and reward r for each possible action a and not just the action $a = \pi(x, w)$ dictated by the policy. This requires drawing more samples during database construction, but it restores the independence of $\tilde{w}$ from $\tilde{x}$.

It is convenient to collect together all the simulated successor states and rewards into *transition sets*. Let $B(x, w)$ denote the transition set of tuples $\{(x, w, a, x', r)\}$ generated by simulating each action a in state (x, w). Given a transition set B, it is useful to define selector notation as follows. Subscripts of B constrain the set of matching tuples and superscripts indicate which variable is extracted from the matching tuples. Hence, $B_a^{x'}$ denotes the result state x' for the tuple in B that matches action a. With this notation, Algorithm 9.2 describes the process of populating the database with transition sets.

Algorithm 9.2. Populating D for MFMCi by sampling whole trajectories.

Input Parameters: Policy π, horizon h, trajectory count n, transition
simulator f_x, reward simulator f_r, exogenous distribution $P(w)$,
stochasticity distribution $P(z)$

Returns: nh transition sets B

$D \leftarrow \emptyset$

while $|D| < nh$ **do**

 $x = f_x(\cdot, \cdot, \cdot, \cdot)$ // Draw initial Markov state

 $l = 0$

 while $l < h$ **do**

  $B \leftarrow \emptyset$

  $w \sim P(w)$

  $z \sim P(z)$

  for $a \in A$ **do**

   $r \leftarrow f_r(x, a, w, z)$

   $x' \leftarrow f_x(x, a, w, z)$

   $B \leftarrow B \cup \{(x, w, a, r, x')\}$

  end

  append(D,B)

  $x \leftarrow B^{x'}_{\pi(x,w)}$

  $l \leftarrow l + 1$

 end

end

return(D)

Algorithm 9.3 gives the pseudocode for MFMCi. To estimate the cumulative return of policy π, we call MFMCi n times without database replacement and compute the mean of the cumulative rewards of the resulting trajectories.

Fonteneau et al. (2010) apply MFMC to estimate the expected cumulative return of a new policy π and derived bias and variance bounds on the MFMC value estimate. We reworked this derivation (McGregor et al., 2017a) to provide analogous bounds for MFMCi. The MFMC bounds depend on assuming Lipschitz smoothness of the state, policy, and reward spaces and bound the error that can be introduced at each time step by assuming the database contains transitions across the whole state–action space. MFMCi improves on these bounds by eliminating the need for the Lipschitz assumption on the policy space and exogenous state space variables.

With the MFMCi surrogate, it becomes possible to quickly generate whole trajectories from arbitrary policies. In our experimental section, we will

---

Algorithm 9.3. MFMCi

Input Parameters: Policy π, horizon h, starting state x_0, distance metric
$\Delta_i(\cdot, \cdot)$, database D
Returns: $(x_0, w, a, r)_1, \ldots, (x', w', a', r')_h$
$t \leftarrow \emptyset$
$x \leftarrow x_0$
while $length(t) < h$ **do**
$\quad \hat{B} \leftarrow \operatorname{argmin}_{B \in D} \Delta_i(x, B^{x'})$
$\quad \hat{w} \leftarrow \hat{B}^w$
$\quad a \leftarrow \pi(x, \hat{w})$
$\quad r \leftarrow \hat{B}^r_a$
$\quad \operatorname{append}(t, (x, w, a, r))$
$\quad D \leftarrow D \setminus \hat{B}$
$\quad x \leftarrow B^{x'}_a$
end
return(t)

---

empirically demonstrate how MFMCi improves on an MFMC baseline for visualizing policies within WildFireAssistant. Then we will optimize policies from the MFMCi surrogate with a fast black box optimization method and evaluate the resulting policies directly within the OCWS.

Experimental Evaluation

In our experiments we evaluate the quality of trajectory visualizations and then an optimization method invoking the MFMCi surrogate.

Evaluation of Visualization Fidelity

We constructed three policy classes that map fire ignitions to fire suppression decisions. We label these policies INTENSITY, FUEL, and LOCATION. The INTENSITY policy suppresses fires based on the weather conditions at the time of the ignition and the number of days remaining in the fire season. The FUEL policy suppresses fires when the landscape accumulates sufficient high-fuel pixels. The LOCATION policy suppresses fires that are ignited in the top half of the landscape, but allows fires on the bottom half of the landscape to burn. These policies approximate scenarios in which the goal is to prevent catastrophic fires or the destruction of structures located on the north side of the landscape.

We focus on sampling database states that are likely to be entered by future policy queries by seeding the database with one trajectory for each of 360 policies whose parameters are chosen according to a grid over the INTENSITY policy space. The INTENSITY policy parameters include a measure of the weather conditions at the time of ignition, known as the energy release component (ERC) and a measure of the seasonal risk in the form of the calendar day. These measures are drawn from $[0, 100]$ and $[0, 180]$, respectively.

One of our goals is to determine whether MFMCi can generalize from state transitions generated from the INTENSITY policy to accurately simulate state transitions under the FUEL and LOCATION policies. We selected these policy classes because they are functions of different components of the Markov and exogenous state such that knowing the action selected within one of the policy classes will not indicate the action selected by the other policy classes. We evaluate MFMCi by generating 30 trajectories for each policy from the ground truth simulator.

For our distance metric Δ_i, we use a weighted Euclidean distance computed over the mean/variance standardized values of the following landscape features: *Canopy Closure, Canopy Height, Canopy Base Height, Canopy Bulk Density, Stand Density Index, High Fuel Count, and Stand Volume Age.* All of these variables are given a weight of 1. An additional feature, the time step (*Year*), is added to the distance metric with a very large weight to ensure that MFMCi will only stitch from one state to another if the time steps match. Introducing this non-stationarity ensures we exactly capture landscape growth stages for all pixels that do not experience fire.

Our choice of distance metric features is motivated by our key insight that the risk profile (the likely size of a wildfire) and the vegetation profile (the total tree cover) are easy to capture in low dimensions. If we instead attempt to capture the likely size of a *specific* fire on a landscape, we need a distance metric that accounts for the exact spatial distribution of fuels on the landscape. Our distance metric successfully avoids directly modeling spatial complexity while still generating accurate visualizations and estimators of the discounted reward.

We quantitatively evaluate the quality of the surrogate MDPvis fan charts by defining visual fidelity error as the difference in vertical position between the MFMCi median and the Monte Carlo sampled median (see Figure 9.5). More formally, we define error(v, t) as the offset between the correct location of the median and its MFMCi-modeled location for state variable v in time step t. We normalize the error by the height of the fan chart for the rendered policy $(H_v(\pi))$. The weighted error is thus $\sum_{v \in S} \sum_{t=0}^{h} \frac{\text{error}(v,t)}{H_v(\pi)}$.

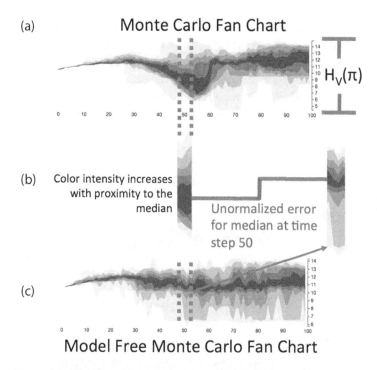

Figure 9.5 (a) A fan chart generated by Monte Carlo simulations from the expensive simulator. (b) A fan chart generated from the MFMC surrogate model. *x*-axis is the time step and *y*-axis is the value of the state variable at each time step. Each change in color shows a quantile boundary for a set of trajectories generated under policy π. (b) Error measure is the distance between the median of the Monte Carlo simulations (left) and the median of the MFMC/MFMCi surrogate simulations (right). The error is normalized across fan charts according to $H_v(\pi)$, which is the Monte Carlo fan chart height for policy π and variable v.

This error is measured for 20 variables related to the counts of burned pixels, fire suppression expenses, timber loss, timber harvest, and landscape ecology.

We evaluated the visual fidelity for both MFMC (including exogenous variables in the distance metric) and MFMCi. We also compare against two baselines that explore the upper and lower bounds of the visual error. First, we show that the lower bound on visual error is not zero. Although each policy has true quantile values at every time step, estimating these quantiles with 30 trajectories is inherently noisy. The computational expense of the ground truth simulator prevents estimating its visual fidelity error directly, instead we find the average achievable visual fidelity error by bootstrap resampling the

30 ground truth trajectories. Second, we check whether the error introduced by stitching is worse than visualizing a set of random database trajectories. Thus the bootstrap resample forms a lower bound on the error, and comparison to the random trajectories detects stitching failure.

Figures 9.6 and 9.7 plot the visual fidelity error when simulating LOCA-TION and FUEL policies, respectively, from the database of INTENSITY policy

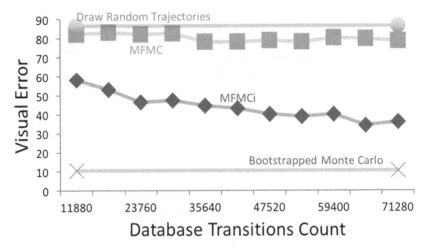

Figure 9.6 Visual fidelity errors for an ignition *location* policy class. Fires are always suppressed if they start on the top half of the landscape, otherwise they are always allowed to burn.

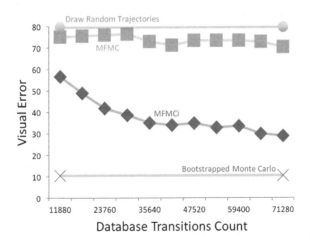

Figure 9.7 Visual fidelity errors for a *fuel* accumulation policy class. Fires are always suppressed if the landscape is at least 30 percent in high fuels, otherwise the fire is allowed to burn.

trajectories. The ideal learning curve should show a rapid decrease in visual fidelity error as $|D|$ grows. When D is small, the error is very high. MFMC is unable to reduce this error as D grows, because its distance metric does not find matching fire conditions for similar landscapes. In contrast, because the MFMCi methods are matching on the smaller set of Markov state variables, they are able to find good matching trajectories.

In summary, our experiments show that MFMCi generalizes across policy classes and that it requires only a small number of database trajectories to accurately reproduce the median of each state variable at each future time step. Having specified a surrogate that quickly generates trajectories, we now turn to supporting optimization from these trajectories.

Evaluation of Policy Optimization

WildFireAssistant requires an optimization method that is fast and can optimize any reward function specified by forest managers. We employ SMAC (Hutter et al., 2010), a black box optimization algorithm originally developed for tuning the hyperparameters of algorithms.

SMAC is similar to Bayesian methods for black box optimization. However, unlike those methods, SMAC does not employ a Gaussian process to model the black box function. Instead, it fits a random forest ensemble (Breiman, 2001). This has three important benefits. First, it does not impose any smoothness assumption on the black box function. We will see below that wildfire policies are naturally expressed in the form of decision trees, so they are highly non-smooth. Second, SMAC does not require the design of a Gaussian process kernel. This makes it more suitable for application by end users such as forest managers. Third, the CPU time required for SMAC scales as $O(n \log n)$ where n is the number of evaluations of the black box function, whereas standard GP methods scale as $O(n^3)$ because they must compute and invert the kernel matrix.

Let Π be a class of deterministic policies with an associated parameter space Θ. Each parameter vector $\theta \in \Theta$ defines a policy $\pi_\theta : S \mapsto A$ that specifies what action to take in each state. Let $\tau = \langle s_0, s_1, \ldots, s_h \rangle$ be a trajectory generated by drawing a state $s_0 \sim P_0(s_0)$ according to the starting state distribution and then following policy π_θ for h steps. Let $\rho = \langle r_0, \ldots, r_{h-1} \rangle$ be the corresponding sequence of rewards. Both τ and ρ are random variables because they reflect the stochasticity of the starting state and the probability transition function. Let V_θ define the expected cumulative discounted return of applying policy π_θ starting in a state $s_0 \sim P_0(s_0)$ and executing it for h steps:

$$V_\theta = \mathbb{E}_\rho[r_0 + \gamma r_1 + \gamma^2 r_2 + \cdots + \gamma^{h-1} r_{h-1}].$$

The goal of "direct policy search" is to find θ^* that maximizes the value of the corresponding policy:

$$\theta^* = \underset{\theta \in \Theta}{\operatorname{argmax}} V_\theta.$$

Sequential model-based optimization methods (Kushner, 1964; Zilinskas, 1992; Mockus, 1994; Hutter et al., 2010; Srinivas et al., 2010; Wilson et al., 2014; Wang et al., 2016) construct a model of V_θ called a policy value model and denoted $PVM(\theta)$. The PVM estimates both the value of V_θ and a measure of the uncertainty of that value. The basic operation of sequential model-based optimization methods is to select a new point θ at which to query the PVM, observe the value of V_θ at that point (e.g., by simulating a trajectory τ using π_θ), and then update the PVM to reflect this new information. In Bayesian optimization, the PVM is initialized with a prior distribution over possible policy value functions and then updated after gathering observations by applying Bayes' rule. The new points θ are selected by invoking an *acquisition function*.

SMAC (Hutter et al., 2010) is a sequential model-based optimization method in which the PVM is a random forest of regression trees. The estimated value of V_θ is obtained by "dropping" θ through each of the regression trees until it reaches a leaf in each tree and then computing the mean and the variance of the training data points stored in all of those leaves. In each iteration, SMAC evaluates V_θ at ten different values of θ, adds the observed values to its database R of (θ, V_θ) pairs, and then rebuilds the random forest.

SMAC chooses five of the ten θ values with the goal of finding points that have high "generalized expected improvement." The (ordinary) expected improvement at point θ is the expected increase in the maximum value of the PVM that will be observed when we measure V_θ under the assumption that V_θ has a normal distribution whose mean is μ_θ (the current PVM estimate of the mean at θ) and whose variance is σ_θ^2 (the PVM estimate of the variance at θ). The expected improvement at θ can be computed as

$$EI(\theta) := \mathbb{E}\big[I(\theta)\big] = \sigma_\theta\big[z \cdot \Phi(z) + \phi(z)\big], \qquad (9.2)$$

where $z = \frac{\mu_\theta - f_{max}}{\sigma_\theta}$, f_{max} is the largest known value of the current PVM, Φ denotes the cumulative distribution function of the standard normal distribution, and ϕ denotes the probability density function of the standard normal distribution (Jones et al., 1998).

The generalized expected improvement (GEI) is obtained by computing the expected value of $I(\theta)$ raised to the gth power. In SMAC, g is set to 2. Hutter et al. (2010) show that this can be computed as

$$GEI(\theta) = \mathbb{E}\big[I^2(\theta)\big] = \sigma_\theta^2\big[(z^2 + 1) \cdot \Phi(z) + z \cdot \phi(z)\big]. \qquad (9.3)$$

Ideally, SMAC would find the value of θ that maximizes $GEI(\theta)$ and then evaluate V_θ at that point. However, this would require a search in the high-dimensional space of Θ, and it would also tend to focus on a small region of Θ. Instead, SMAC employs the following heuristic strategy to find ten candidate values of θ. First, it performs a local search in the neighborhood of the ten best-known values of θ in the PVM. This provides ten candidate values. Next, it randomly generates another 10,000 candidate θ vectors from Θ and evaluates the GEI of each of them. Finally, it chooses the five best points from these 10,010 candidates and five points sampled at random from the 10,000 random candidates, and evaluates V_θ at each of these ten points. This procedure mixes "exploration" (the five random points) with "exploitation" (the five points with maximum GEI), and it has been found empirically to work well.

Hutter et al. (2010) prove that the SMAC PVM is a consistent estimator of V and that given an unbounded number of evaluations of V, it finds the optimal value θ^*.

In our experimental evaluation, we optimize and validate policies for the two different reward functions with components shown in Table 9.1. These two reward functions may approximate a homeowner, and a proposed composite reward function that may be representative of some combination of homeowner, timber company, naturalist, and recreational stakeholder interests.

The reward functions are compositions of five different reward components. The *Suppression* component gives the expenses incurred for suppressing a fire. Fire suppression expenses increase with fire size and the number of days the fire burns. Without fire suppression effort, the fire suppression costs are zero, but the fire generally takes longer to self-extinguish. *Timber* harvest values

Table 9.1. *Components of each reward function. The "homeowner" constituency only cares about air quality and recreation. The "composite" reward function takes an unweighted sum of all the costs and revenues realized by forest stakeholders. Additional reward functions can be specified by forest managers interactively within WildFireAssistant*

	Suppression costs	Timber revenues	Ecology target	Air quality	Recreation target
Composite	✓	✓	✓	✓	✓
Homeowners	-	-	-	✓	✓

sum the sale price for board feet of timber. *Ecological* value is a function of the squared deviation from an officially specified target distribution of vegetation on the landscape, known as the "restoration target." *Air quality* is a function of the number of days a wildfire burns. When fires burn, the smoke results in a large number of homeowner complaints. We encode this as a negative reward for each smoky day. Finally, the *Recreation* component penalizes the squared deviation from a second vegetation target distribution – namely, one preferred by people hiking and camping. If we optimize for any single reward component, the optimal policy will tend to be one of the trivial policies "suppress-all" or "letburn-all." When multiple reward components are included, the optimal policy still tends to either suppress or let burn most fires by default, but it tries to identify exceptional fires where the default should be overridden. See Houtman et al. (2013) for a discussion of this phenomenon.

A natural policy class in this domain takes the form of a binary decision tree as shown in Figure 9.8. At each level of the tree, the variable to split on is fixed

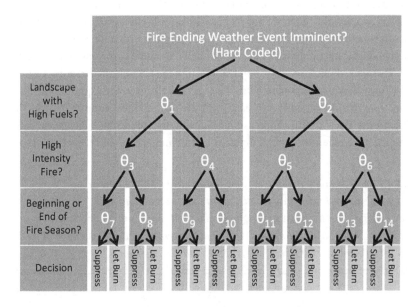

Figure 9.8 The layers of the decision tree used to select wildfires for suppression. The top layer splits on whether the fire will likely be extinguished by a storm in the next eight days regardless of the suppression decision. The next layers then have 14 parameters for the number of pixels that are in high fuel (parameters 1 and 2, $[0, 1000000]$), the intensity of the weather conditions at the time of the fire (3 through 6, $[0, 100]$), and a threshold that determines whether the fire is close to either the start or end of the fire season (7 through 14, $[0, 90]$).

in this policy class. With the exception of the very first split at the root, which has a hard-coded threshold, the splitting thresholds $\theta_1, \ldots, \theta_{14}$ are all adjusted by the policy optimization process. Moving from the top layer of the tree to the bottom, the tree splits first on whether the fire will be extinguished within the next eight days by a "fire-ending weather event" (i.e., substantial rain or snowfall). The threshold value of 8 is fixed (based on discussions with forest managers and on the predictive scope of weather forecasts). The next layer splits on the state of fuel accumulation on the landscape. The fuel level is compared either to θ_1 (left branch, no weather event predicted within eight days) or θ_2 (right branch; weather predicted within eight days). When the fuel level is larger than the corresponding threshold, the right branch of the tree is taken. The next layer splits on the intensity of the fire at the time of ignition. In this fire model, the fire intensity is quantified in terms of the ERC, which is a composite measure of dryness in fuels. Finally, the last layer of the tree asks whether the current date is close to the start or end of the fire season. Our study region in eastern Oregon is prone to late spring and early fall rains, which means fires near the boundary of the fire season are less likely to burn very long.

We apply SMAC with its default configuration. Optimization details are provided by McGregor et al. (2017b). Every query to the MFMCi surrogate generates 30 trajectories, and the mean cumulative discounted reward of these is returned as the observed value of V_θ.

Figure 9.9 shows the results of applying SMAC to find optimal policies for the two reward functions. The left column of plots show the order in which SMAC explores the policy parameter space. The vertical axis is the estimated cumulative discounted reward, and the point that is highest denotes the final policy output by SMAC. Line dashes are policy parameter vectors chosen by the GEI acquisition function, whereas circles are parameter vectors chosen by SMAC's random sampling process. Notice that in all cases, SMAC rapidly finds a fairly good policy. The right column of plots gives us some sense of how the different policies behave. Each plot shows the percentage of fires that each policy suppresses. In Figure 9.9(b), we see that the highest-scoring policies allow almost all fires to burn, whereas in Figure 9.9(d), the highest-scoring policies suppress about 80 percent of the fires.

Let us examine these policies in more detail. The optimal policy for the *composite* reward allows most wildfires to burn, but the *homeowner* reward policy suppresses most wildfires. The *homeowner* constituency reward function seeks to minimize smoke (which suggests suppressing all fires) and maximize recreation value (which suggests allowing fires to burn the understory occasionally). We can see in Figure 9.9(d) that the best policy found by SMAC allows 20 percent of fires to burn and suppresses the remaining 80 percent.

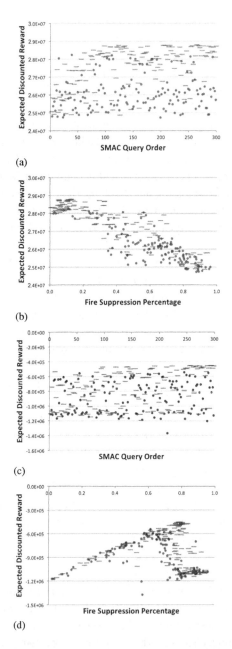

Figure 9.9 Average reward achieved for 30 trajectories. Horizontal lines are selected by the EI heuristic and circles are randomly sampled points. (a,b) Composite reward function; (c,d) Homeowner reward function.

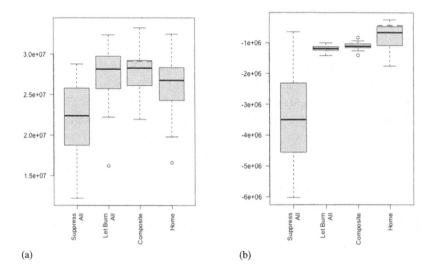

(a)   (b)

Figure 9.10 Each set of box charts show the performance of various policies for a constituency. The individual box plots show the expected discounted reward for each of the policies optimized for a constituency, as well as the hard-coded policies of Suppress All and Let Burn All. The dashed lines indicate the expected discounted reward estimated by MFMCi. (a) Policies for composite reward function; (b) policies for homeowner reward function.

These results agree with our intuition and provide evidence that SMAC is succeeding in optimizing these policies. However, the expected discounted rewards in Figure 9.9 are estimates obtained from the modified MFMC surrogate model. To check that these estimates are valid, we invoked each optimized policy on the full simulator at least 50 times and measured the cumulative discounted reward under each of the reward functions. We also evaluated the Suppress All and Let Burn All policies for comparison. The results are shown in Figure 9.10.

Each panel of boxplots depicts the range of cumulative returns for each policy on one reward function. For the policy that SMAC constructed, we also plot a dashed red line showing the MFMCi estimate of the return. In all cases, the estimates are systematically biased high. This is to be expected, because any optimization against a noisy function will tend to exploit the noise and, hence, overestimate the true value of the function. Nonetheless, the MFMCi estimates all fall near the interquartile range of the full simulator estimates. This confirms that the MFMC estimates are giving an accurate picture of the true rewards.

Conclusion

Previous work on high-fidelity wildfire management (Houtman et al., 2013) has focused only on *policy evaluation*, in which the full simulator was applied to evaluate a handful of alternative policies. We report the first successful *policy optimization* for wildfire suppression at scale. Moreover, the MFMCi surrogate executes quickly enough to support optimization within WildFireAssistant, which provides a basis for forest managers to discover the long-term consequences of present-day decisions.

Our forestry economics collaborators inform us that WildFireAssistant has greatly accelerated development of their MDP research. For future work we would like to deploy MDPvis to the US Forest Service. We believe we can build on our proof-of-concept by optimizing for entire US Forest Service regions.

Acknowledgments

This material is based upon work supported by the National Science Foundation under grant numbers 1331932 and 0832804. Any opinions, findings, and conclusions or recommendations expressed in this material are those of the authors and do not necessarily reflect the views of the National Science Foundation.

References

Abbeel, P., Ganapathi, V., and Ng, A.Y. 2005. Learning Vehicular Dynamics, with Application to Modeling Helicopters. *Advances in Neural Information Processing Systems (NIPS)*, 1–8. Neural Information Processing Systems Foundation, Inc.

Ager, A.A., Finney, M.A., Kerns, B.K., and Maffei, H. 2007. Modeling Wildfire Risk to Northern Spotted Owl (*Strix occidentalis caurina*) habitat in Central Oregon, USA. *Forest Ecology and Management*, **246**(1 special issue), 45–56.

Arca, B., Ghisu, T., Spataro, W., and Trunfio, G.A. 2013. GPU-Accelerated Optimization of Fuel Treatments for Mitigating Wildfire Hazard. *Procedia Computer Science*, **18**, 966–975.

Bellman, R. 1957. *Dynamic Programming*. Princeton, NJ: Princeton University Press.

Breiman, L. 2001. Random Forests. *Machine Learning*, **45**(1), 5–32.

Dilkina, B., Houtman, R., Gomes, C.P., et al. 2016. Trade-offs and Efficiencies in Optimal Budget-Constrained Multispecies Corridor Networks. *Conservation Biology*, **31**(1), 192–202.

Dixon, G. 2002. *Essential FVS: A User's Guide to the Forest Vegetation Simulator*. Fort Collins, CO: USDA Forest Service.

Egan, T. 2005 (December). *6* Arrested Years After Ecoterrorist Acts. *New York Times*.

Endert, A., Hossain, M.S., Ramakrishnan, N., et al. 2014. The Human is the Loop: New Directions for Visual Analytics. *Journal of Intelligent Information Systems*, **43**(3), 411–435.

Finney, M.A. 1998. *FARSITE: Fire Area Simulator: Model Development and Evaluation*. Missoula, MT: USDA Forest Service.

Fonteneau, R., Murphy, S.A, Wehenkel, L., and Ernst, D. 2010. Model-Free Monte Carlo-Like Policy Evaluation. *Proceedings of the Thirteenth International Conference on Artificial Intelligence and Statistics (AISTATS 2010)*, 217–224. AI & Statistics.

Fonteneau, R., Murphy, S.A., Wehenkel, L., and Ernst, D. 2013. Batch Mode Reinforcement Learning Based on the Synthesis of Artificial Trajectories. *Annals of Operations Research*, **208**(1), 383–416.

Forest History Society. 2017. *U.S. Forest Service Fire Suppression*. Durham, NC: Forest History Society.

Houtman, R.M., Montgomery, C.A., Gagnon, A.R., et al. 2013. Allowing a Wildfire to Burn: Estimating the Effect on Future Fire Suppression Costs. *International Journal of Wildland Fire*, **22**(7), 871–882.

Hutter, F., Hoos, H.H., and Leyton-Brown, K. 2010. Sequential Model-Based Optimization for General Algorithm Configuration (Extended Version). *Proceedings of the 5th international conference on Learning and Intelligent Optimization*, 507–523. Springer.

Jones, D.R., Schonlau, M., and Welch, W.J. 1998. Efficient Global Optimization of Expensive Black-Box Functions. *Journal of Global Optimization*, **13**, 455–492.

Keim, D., Andrienko, G., Fekete, J.-D., et al. 2008. Visual Analytics: Definition, Process and Challenges. In *Information Visualization: Human-Centered Issues and Perspectives*, 154–175. New York: Springer.

Kushner, H.J. 1964. A New Method of Locating the Maximum Point of an Arbitrary Multipeak Curve in the Presence of Noise. *Journal of Basic Engineering*, **86**, 97–106.

McGregor, S., Buckingham, H., Dietterich, T.G., et al. 2015. Facilitating Testing and Debugging of Markov Decision Processes with Interactive Visualization. In: *IEEE Symposium on Visual Languages and Human-Centric Computing*. IEEE.

McGregor, S., Buckingham, H., Dietterich, T.G., et al. 2016. Interactive Visualization for Testing Markov Decision Processes: MDPVIS. *Journal of Visual Languages and Computing*, **39**, 93–106.

McGregor, S., Houtman, R., Montgomery, C., Metoyer, R., and Dietterich, T.G. 2017a. Factoring Exogenous State for Model-Free Monte Carlo. *ArXiv*.

McGregor, S., Houtman, R., Montgomery, C., Metoyer, R., and Dietterich, T.G. 2017b. Fast Optimization of Wildfire Suppression Policies with SMAC. *ArXiv*.

Mockus, J. 1994. Application of Bayesian Approach to Numerical Methods of Global and Stochastic Optimization. *Journal of Global Optimization*, **4**, 347–365.

National Interagency Fire Center. 2009. Guidance for Implementation of Federal Wildland Fire Management Policy. Federal Guidance.

Puterman, M. 1994. *Markov Decision Processes: Discrete Stochastic Dynamic Programming*. New York: Wiley-Interscience.

Sacha, D., Stoffel, A., Stoffel, F., et al. 2014. Knowledge Generation Model for Visual Analytics. *IEEE Transactions on Visualization and Computer Graphics*, **20**(12).

Sedlmair, M., Heinzl, C., Bruckner, S., Piringer, H., and Möller, T. 2014. Visual Parameter Space Analysis: A Conceptual Framework. *IEEE Transactions on Visualization and Computer Graphics*, **20**(12).

Srinivas, N., Krause, A., Kakade, S.M., and Seeger, M. 2010. Gaussian Process Optimization in the Bandit Setting: No Regret and Experimental Design. *Proceedings of the 27th International Conference on Machine Learning (ICML 2010)*, 1015–1022. Omnipress.

Tephens, S.L., and Ruth, L.W. 2005. Federal Forest-Fire Policy in the United States. *Ecological Applications*, **15**, 532–542.

The National Wildfire Coordinating Group. 2009. S-520 – Advanced Incident Management. In: *Manual for Wildland Fire Decision Support System (WFDSS)*, 1–8. National Wildre Coordinating Group

United Nations. 2017. *Goal 15: Sustainably Manage Forests, Combat Desertification, Halt and Reverse Land Degradation, Halt Biodiversity Loss*. https://unstats.un.org/sdgs/report/2016/goal-15/

United States Department of Agriculture. 2015. The Rising Cost of Fire Operations: Effects on the Forest Service's Non-Fire Work. Washington, DC: United States Department of Agriculture.

Wang, Z., Hutter, F., Zoghi, M., Matheson, D., and de Freitas, N. 2016. Bayesian Optimization in High Dimensions via Random Embeddings. *Journal of Artificial Intelligence Research*, **55**, 361–387.

Western Regional Climate Center. 2011. *Remote Automated Weather Stations (RAWS)*. Reno, NV: Western Regional Climate Center.

Wilson, A., Fern, A., and Tadepalli, P. 2014. Using Trajectory Data to Improve Bayesian Optimization for Reinforcement Learning. *Journal of Machine Learning Research*, **15**, 253–282.

Zilinskas, A. 1992. A Review of Statistical Models for Global Optimization. *Journal of Global Optimization*, **2**, 145–153.

10

Probabilistic Inference with Generating Functions for Animal Populations

Daniel Sheldon, Kevin Winner, and Debora Sujono

Introduction

Estimating the size and demographic parameters of animal populations is key to effective conservation. This is commonly done by using counts of animals made by human observers to estimate the parameters of a population model. When some variables from the population model are not directly observed – for example, the number of animals that are *not* detected by the observer, or the number of animals that leave a habitat patch between two consecutive surveys – an inference algorithm is required to reason about hidden events while fitting the model.

Probabilistic inference is a challenging computational problem, and a great deal of AI research over the last 20 years has been devoted to developing efficient and general probabilistic inference algorithms. Despite great advances, models can still be "hard" for several reasons. One reason is model size and complexity, for example, as measured by the number of variables and the number, structure, and type of functional relationships among variables. There is a natural trend toward more complex models in ecology as we collect large and diverse datasets through efforts such as citizen science [Sullivan et al., 2009]. Developing efficient probabilistic inference algorithms to reason about complex ecological models from growing data resources is an important research direction.

This chapter will focus on a second property of population models that can make inference difficult: the presence of count variables to represent the unknown population size. A simple example is the *N-mixture* model [Royle, 2004] illustrated in Figure 10.1. Here, the variable n is an integer representing the unknown number of animals in a patch of habitat; because this number is not directly observed, it is a *latent* variable. An observer visits the patch K times, and the variable y_k represents the number of animals she is able to

$$n \in \{0, 1, 2, 3, \ldots\}$$

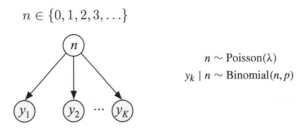

$n \sim \text{Poisson}(\lambda)$

$y_k \mid n \sim \text{Binomial}(n, p)$

Figure 10.1 The N-mixture model [Royle, 2004]. The latent variable n represents the unknown number of animals in a habitat patch. The observed (shaded) variables $y_1, \ldots, y_K$ represent the number detected by an observer during repeated surveys of the habitat patch. During each survey, each animal is detected with probability p.

detect during the kth survey; these are the *observed* variables. This model is very simple by typical measures of complexity, but, surprisingly, until very recently there was *no known exact inference algorithm* for this model. The computational challenge arises because the algorithm must reason about the infinite number of possible values (any non-negative integer) for the latent variable. Widely used estimation procedures for population models with latent count variables all resort to some form of approximation, usually by assuming an *a priori* upper bound on the population size. This has several drawbacks. First, it places a burden on the modeler, when we would like to let the data speak for themselves. Second, it interacts poorly with estimation of the detection probability, which determines the approximate "multiplier" between the observed counts and the true population size; we demonstrate pathologies related to this later in the chapter. Finally, this method is slow, especially when reasoning about populations over time. We desire *fast* algorithms for basic building blocks like the N-mixture model, so that we may use our growing data resources to design and fit more complex models of populations over time and space.

This chapter will summarize recent AI advances that provide the first exact and efficient algorithms for models with latent count variables. The key idea is to express probability distributions over count variables using *probability generating functions* (PGFs), and then to implement traditional inference algorithms using this novel representation. PGFs allow us to compactly represent distributions of interest even though they have an infinite number of possible values. The resulting algorithms are exact, substantially faster than existing approximate approaches, and they avoid misleading statistical inferences caused by *a priori* upper bounds on the population size.

The goal of the chapter is to present an overview of the main ideas and illustrate their impact on ecological models. Readers are referred to the papers by Winner and Sheldon [2016] and Winner et al. [2017] for additional details.

Population Models and Estimation

We will introduce the ecological and computational problem in more depth using Royle's N-mixture model. Recall that n is the unobserved population size, and $y_1, \ldots, y_K$ are the counts conducted by the observer. We encode uncertainty about these values, as well as some beliefs about the mechanisms that generated them, through a probabilistic model. The model is shown in Figure 10.1. The variables $y_1, \ldots, y_K$ are shaded to indicate that they are observed. The arrows represent the dependencies of the model: the observed counts depend on the unobserved population size. The population size n is assumed to be a Poisson random variable with (unknown) mean λ. The Poisson distribution is selected as a canonical distribution for count variables; our methods are not tied to this particular choice nor do we make any particular mechanistic interpretation of it. For the observations, we assume the observer detects each animal independently with probability p, so that y_k is distributed according to the binomial distribution with n trials (the number of animals) and success probability p (the probability of detecting each one).

The scientist wishes to answer questions like "How many animals were present?" or "What is the probability of detecting an animal that is present?" Often, the model will be simultaneously applied to many different habitat patches, where the mean number of animals λ is either shared across patches, or modeled as $\lambda = f(x)$, where x is a vector of covariates that describe the habitat and other features of the patch. In this case the probability distribution over n is used to model variability among patches. The scientist can then answer questions such as: "What is the typical population size of patches in my district?" or "How does population size relate to measures of habitat quality?" For examples, see Royle [2004]. We will focus on the single-patch model because the computational considerations are the same across all of these modeling variations.

A key to answering each of the above questions is *probabilistic inference* in the model: answering queries about the probability of some variables in the model given some other variables that are observed. Suppose the observer visits the patch three times and observes $y_1 = 2, y_2 = 5, y_3 = 3$ (these are the number of animals detected in each visit). If $\lambda = 20$ and $p = 0.25$, the probability of observing these values is 0.0034; if $\lambda = 10$ and $p = 0.25$, the probability is 0.0025. Based on this, we believe the first setting of parameters is more likely. The principle of maximum likelihood is to set the unknown model parameters to the ones that maximize the probability of the observed variables. So, we can see that calculating the likelihood $p(y_1, \ldots y_K) := p(y_{1:K})$ – the probability of all observed values – is a key computational problem. Solving this problem will allow us to use numerical optimization routines to find the parameters λ and p that maximize the likelihood, and it is also a basic building block of *posterior queries* about the model, such as "What is the probability there were five animals in the patch, given my observations?"

So, let us focus on the problem of computing the likelihood $p(y_{1:k})$ for fixed λ and p. Since our model was specified in terms of the joint probability of *all* the variables, we must apply the rules of probability to sum over all possible values of n:

$$\text{Likelihood}: \qquad p(y_{1:K}) = \sum_{n=0}^{\infty} p(n, y_{1:K}).$$

Each term of the sum on the right-hand side is easily computed from the model specification. The nth term is the joint probability $p(n, y_{1:K})$, which, according to the model we have defined, is equal to $p(n) \prod_{k=1}^{K} p(y_k \mid n)$, where $p(n) = \frac{\lambda^n e^{-\lambda}}{n!}$ is Poisson prior probability that there are n animals present, and $p(y_k \mid n) = \binom{n}{y_k} p^{y_k} (1 - p)^{n-y_k}$ is the probability that y_k animals are observed on the kth visit, given that there are actually n animals present. However, even though we can compute each term easily, we can't compute the likelihood directly because there are an infinite number of terms! More generally, we lack general computational tools to efficiently manipulate distributions over an infinite number of terms, and this prevents us from applying well known probabilistic inference algorithms.

A Change of Representation: Probability Generating Functions

The main idea of our approach is to work instead using a different representation of the probability distribution: a *probability generating function*, or PGF. The PGF is a transformation of a probability distribution $q(n)$ over nonnegative integers defined as follows:

$$\{q(n) : n = 0, 1, 2, \ldots\} \qquad \Longrightarrow \qquad F(s) = \sum_{n=0}^{\infty} q(n) s^n$$

Probability distribution   PGF

The PGF uses the probability values as coefficients of a power series (i.e., a polynomial with an infinite number of terms) in the new variable s, and it is a function that maps s to another real number whenever the series converges. It is well known that this transformation preserves all the information about the probability distribution. That is, if we know $F(s)$, we can recover all of the original probability values.[1] At first glance, it is not clear what this buys us. We have switched from an infinite sequence of probability values to a power series with an infinite number of terms. The important observation is that it may be possible to find a *compact* representation of the PGF. For example, for the Poisson distribution, for any value of s, the infinite sum on the right-hand side converges and we have:

$$\left\{ p(n) = \frac{\lambda^n e^{-\lambda}}{n!} : n = 0, 1, 2, \ldots \right\} \implies F(s) = \sum_{n=0}^{\infty} \frac{\lambda^n e^{-\lambda}}{n!} s^n = e^{\lambda(s-1)}.$$

This is now a simple, compact representation of the entire probability distribution. It should not be a surprise that we can do this for the Poisson distribution, since we already had a compact formula for the probability values.

We will show that it is possible to compute compact representations of PGFs for probability distributions that arise during inference algorithms. Returning to the previous N-mixture model example, consider the distribution $p(n, y_1 = 2, y_2 = 5, y_3 = 3)$. We will describe how to algorithmically compute a formula for the PGF, which in this example is:

$$\begin{aligned}
F(s) &= \sum_{n=0}^{\infty} p(n, y_1 = 2, y_2 = 5, y_3 = 3) s^n \\
&= \left(0.0061 s^5 + 0.1034 s^6 + 0.5126 s^7 \right. \\
&\quad \left. + 1.0000 s^8 + 0.8023 s^9 + 0.2184 s^{10} \right) \\
&\quad \times \exp(8.4375 s - 15.4101).
\end{aligned} \tag{10.1}$$

Although this expression appears somewhat complex – it is a polynomial of degree ten times an exponential function – it is a tractable and exact representation of the distribution $p(n, y_{1:K})$.

Importantly, given the PGF, it is easy to solve our original problem of computing the likelihood – we simply evaluate the PGF at $s = 1$. From the series representation, we know that $F(1) = \sum_{n=0}^{\infty} p(n, y_{1:K}) 1^n$ is the sum over all terms in the series, which is equal to the likelihood $p(y_{1:K})$. We can compute $F(1)$ efficiently by substituting $s = 1$ in the compact representation.

---

[1] Specifically, we do this using the derivatives of F at zero: $q(n) = F^{(n)}(0)/n!$

For example, we find that $p(y_1 = 2, y_2 = 5, y_3 = 3) = 0.0025$ by substituting $s = 1$ in the right-hand side of equation 10.1.

We have now seen the main elements of our new approach for probabilistic inference. Given a probability model, we will devise an algorithm to compute a compact representation of the PGF for the distribution $p(n, y_{1:K})$, where n is a single latent variable and $y_{1:K}$ are all of the observed variables. Then we will compute the likelihood by evaluating $F(1)$ using our compact representation. What remains is to describe the mathematical and computational operations needed to find the compact representation of the PGF for models of interest. We summarize these steps in the following sections.

The PGF Forward Algorithm

Our goal is to algorithmically manipulate PGFs to compute the likelihood of population models. We would like to do this for a reasonably broad class of models that includes the N-mixture model and other models that are used in practice by ecologists. To this end, we will describe a class of models called *integer hidden Markov models* (HMMs) for partially observed populations that change over time through processes such as immigration, mortality, and reproduction. Integer HMMs map closely onto *open metapopulation models* from statistical population ecology [Dail and Madsen, 2011] and (latent) *branching processes* from applied mathematics and epidemiology [Watson and Galton, 1875; Heathcote, 1965].

The Integer HMM

Figure 10.2 illustrates the model. This extends the N-mixture model so the number of animals in the patch can change over time. The variable n_k is the

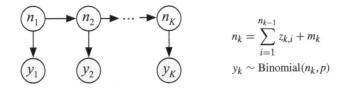

$$n_k = \sum_{i=1}^{n_{k-1}} z_{k,i} + m_k$$

$$y_k \sim \text{Binomial}(n_k, p)$$

Figure 10.2 The integer HMM model. The variable n_k represents the size of the population in the kth time period. The variable y_k represents the number of individuals counted by an observer during that time period. The population changes over time through immigration and emigration, mortality, and reproduction.

size of the population at time k, which, again, is not observed. The variable y_k is the number detected by the observer. As before, we assume that each individual is detected with probability p. The population size n_k now depends probabilistically on the population size from the previous time step as follows. First, for all i, the ith individual from the previous time step contributes $z_{k,i}$ individuals to the present time step, where $z_{k,i} \sim P_Z$ is an independent random variable drawn from the common *offspring distribution* P_Z. Here, the "offspring" can include the individual itself, to model the event that it survives from one generation to the next and remains in the patch; they can also include true offspring, to model reproduction. In this way, the modeler can model emigration, mortality, and reproduction by the appropriate choice of offspring distribution. In practice, the modeler would model these processes separately and then follow standard procedures to determine the offspring distribution P_Z. We assume only that the PGF $F(s)$ of the offspring distribution is available. In addition to the "offspring" from previous time steps, m_k new individuals enter the population, where m_k is a random variable from the *immigration distribution*. The modeler is free to select any count-valued immigration distribution; we assume only that that the PGF $G(s)$ is specified. The model can easily be extended to allow these distributions to vary over time.

The Forward Algorithm

The forward algorithm is a classical algorithm to compute the likelihood in a hidden Markov model [Rabiner, 1989]. We will adapt it to use PGFs in its internal representation to compute the likelihood in integer HMMs. The algorithm is illustrated schematically in Figure 10.3. It proceeds in steps that model the joint distributions of different subsets of the variables. In the figure, the shaded boxes indicate which variables are modeled at each step. The fundamental distributions of interest are those of the form $p(n_k, y_{1:k})$ – of the hidden variable n_k and the observations $y_{1:k}$ up to and including the corresponding time step – which we denote as $\alpha_k(n_k)$ and are called the *messages*. The left-most figure shows the message $\alpha_{k-1}(n_{k-1})$ for the $k-1$st time step, and the right-most plot shows the message $\alpha_k(n_k)$ for the kth time step. A recurrence is used to compute the message for the current time step from the previous one. We have split the recurrence into two steps: (1) the *prediction* step, where the observations up until time $k - 1$ are used to predict n_k, resulting in the intermediate quantity $\gamma_k(n_k) := p(n_k, y_{1:k-1})$ (illustrated in the middle figure); and (2) the *evidence* step, where the observation at time k

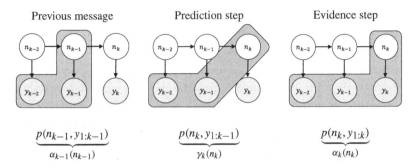

Previous message   Prediction step   Evidence step

$$\underbrace{p(n_{k-1}, y_{1:k-1})}_{\alpha_{k-1}(n_{k-1})} \qquad \underbrace{p(n_k, y_{1:k-1})}_{\gamma_k(n_k)} \qquad \underbrace{p(n_k, y_{1:k})}_{\alpha_k(n_k)}$$

Figure 10.3 Illustration of the forward algorithm. The algorithm utilizes a recurrence to compute the current message $\alpha_k(n_k)$ (right) starting from the message $\alpha_{k-1}(n_{k-1})$ at the previous time step (left). Each message represents the joint distribution of a subset of variables that includes one hidden variable and a prefix of the observed variables – the shaded boxes show the subset corresponding to each message. The recurrence utilizes an intermediate prediction step that creates the message $\gamma_k(n_k)$ (middle).

is used to update the distribution and obtain $\alpha_k(n_k)$. The two steps are defined formally as follows:

$$\text{Predict}: \qquad \gamma_k(n_k) = \sum_{n_{k-1}} \alpha_{k-1}(n_{k-1}) p(n_k \mid n_{k-1}),$$

$$\text{Evidence}: \qquad \alpha_k(n_k) = \gamma_k(n_k) p(y_k \mid n_k).$$

Starting from a base case, all α messages can be computed in a single forward pass using this recurrence. The likelihood is obtained by summing over all values of the final message.

The PGF Forward Algorithm

The forward algorithm recurrence is mathematically correct even for integer HMMs, but the limits of the summation in the prediction step are infinite, and there are an infinite number of terms in each message, so it cannot be implemented directly. Instead, we will modify the algorithm to work with the PGFs of the α and γ messages, which are defined (using the corresponding capital letters) as $A_k(s_k) = \sum_{n_k=0}^{\infty} \alpha_k(n_k) s_k^{n_k}$ and $\Gamma_k(u_k) = \sum_{n_k=0}^{\infty} \gamma_k(n_k) u_k^{n_k}$. An equivalent recurrence for the PGFs is derived in [Winner et al., 2017]:

$$\text{Predict}: \qquad \Gamma_k(u_k) = A_{k-1}\big(F(u_k)\big) \cdot G(u_k)$$

$$\text{Evidence}: \qquad A_k(s_k) = \frac{(s_k \rho_k)^{y_k}}{y_k!} \cdot \Gamma_k^{(y_k)}\big(s_k(1 - \rho_k)\big).$$

We do not provide details of how these formulas are derived. The formula in the prediction step follows from the model definition (see Figure 10.2) by fairly standard and elementary manipulations of PGFs, and is well known in the literature on branching processes [Heathcote, 1965]. The formula in the evidence step may appear surprising. It includes the y_kth derivative of the function Γ_k from the prediction step. This formula was derived by Winner and Sheldon [2016]. The derivatives are related to the selection of particular terms in the joint PGF of n_k and y_k corresponding to the observed value of y_k.

The likelihood is recovered by evaluating the final PGF at the input value one:

$$\text{Likelihood:} \quad p(y_{1:K}) = A_K(1).$$

It remains to discuss how to efficiently implement the PGF recurrence.

Implementing the Recurrence: Computation with PGFs

We provide a high-level overview of the techniques to algorithmically manipulate PGFs.

Symbolic Manipulation of PGFs

An obvious approach to try first is to write down the mathematical formula for the first PGF, $A_1(s_1)$, which will always have a simple form, and then observe how this formula changes when the prediction and evidence steps are repeatedly applied. In the best case, one will be able to simplify each successive PGF into a tractable mathematical expression. In Winner and Sheldon [2016], we successfully followed this *symbolic* approach for a restricted class of models called *Poisson HMMs*. In Poisson HMMs, the immigration distribution is Poisson and the offspring distribution is Bernoulli, which models survival but is not able to model reproduction. In this case we showed that each PGF has a form similar to the one shown in Figure 10.4(a). Specifically, each PGF can be written in the form $f(s) \exp(as + b)$, where f is a bounded degree polynomial. Thus, it can be represented compactly by the polynomial coefficients and the scalars a and b, and these can be computed efficiently from the representation of the PGF in the previous time step.

Circuit Representation

Although the symbolic representation is efficient, it does not seem to extend to a broader class of models, including variations commonly used by ecologists

$$F(s) = \Big(0.0061s^5 + 0.1034s^6 + 0.5126s^7$$
$$+ 1.0000s^8 + 0.8023s^9 + 0.2184s^{10}\Big)$$
$$\times \exp(8.4375s - 15.4101)$$

(a)

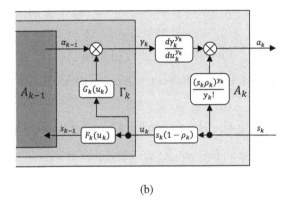

(b)

Figure 10.4 Algorithmic manipulation of PGFs. Winner and Sheldon [2016] showed how to compute compact symbolic representations of PGFs that appear in the forward algorithm for a restricted class of models with Poisson latent variables. Winner et al. [2017] showed how to use a circuit representation and automatic differentiation to evaluate the final PGF to compute the likelihood. (a) Symbolic representation; (b) circuit representation.

[Dail and Madsen, 2011]. For example, it is common to model immigration using the negative binomial distribution instead of the Poisson. In this and other cases, the mathematical expressions for PGFs grow rapidly more complex in each iteration and do not appear to simplify to a tractable form. In Winner et al. [2017], we developed a much more general approach that does not attempt to represent PGFs symbolically, but instead models them using a circuit or *computation graph*. Since each PGF recursively calls the previous one in the recurrence, this circuit consists of recursively nested circuits (see Figure 10.4(b)). Because the recurrence involves *derivatives* of prior PGFs, the circuit cannot be evaluated using simple arithmetic operations alone. In Winner et al. [2017] we developed novel techniques based on automatic differentiation [Griewank and Walther, 2008] to compute the nested, higher-order, derivatives required to evaluate $A_K(1)$.

Demonstration and Experiments

So far we have given an overview of the PGF forward algorithm, a novel algorithm that leads to the first exact inference algorithms for ecological models with latent count variables. In this section, we will examine the practical capabilities of the algorithm by comparing it to the previously available approximate algorithms, and through two case studies.

Running Time

Our new exact algorithms are substantially faster than existing *approximate* algorithms. Figure 10.5(a) shows the running time of the symbolic version of the PGF forward algorithm for Poisson HMMs [Winner and Sheldon, 2016] compared with two versions of an approximate algorithm that is currently used in practice [Royle, 2004; Dail and Madsen, 2011; Fiske and Chandler, 2011]. The approximate algorithm places an *a priori* upper bound N_{max} on the population size, and then uses the standard forward algorithm [Rabiner, 1989] to compute the approximate likelihood. We refer to this as the *truncated* forward algorithm, denoted FA in the figure. Our algorithm is denoted PGFFA. The running time of PGFFA grows with the magnitude of the observed counts. The running time of the truncated forward algorithm grows with the truncation parameter N_{max}: smaller values are faster, but may underestimate the likelihood. Selecting N_{max} large enough to yield correct likelihoods but small enough to be fast is known to be difficult [Couturier et al., 2013; Dennis et al., 2015]. We evaluated two strategies to select N_{max}: an *oracle* strategy that runs prior experiments to find an optimal setting of N_{max} ("FA – Oracle"), and a heuristic based on the prior Poisson distribution ("FA – Poiss"). We simulated data from a Poisson HMM parameterized based on a model for insect populations [Zonneveld, 1991], and then measured the time for each algorithm to compute the likelihood in this model. We varied two parameters over a range of different values: the parameter Λ controls the overall population size, and the parameter ρ is the detection probability. (For further details, see Winner and Sheldon [2016].) The running time is plotted relative to $\Lambda\rho$, which is the expected total number of individuals observed, on a log–log scale. We can see that the PGFFA running time indeed scales with the magnitude of the observations, and is 2–3 orders of magnitude faster than the truncated algorithms.

Avoiding Pathologies in Parameter Estimation

The next experiment highlights a pathology of the truncated algorithm that is avoided by our exact algorithms. We simulated data from the N-mixture

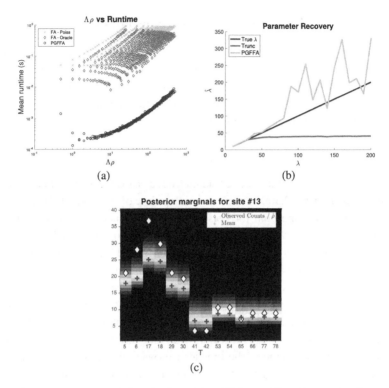

Figure 10.5 Experimental evaluation of the PGF forward algorithm: (a) running time PGF forward (PGFFA) versus two versions of the truncated forward algorithm (FA – Oracle, FA – Poiss) for a Poisson HMM (see text). (b) Parameter recovery via maximum-likelihood using the PGF forward algorithm avoids a pathology that affects the corresponding procedure using the truncated forward algorithm. (c) Illustration of inferences from a fitted model for the northern dusky salamander. The horizontal axis represents months since the beginning of the study period; surveys are conducted only in June and July so time steps are not consecutive. The vertical axis represents the number of individuals, with crosses showing the posterior mean, and shading intensity illustrating the posterior probability. The diamonds represent a coarse estimate made by dividing the observed count by the detection probability.

model and attempted to recover the parameter values λ (population size) and ρ (detection probability) by numerically maximizing the likelihood, using both the PGF forward algorithm and the truncated forward algorithm as subroutines to compute the likelihood. For the truncated algorithm, the modeler must select N_{max} without knowing the true values of the parameters – we assume she heuristically sets N_{max} to be approximately five times the average observed count based on her belief that the detection probability is not too small and this will capture most of the probability mass. We varied λ and ρ inversely proportionally to each other so that their product $\lambda\rho$, which is the expected number of observed animals, is held constant at ten. We therefore fixed $N_{max} = 50$ to be five times this observed number.

Figure 10.5(b) shows that as the true λ approaches and surpasses $N_{max} = 50$, the truncated method cuts off significant portions of the probability mass and severely underestimates λ. This artificially reinforces the modeler's prior belief that the true detection probability is "not too small," even when the true detection probability approaches zero! In contrast, estimation with the exact likelihood does not show this bias. It does show significantly increased variance as λ increases and $\rho \to 0$. In fact, this variance is a property of the true likelihood, but is artificially suppressed by the truncated algorithm. It is well-known in this and related models that, without enough data, it is difficult to tease apart the population size and detection probability, especially as the true detection probability goes to zero (e.g., see Dennis et al. [2015]). The variance seen here is a byproduct of the fact that the parameters are *actually* poorly determined as $\rho \to 0$. The truncated algorithm artificially stabilizes the estimation procedure by expressing a hidden bias toward smaller population sizes.

Dusky Salamander Case Study

Figure 10.5(c) shows the results from a case study to model the abundance of northern dusky salamanders at 21 sites in the mid-Atlantic USA using data from Zipkin et al. [2014]. The data consist of 14 counts at each site, conducted in June and July over seven years. Six sites were excluded because no salamanders were observed. We first fit a Poisson HMM by numerically maximizing the likelihood as computed by the PGF forward algorithm. Arrivals are modeled as a homogeneous Poisson process, and survival is modeled by assuming individual lifetimes are exponentially distributed. The fitted parameters indicated an arrival rate of 0.32 individuals per month, a mean lifetime of 14.25 months, and detection probability of 0.58.

We then investigate the posterior distribution over the number of animals at each time step. We may wish to use the model to make fine-grained inferences about the population status at individual sites over time. In the figure, the horizontal axis represents time (in months) and the vertical axis is the population size. The cross represents the posterior mean for the population size at the given time step (given all observations), and the shading intensity represents the posterior probability of different values; the "spread" of this posterior distribution helps quantify our posterior uncertainty under the modeling assumptions we have made. The diamonds represent a coarse estimate of the population size at each time step made by dividing the observed count by the estimated detection probability. In contrast to the coarse estimates, the posterior distribution varies more smoothly over time, because it models the counts as being coupled through time by the processes of survival and immigration.

Computationally, querying the posterior distribution in this way requires computation of the *posterior marginals*, which are the distributions $p(n_k \mid y_{1:K})$ of each latent variable given *all* of the observed data (both preceding and following the focal time period). A variant of the PGF forward algorithm can also compute these marginals [Winner and Sheldon, 2016].

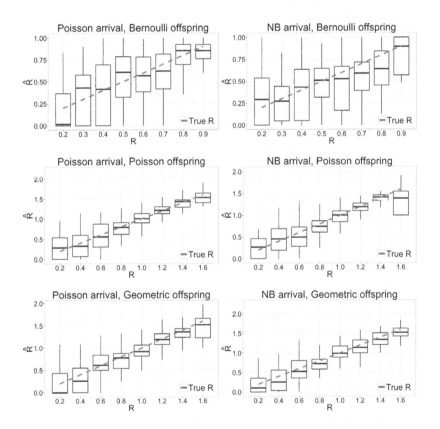

Figure 10.6 Accuracy of estimates for the mean R of the offspring distribution in different models. Rows, from top to bottom: Bernoulli offspring, Poisson offspring, geometric offspring. Columns, from left to right: Poisson immigration, negative binomial immigration. For each model combination and true value of R, box plots summarize the estimated values from 50 independent trials.

The Model Zoo

A major advance of Winner et al. [2017] was the ability to perform inference in a much wider class of models by using circuits and automatic differentiation to evaluate the PGFs. To demonstrate the advantages of this flexibility, we used this version of the algorithm within an optimization routine to compute maximum likelihood estimates (MLEs) for a variety of models with different immigration and offspring distributions. In each experiment, we generated a dataset of independent samples from each model and then used a numerical optimization procedure to find the parameters that maximize the likelihood of the observations. We varied the immigration and offspring distributions as well as the mean R of the offspring distribution. We fixed the mean of the immigration distribution to $\lambda = 6$ across all models, and the detection probability to $p = 0.6$. The quantity R is known as the "basic reproduction number," or the average number of offspring produced by a single individual, which is a key measure of population viability and hence important to estimate. Each panel in Figure 10.6 shows the distribution of the 50 maximum-likelihood estimates for R versus the true values of R for a different model. The estimated values closely track the true values. This shows that the PGF forward algorithm can be applied within likelihood maximization routines to successfully fit the parameters of a wide class of models.

Conclusion

Effective conservation requires effective assessment and monitoring of animal populations. Population sizes and demographic rates are commonly estimated by fitting probabilistic population models to observational data. However, these models expose a gap in our probabilistic inference toolkit. They often contain latent count variables to represent unknown population sizes, and, despite many years of research in the area of probabilistic inference, until recently there was no known algorithm to exactly compute the likelihood in models with latent count variables.

This chapter summarizes recent advances in the AI research area of probabilistic inference motivated by this gap. We described how the forward algorithm, a standard inference algorithm for hidden Markov models, can be adapted to use *probability generating functions* as its internal representation of probability distributions, which then leads to the first efficient and exact inference algorithms for this class of models.

We recommend several directions forward. From a technical standpoint, the forward algorithm is an example of a *message passing* inference algorithm

[Pearl, 1986; Lauritzen and Spiegelhalter, 1988; Jensen et al., 1990; Shenoy and Shafer, 1990]. We have shown how to extend the forward algorithm to a broad class of models with latent count variables by using PGFs to represent messages. Extending this idea to more structurally complex models by doing the analogous thing for general-purpose message-passing algorithms, and, more generally, exploring the potential uses of PGFs for probabilistic inference, is an interesting technical research direction. Developing techniques to compute the *gradient* of the log-likelihood in addition to the likelihood, which would facilitate learning and parameter estimation in ecological models, is another promising research direction.

From the application standpoint, we envision extending models such as the N-mixture model and the integer HMM, which assume independence across sites, by using them as the basic building blocks of spatio-temporal models that also model the interdependence among sites. Our hypothesis is that increasing volumes of data available from citizen science projects and other technological advances provide evidence about spatio-temporal patterns and interactions among populations. These models will have many more variables and interactions, and will present increasingly difficult challenges in the area of probabilistic inference. We recommend continued interactions among ecologists and AI researchers to design these models, together with efficient algorithms to reason about them.

References

Couturier, T., M. Cheylan, A. Bertolero, G. Astruc, and A. Besnard. Estimating abundance and population trends when detection is low and highly variable: a comparison of three methods for the Hermann's tortoise. *Journal of Wildlife Management*, 77(3):454–462, 2013.

Dail, D. and L. Madsen. Models for estimating abundance from repeated counts of an open metapopulation. *Biometrics*, 67(2):577–587, 2011.

Dennis, E.B., B.J.T. Morgan, and M.S. Ridout. Computational aspects of N-mixture models. *Biometrics*, 71(1):237–246, 2015.

Fiske, I.J. and R.B. Chandler. unmarked: an R package for fitting hierarchical models of wildlife occurrence and abundance. *Journal of Statistical Software*, 43:1–23, 2011.

Griewank, A. and A. Walther. *Evaluating derivatives: principles and techniques of algorithmic differentiation*. Philadelphia, PA: SIAM, 2008.

Heathcote, C.R. A branching process allowing immigration. *Journal of the Royal Statistical Society. Series B (Methodological)*, 27(1):138–143, 1965.

Jensen, F.V., S.L. Lauritzen, and K.G. Olesen. Bayesian updating in causal probabilistic networks by local computations. *Computational Statistics Quarterly*, 4:269–282, 1990.

Lauritzen, S.L. and D.J. Spiegelhalter. Local computations with probabilities on graphical structures and their application to expert systems. *Journal of the Royal Statistical Society. Series B (Methodological)*, 50(2):157–224, 1988.

Pearl, J. Fusion, propagation, and structuring in belief networks. *Artificial Intelligence*, 29(3):241–288, 1986.

Rabiner, L. A tutorial on hidden Markov models and selected applications in speech recognition. *Proceedings of the IEEE*, 77(2):257–286, 1989.

Royle, J.A. N-mixture models for estimating population size from spatially replicated counts. *Biometrics*, 60(1):108–115, 2004.

Shenoy, P.P. and G. Shafer. Axioms for probability and belief-function propagation. In *Uncertainty in Artificial Intelligence*, 4:169–198, 1990.

Sullivan, B.L., C.L. Wood, M.J. Iliff, et al. ebird: A citizen-based bird observation network in the biological sciences. *Biological Conservation*, 142(10):2282–2292, 2009.

Watson, H.W. and F. Galton. On the probability of the extinction of families. *The Journal of the Anthropological Institute of Great Britain and Ireland*, 4:138–144, 1875.

Winner, K. and D. Sheldon. Probabilistic inference with generating functions for Poisson latent variable models. *Advances in Neural Information Processing Systems*, 29, 2016.

Winner, K., D. Sujono, and D. Sheldon. Exact inference for integer latent-variable models. In *Proc. of the 34th International Conference on Machine Learning (ICML)*, pages 3761–3770, 2017.

Zipkin, E.F., J.T. Thorson, K. See, et al. Modeling structured population dynamics using data from unmarked individuals. *Ecology*, 95(1):22–29, 2014.

Zonneveld, C. Estimating death rates from transect counts. *Ecological Entomology*, 16 (1):115–121, 1991.

11

Engaging Citizen Scientists in Data Collection for Conservation

Yexiang Xue and Carla P. Gomes

Introduction

Big data is becoming increasingly important for monitoring large-scale and complex spatial and temporal ecological processes to support informed decision-making in computational sustainability [Gomes 2009]. Historically, data collection methods for conservation typically involved many hours of field work performed by professional researchers, which could not scale up to meet today's conservation goals. Citizen science programs, on the other hand, engage the general public in the data collection process. With the active participation of thousands of volunteers, citizen science programs have been very successful at collecting rich datasets for conservation, enabling the possibility of conducting ecological surveys across multiple years and at large continental scales. Over the last few years, there have been several successful citizen science programs. For example, in biology, citizen scientists help with bird and arthropod research using eBird [Sullivan et al. 2009] and BugGuide [www.bugguide.net.]. In environmental studies, citizen scientists contribute to monitoring coral bleaching conditions [Marshall et al. 2012]. To attract more people to contribute data, the success of citizen science programs relies on tapping into the intrinsic motivations of citizen scientists. The citizen scientists' contribution cycle is shown in Figure 11.1. The self-fulfillment brought by participation while contributing to science keeps citizen scientists engaged, in return accelerating the whole contribution cycle. In this chapter, we illustrate effective ways to engage citizen scientists in data collection for conservation (Figure 11.2). Our approaches are motivated by our collaborations with two citizen science programs: the eBird and Nchioto projects.

eBird is a citizen science program of the Cornell Lab of Ornithology which engages the general public in bird conservation. To understand the distribution and migration of birds, eBird enlists bird watchers to identify

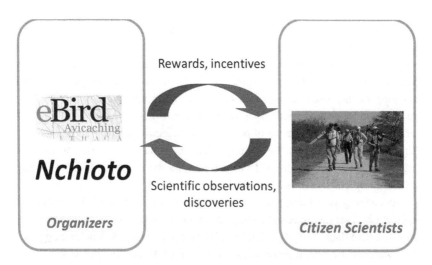

Figure 11.1 Citizen science program cycle. The organizer of a citizen science program uses reward and incentives to stimulate participation. Citizen scientists contribute scientific observations and discoveries to the organizers. Citizen Scientists' photo is from Steve Hillebrand at the U.S. Fish and Wildlife Service. Avicaching banner credit: Ian Davies and Christopher Wood at the Cornell Lab of Ornithology.

Figure 11.2 Three effective ways to engage citizen scientists in scientific discovery.

bird species, a task that is still beyond the capacity of automated technology. Bird watchers report their observations to the centralized eBird database via online checklists that include detailed information about the observed birds, such as the name of the species, number of individuals, gender, and time and location of the observation. eBird has been enormously successful. To date, more than 360,000 individuals have volunteered more than 400 million bird observations, which in terms of person-hours is equivalent to building several Empire State Buildings. Since 2006, eBird data have been used to study a variety of scientific questions, from highlighting the impact of climate change to designing conservation plans [Kelling et al. 2012].

Avicaching is a game that we developed to incentivize bird watchers to collect observations in remote and under-sampled locations in order to reduce bias in eBird data [Xue et al. 2016a, 2016b]. Specifically, Avicaching engages bird watchers by providing rewards in the form of Avicaching points for observations made in remote and under-sampled locations. In a friendly competitive environment, bird watchers compete for Avicaching points through an online leaderboard. At the end of the season, Avicaching players have the chance to win birding gear based on how many points each bird watcher has earned. Avicaching has been very successful among birding communities. In a field study conducted in Tompkins and Cortland County in New York in 2015, the Avicaching game shifted approximately 20 percent of birding effort from traditional hotspots to Avicaching locations, which had not been visited prior to the Avicaching game.

We have also developed Bird-Watcher Assistant [Xue et al. 2013], to further boost eBird participation and scientific discovery. The success of eBird is in part due to a series of service tools for record-keeping, exploration, and visualization, which nurture and reward participation. Bird-Watcher Assistant recommends interesting birding sites in which a diverse set of bird species might be seen. The Bird-Watcher Assistant particularly engages beginner bird watchers, who rely on eBird tools to discover interesting sites. In addition, we recommend locations that are seldom visited through Bird-Watcher Assistant, which helps expand the spatial coverage of eBird into less-populated regions. Recommending tasks that are rewarding to citizen scientists with Bird-Watcher Assistant creates a positive feedback loop, bringing in greater participation, which in turn results in more data, better models, and leads to more accurately recommended tasks.

Nchioto is a crowdsourcing project of the International Livestock Research Institute (ILRI) to monitor rangeland and vegetation conditions in Eastern Africa [Jensen et al. 2017a; Naibei et al. 2017]. In a collaboration with ILRI, we developed AI solutions to incentivize participation in the program.

Nchioto relies on local pastoralists, who live on rangeland themselves, to report information on rangeland and vegetation conditions via an intuitive cellphone application. Nchioto distributes incentives in a monetary form to stimulate participation in under-sampled areas. With a crowdsourcing program, it is important to quantify its elasticity in terms of the reward value, i.e., the extent to which citizen scientists are willing to deviate from their normal everyday path to participate in our data collection program as a function of the rewards. In our work, we showed the potential of large-scale crowdsourcing of environmental information from low-literacy populations, such as the local pastoralists in Eastern Africa. In particular, we showed that participants respond to incentives in a rational way, increasing our confidence that optimally designed incentive schemes will be useful in driving the crowd toward important tasks.

Our tools to support citizen scientists are supported with novel advances in AI technology. In the Nchioto and Avicaching programs, we study the problem of optimal incentive allocation under a game-theoretic setting, taking into account the fact that citizen scientists have their own utility functions, which may not align with the organizers' objectives. Game-theoretic formulations for conservation problems have also been studied in a few related works [Fang et al. 2017; Yadav et al. 2017]. In both applications, we use novel machine learning and constraint programming techniques to capture the citizen scientists' elasticity to rewards and to compute the optimal reward allocation. To solve the two-stage game in both Nchioto and Avicaching programs, we embed agents' decision problem as linear constraints in the master problem, solved by the organizer, therefore reducing a bi-level optimization to a single optimization. In the Bird-Watcher Assistant application, we introduce novel algorithms that assist citizen scientists by recommending locations within a travel budget in which a diverse set of species can be observed. We formalize the problem of recommending these locations as a probabilistic maximum coverage problem, which can be solved by submodular maximization subject to radius locality constraints. We propose several novel algorithms that have constant approximation guarantees and validate their effectiveness empirically.

This chapter is organized as follows. In the next section we describe the Nchioto application, in which we use extrinsic incentives to motivate local pastoralists to monitor vegetation conditions in Eastern Africa. In the third section, we present the eBird Avicaching game and in the fourth section Bird-Watcher Assistant, another tool to further boost eBird participation and scientific discovery. The three sections are organized to illustrate three effective ways to engage citizen scientists, as shown in Figure 11.2. We conclude with a discussion of the relationship among the three incentives and future directions.

Nchioto: Engaging Pastoralists in Eastern Africa with Extrinsic Incentives

The global spread of low-cost mobile phones allows us to communicate effectively in remote and underdeveloped areas. Integrating today's citizen science programs with mobile phones allows us to overcome the gaps in infrastructure that limit the effectiveness of traditional data collection methods. In Kenya, for example, over 80 percent people have access to cellphones, and the percentage of smartphone users is approximately 20 percent and growing.

In collaboration with scientists from the ILRI, we studied the problem of monitoring local vegetation conditions at high spatial and temporal resolution, aggregating responses from local citizen scientists via smartphones. The study area was a 150 km by 155 km region in central Kenya. We recruited volunteers among local pastoralists who spent most of their time herding livestock. We gave pastoralists cellphones, which they used to report vegetation conditions of the local landscape while they were actively herding livestock. Our goal in this study was to see to what extent we could rely on cellphone users on the ground to conduct land survey and monitoring tasks.

Nchioto is a cellphone application that we developed for pastoralists (or herders) to characterize the forage conditions using a short, visually oriented, and geolocated survey (see Figure 11.3) [Jensen et al. 2017a, 2017b; Naibei et al. 2017]. The vegetation survey first asked a few questions, such as whether grass in this area was dense, sparse, or absent; what was the color of the grass; and whether the grass was edible by animals. After these questions, the survey asked participants to estimate the carrying capacity, i.e., the number of livestock that could be supported with the available grass in the local area. All the questions were shown using a graphical interface to overcome language barriers. Questions of similar purpose were asked from different perspectives to guarantee consistency. As the last step, pastoralists were asked to take a picture of the location that they were characterizing before they submitted their report.

Nchioto used extrinsic monetary motivation to stimulate participation. We developed a reward map (Figure 11.3(b)), which gave participants different monetary rewards for observations made in different areas. Through the reward map, participants could see clearly which reward zone they were currently in and information about nearby reward zones. The reward map was based on an AI algorithm, which assigns reward points in an intelligent way to motivate participants toward remote areas where observations are needed the most. The whole reward map was integrated into the Nchioto application.

Through field experiments with interleaved reward treatments, we have been able to capture the reward elasticity of citizen scientists, which captures

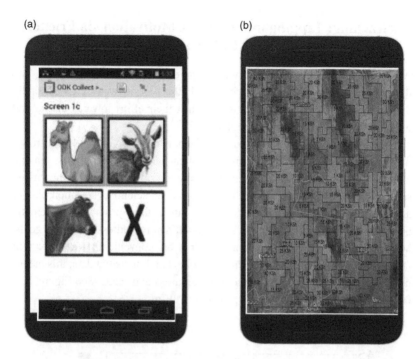

Figure 11.3 The intuitive Nchioto interface allows participants to submit reports monitoring vegetation conditions on the ground via smart phones. (a) The Nchioto interface asks the participants whether the grass on the ground is edible for certain types of animals using graphics that overcomes language barriers. (b) Nchioto shows a map of rewards, motivating participants to conduct land surveys in remote regions with high monetary rewards. Image credit: Andrew Mude, Nathan Jensen at the International Livestock Research Institute.

the percentage increase in participation per unit of reward increase. In terms of individual-level elasticity, we observed that increasing the amount of reward leads to an increase in submissions. In terms of aggregate-level elasticity, we observed that a spatial variant reward treatment designed with AI algorithm, where rewards were biased toward remote and under-sampled locations, performed better than a uniform reward treatment in pushing the crowd to remote areas [Jensen et al. 2017a].

In summary, our results demonstrate that large-scale crowdsourcing of environmental information from low-literacy populations can be feasible. Furthermore, we showed that participants respond to incentives in a rational way, demonstrating the potential impact of optimally designed incentive schemes in driving the crowd toward the most useful tasks.

Avicaching: Tapping into Intrinsic Motivation via Friendly Competition for Uniform Data Collection

Aside from monetary incentives, we engage citizen scientists by tapping into their intrinsic motivation for participation. In this section, we discuss a friendly competition among citizen scientists to shift their effort toward remote and under-sampled areas to reduce the data bias.

Data bias is a common problem in citizen science. To attract large groups of participants, citizen science projects often have few restrictions, leaving many decisions about where, when, and how to collect data up to the citizen scientists. As a result, the data collected by citizen scientists are often biased, aligned with their personal preferences, rather than providing systematic observations across various experimental settings to address scientific goals. Moreover, since participants volunteer their effort, convenience is an important factor that often determines how data are collected. For spatial data, this means more searches occur in areas close to urban areas and roads. See Figure 11.4 for an illustration of the data bias problem in eBird.

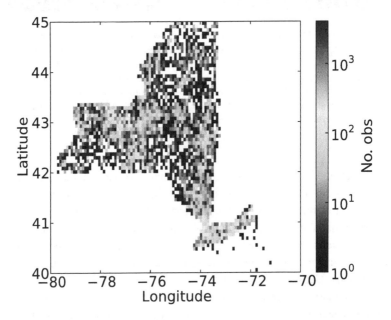

Figure 11.4 Highly biased distribution of eBird observations. This picture shows the number of observations in New York State from May 1 to September 1, 2011. A few locations receive orders of magnitude more observations than other locations.

Citizen scientists often join the program with very commendable goals; they would like to contribute in a meaningful way to science. The best way to motivate them, in this case, is to nurture their intrinsic motivation, by creating ranked lists and milestones, which will engage them in a healthy, competitive environment, to see more and rare bird species.

To address the data bias problem in citizen science, and particularly in eBird, we proposed a game called Avicaching, which motivates the participants by tapping into their intrinsic motivation via friendly competition (see Figure 11.5). We reward citizen scientists with additional Avicaching points for observations conducted in remote and under-sampled areas. Avicaching points, in this case, represent how much effort each bird watcher has expended. We maintain a leaderboard to document how many Avicaching points each

Figure 11.5 The Avicaching game motivates bird watchers to explore remote and under-sampled locations by tapping into their intrinsic motivation via a friendly competition. Bird watchers compete on how many Avicaching points they have earned in an online ranking list (a reward map in the lower left; a ranking list in the lower right). At the end of each season, bird watchers have an opportunity to win birding gear in a lottery drawn based on the number of Avicaching points earned. Avicaching banner credit: Ian Davies and Christopher Wood at the Cornell Lab of Ornithology.

participant has earned, viewable by all participants. At the end of the season, Avicaching players have the chance of winning a prize, such as a pair of binoculars, which is determined by how many Avicaching points one has earned.

The Avicaching game is supported by novel AI technologies in multi-agent systems and game theory. We formalize Avicaching as a two-stage game, which can be represented by the following bi-level optimization:

$$
\begin{aligned}
\text{(Organizer)} : \quad & r \leftarrow \operatorname{argmin}_r V_{\text{org}}(v, r), \\
\text{subject to} \quad & B_{\text{org}}(r), \\
& v \leftarrow \operatorname{argmax}_v U_a(v, r) \qquad \text{(Agents)} \\
& B_a(v).
\end{aligned}
\tag{11.1}
$$

The agents of this game are citizen scientists, who maximize their total utility function $U_a(v, r)$, which includes their intrinsic utilities, combined with the incentives distributed by the game organizer, subject to a budget constraint $B_a(v)$. v is the optimal action of the agents, which in this game is the set of locations that agents choose to visit. r denotes a vector of rewards that the organizer allocates to different locations. The agents' intrinsic utilities include the birding quality of the location, such as how many bird species can be seen in one location, as well as the convenience factor of the location. The organizer in our two-stage game corresponds to an organization with notable influence on the citizen scientists, such as the eBird program. The organizer factors in the reasoning of the citizen scientists to propose an optimal incentive allocation r which maximizes his/her objective function $V_{\text{org}}(v, r)$. In our setting, since the organizer would like to induce a uniform data collection process, $V_{\text{org}}(v, r)$ is an objective function that measures the spatial and temporal uniformity of the data collected.

There are two aspects to consider in solving the two-stage game. The first aspect is to design a behavioral model in order to learn citizen scientists' utility function $U_a(v, r)$. Citizen scientists do not reveal their reward preferences to the organizer directly. Instead, the organizer must infer the agents' utility functions based on their response to different reward treatments. According to the formulation in equation 11.1, v is the response that maximizes the citizen scientists' utility function. Assuming v^* is the optimal response of one agent, the following inequalities

$$
U_a\left(v^*, r\right) \geq U_a(v, r)
\tag{11.2}
$$

hold for every action v that the agent can possibly take. Motivated by this idea, we formalize the problem of fitting the behavioral model as a structured learning problem, in which we search for model parameters that satisfy as many inequalities of type 11.2 as possible. We first proposed a structural SVM approach for behavioral modeling [Xue et al. 2016a]. We also proposed a refined dynamic discrete choice model [Xue et al. 2016b]. We refer the reader to these two papers for mathematical details.

The second aspect is to solve the two-stage game, given the behavioral model of the agents. This is challenging because it is a bi-level optimization, in which the organizer needs to solve his/her own optimization problem, taking into account that agents are also optimizing for their own reward functions. In other words, there is a sub-optimization (shown in the box of equation 11.1) embedded in the global optimization problem. We devised several novel algorithms to solve the two-stage game.

Our novel contribution is to embed (an approximation of) the agents' problems into the organizer's problem. The core idea is to approximate the agents' reasoning process with a tractable algorithm. We then compile this algorithm as a set of linear constraints. The compilation process mimics exactly the execution of the algorithm, introducing one constraint for each operation. After obtaining all the linear constraints, we embed them in the bi-level optimization, collapsing the entire problem to a single optimization. To be more specific, we consider different objectives for the organizer, corresponding to different measures of data uniformity, using mixed integer programming and mixed integer quadratic programming formulations. We also consider different levels of rationality for the agents. For the scenario in which the agents have unbounded rationality, we developed an iterative row generation method to avoid the potentially exponential number of constraints induced by agents' optimization problems. We also consider the case in which the agents have bounded rationality. In this scenario, we embed the agent decision process as linear constraints into the global bi-level optimization problem, and therefore the entire problem can be solved by a single optimization.

The Avicaching game has been very popular among citizen scientists and has received an amazing field response. In a study conducted in Tompkins and Cortland Counties in New York in 2015, the Avicaching game was able to shift approximately 20 percent of birding effort from traditional hotspots to Avicaching locations, which had not been visited prior to the Avicaching game. Many participants revealed that indeed it is both the intrinsic motivations to make contributions to science, and the honor and fulfillment of ranking highly in the final list that have kept them competing in the Avicaching game.

Bird-Watcher Assistant: Engaging Participants with Service Tools

Rather than using incentives, in this section we explore the possibility of engaging citizen scientists by developing service tools that render participation more enjoyable and rewarding. Service tools bring value to the citizen science community and are appreciated by the participants. Successful citizen science programs often emphasize service tools to the participants. For example, in eBird, many useful tools have been built over the years, such as eBird bar charts, top 100 lists and Merlin [Wood et al. 2011; http://merlin .allaboutbirds.org.].

We focus on building a set of service tools for recommending interesting birding sites to bird watchers, encapsulated in an application that we call Bird-Watcher Assistant, to further boost participation in eBird. Figure 11.6 shows snapshots of our application on a cellphone. Bird-Watcher Assistant is especially targeted at beginner bird watchers, whose continuous participation depends on discovering interesting birding sites and therefore building reputation and skills within the birding community. To increase their participation,

(a)   (b)

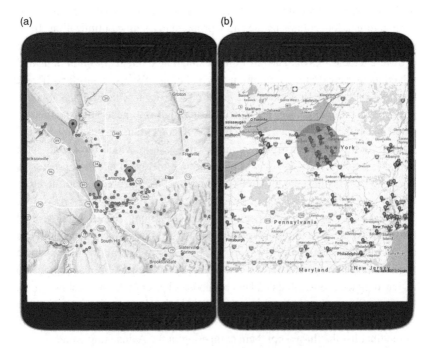

Figure 11.6 Bird-Watcher Assistant brings back value to bird watchers by making birding activities fun and enjoyable. (a) Bird-Watcher Assistant recommends a few locations in a small region under a travel budget. A diverse set of species can be seen by visiting these locations. (b) A large-scale variant in which Bird-Watcher Assistant recommends locations within the travel budget in a sub-region (shown in the blue circle) of the entire area.

we suggest birding sites that they may not have known about, based on their limited experience.

Bird-Watcher Assistant makes use of information from spatio-temporal species distribution models [Fink et al. 2010], which predict species occurrence at a given location and time based on the associations between current eBird observations and local environmental data. These species distribution models inform the selection of the most desirable or useful new tasks for the citizen scientists. Besides engaging participants, another goal is to build a loop for active learning, in which our Bird-Watcher Assistant recommends locations that are most informative for addressing eBird's scientific goal. Active learning is a popular research direction in machine learning and artificial intelligence, where one seeks to select the set of unlabeled data points that would have the most significant impact on the fitted predictive model when added to the labeled training data. In the context of citizen science, however, one cannot simply maximize the information content of the tasks but should take into account the interests of the citizen scientists to make the recommended tasks enjoyable.

In order to improve the bird watchers' chances of seeing a diverse set of species, the Bird-Watcher Assistant is designed to recommend locations based on the solution to the following problem: given a set of locations, select a subset of size k, such that the bird watchers maximize the expected number of observed species by visiting such locations. We consider two variants of this problem: (1) a local-scale variant (Figure 11.5(a)), in which we are choosing among birding sites that are within a given region, for example when planning a birding trip within a county; and (11.2) a large-scale variant (Figure 11.5(b)), in which we want to choose a sub-region (with a given radius) from a given larger region, from which we want to choose the set of locations to visit. For example, bird watchers might want to fly to Colombia and visit a subset of birding sites within a sub-region of Colombia. We formalize the first small-scale problem as the probabilistic maximum coverage problem. Mathematically, it can be represented as:

(probabilistic maximum coverage)

maximize $f(S)$, subject to $|S| \leq k$.

Here, S is the set of locations that we recommend to the user. $f(S)$ is the objective function that captures the expected number of species that one can see by visiting all locations in S. We formalize the second large-scale problem as probabilistic maximum coverage with locality constraints, which is:

(probabilistic maximum coverage with locality constraints)

maximize $f(S)$, subject to $|S| \leq k$ and

all locations in S are covered by a circle of radius r.

In addition to the primary objective of maximizing the expected number of observed species, we also consider a secondary objective that gives preference to birding sites not previously visited, when in the presence of multiple solutions with a comparable number of expected species. This secondary objective helps expand the spatial coverage of eBird by promoting new birding sites, typically in less-populated areas. Observations made at the Bird-Watcher Assistant recommended sites will help mitigate the spatial bias in eBird, where observations are concentrated toward regions with high human density.

The first problem of probabilistic maximum coverage can be formulated as maximizing a submodular function, subject to cardinality constraints. While the problem is NP-hard, we can use the classical $(1 - 1/e)$ approximation algorithm to solve the problem. The second probabilistic maximum coverage with locality constraints problem is a submodular optimization subject to both cardinality and locality constraints, specified by a given radius. To our knowledge, the most similar problem studied previously concerns submodular optimization subject to a path length constraint [Chekuri and Pal 2005; Singh et al. 2009]. The state-of-the-art for that problem is a quasi-polynomial-time algorithm with a logarithmic approximation bound. In contrast, we show that the probabilistic maximum coverage problem with radius locality constraints admits a strongly polynomial $(1 - 1/e)$ approximation bound. The high-level idea of our algorithm is to consider all location sets covered by circles of radius r, and then select the k best locations from each location set. To consider all possible location sets, it turns out to be sufficient to only consider circles of radius r that pass through all pairs of locations that are at most $2r$ apart.

We evaluated the performance of the proposed algorithms in the context of eBird. At the local scale, we considered Tompkins County, NY, the home of the Cornell Lab of Ornithology and eBird. To test the performance of Bird-Watcher Assistant, we compared locations recommended by our model to locations recommended by a set of expert bird watchers. Qualitatively, the locations suggested by our model were judged to be of high quality by the domain experts. Quantitatively, the locations suggested by our model achieve higher expected numbers of species than the locations suggested by the experts. The locations suggested by Bird-Watcher Assistant systematically covered the three most important habitat types for birds while promoting increased spatial coverage of the county. At a larger scale, we considered planning birding trips across multiple states, spanning more than 70,000 potential locations.

Overall, our algorithms are remarkably fast and provide high-quality birding site recommendations.

Conclusion

Citizen science programs are an effective way to engage the general public in data collection for conservation. To make citizen science programs enjoyable, this chapter presented three effective ways to stimulate participation, namely with extrinsic motivation, intrinsic motivation, and service tools. We discussed the Nchioto application, in which we used extrinsic incentives to motivate local pastoralists to monitor vegetation conditions in Eastern Africa. We then described a two-stage game called Avicaching in eBird, where we encouraged bird watchers to conduct bird observations in remote and under-sampled locations, with intrinsic motivations via friendly competitions. In addition, we discussed Bird-Watcher Assistant, a service tool to help bird watchers discover interesting and enjoyable birding locations and to further boost participation and scientific discovery. The success of each of these citizen science programs depends on novel contributions from game theory, machine learning, and combinatorial optimization of artificial intelligence. On the other hand, artificial intelligence benefits enormously from novel problems and concepts from conservation. We see the integration of artificial intelligence and conservation as a very promising interdisciplinary research direction that benefits both fields, showing the great impact of artificial intelligence to conservation.

Acknowledgments

This research was supported by the National Science Foundation (grant numbers OCI-0830944, CCF-0832782, CCF-1522054, ITR-0427914, DBI-1049363, DBI-0542868, DUE-0734857, IIS-0748626, IIS-0844546, IIS-0612031, IIS-1050422, IIS-0905385, IIS-0746500, IIS-1209589, AGS-0835821, CNS-0751152, CNS-0855167, CNS-1059284, DEB-110008, DBI-1356308); ARO grant W911-NF-14-1-0498; the Leon Levy Foundation; and the Wolf Creek Foundation. We acknowledge research collaboration and fieldwork support from colleagues at the International Livestock Research Institute (Nairobi, Kenya), Cornell University, and UC San Diego. We also acknowledge the Atkinson Center for a Sustainable Future's Academic Venture Fund and Australian Aid. We thank the eBird citizen science program, thousands of eBird participants, and the Cornell Lab of Ornithology. We would like to thank Chris Barrett, Richard Bernstein, Eddy Chebelyon, Theodoros Damoulas, Ian Davies, Bistra Dilkina, Daniel Fink, Nathan Jensen, Steve Kelling, Andrew Mude, Oscar Naibei, Russell Toth, and Christopher Wood for their contributions.

References

Chekuri, C., and Pal, M. 2005. A recursive greedy algorithm for walks in directed graphs. In *Proc. of the 46th Annual IEEE Symposium on Foundations of Computer Science*, 245–253. IEEE.

Fang, F.; Nguyen, T.H.; Pickles, R.; et al. 2017. PAWS: a deployed game-theoretic application to combat poaching. *AI Magazine*, 38(1).

Fink, D.; Hochachka, W.M.; Zuckerberg, B.; et al. 2010. Spatiotemporal exploratory models for broad-scale survey data. *Ecological Applications* 20(8):2131–2147.

Gomes. C.P. 2009. Computational sustainability: computational methods for a sustainable environment, economy, and society. *The Bridge* 39(4):5–13.

Jensen, N.; Toth, R.; Xue, Y.; et al. 2017a. Don't follow the crowd: incentives for directed spatial sampling. In *Proc. of the Agricultural and Applied Economics Association*. AAEA.

Jensen, N.; Elizabeth, L.; Chebelyon, E.; Le Bras, R.; and Gomes, C.P. 2017b. Monitoring A, while hoping for A & B: field experimental evidence on multidimensional task monitoring. https://sites.google.com/a/cornell.edu/nathan-jensen.

Kelling, S.; Gerbracht, J.; Fink, D.; et al. 2012. ebird: A human/computer learning network for biodiversity conservation and research. In *Proc. of the 26th AAAI Conference on Artificial Intelligence*, 2229–2236. AAAI Press.

Marshall, N.J.; Kleine, D.A.; and Dean, A.J. 2012. Coralwatch: education, monitoring, and sustainability through citizen science. *Frontiers in Ecology and the Environment* 10:332–334.

Naibei, O; Jensen, N.; Banerjee, R.R.; and Mude A. 2017. Crowdsourcing for rangeland conditions: process innovation and beyond. *ILRI Research Brief* 84:1–4.

Singh, A.; Krause, A.; Guestrin, C.; and Kaiser, W.J. 2009. Efficient informative sensing using multiple robots. *Journal of Artificial Intelligence Research* 34:707–755.

Sullivan, B.L.; Wood, C.L.; Iliff, M.J.; et al. 2009. ebird: a citizen-based bird observation network in the biological sciences. *Biological Conservation* 142(10): 2282–2292.

Wood, C.; Sullivan, B.; Iliff, M.; Fink, D.; and Kelling, S. 2011. ebird: engaging birders in science and conservation. *PLoS Biology* 9(12).

Xue, Y.; Dilkina, B.; Damoulas, T; et al. 2013. Improving your chances: boosting citizen science discovery. In *Proc. of the First AAAI Conference on Human Computation and CrowdSourcing*. AAAI Press.

Xue, Y.; Davies, I.; Fink, D.; Wood, C.; and Gomes, C.P. 2016a. Avicaching: a two stage game for bias reduction in citizen science. In *Proc. of the 2016 International Conference on Autonomous Agents & Multiagent Systems*, 776–785. International Foundation for Autonomous Agents and Multiagent Systems.

Xue, Y.; Davies, I.; Fink, D.; Wood, C.; and Gomes, C. P. 2016b. Behavior identification in two-stage games for incentivizing citizen science exploration. In *Proc. of the 22nd International Principles and Practice of Constraint Programming*. Springer.

Yadav, A.; Chan, H.; Jiang, A.X.; et al. 2017. Maximizing awareness about HIV in social networks of homeless youth with limited information. In *Proc. of the 26th International Joint Conference on Artificial Intelligence*. AAAI Press.

12

Simulator-Defined Markov Decision Processes

A Case Study in Managing Bio-invasions

H. Jo Albers, Thomas G. Dietterich, Kim Hall, Katherine D. Lee,
and Majid A. Taleghan

Introduction

Non-native invasive species (IS) have spread widely in recent decades, invading both land and water systems. These species threaten an ecosystem's ability to house biodiversity and provide ecosystem services (USADA 2013; see also www.fs.fed.us/invasivespecies). For example, the invasion of tamarisk tree in the Rio Grande valley in New Mexico has greatly reduced the amount of water available for native species and for irrigation of agricultural crops (Di Tomaso, 1998)

The goal of IS management is to take actions to eliminate or control the invasive species. Managers typically have multiple actions that they can perform – subject to tight budget constraints. Some actions seek to remove the IS from invaded sites and restore those sites to an uninvaded state. Other actions seek to protect not-yet-invaded sites (Stewart-Koster et al., 2015). To select optimal actions, managers must model the processes by which the invasive species is being introduced to the landscape and the processes by which it spreads. These processes are known as the "dynamics" of the ecosystem. Managers must also develop models of the costs and effects of their management actions. These models can be combined into a single bio-economic model to provide a basis for policy optimization and sensitivity analysis.

Invasive species invade and spread through stochastic spatio-temporal processes that include introduction, reproduction, spatial dispersal, and site invasion. Each of these processes may be spatially heterogeneous and depend on interactions with native species and the degree of invasibility of different sites. Dispersal may involve long-distance "jumps" in which organisms (e.g., seeds, spores) skip over uninvaded sites when moving from one site to another (e.g., by traveling on wind, on water, on an animal, or on a vehicle). The success of management actions is also stochastic. Hence, a bio-economic model that encompasses the full complexity of the IS problem is a complex, stochastic, spatio-temporal model.

The economics literature seeks to inform management decisions by developing decision frameworks that incorporate characteristics of the spatio-temporal spread of IS and using those frameworks to define management plans that are spatially and dynamically optimal. However, the challenges of formulating and optimizing complex stochastic spatio-temporal models have led economists to simplify their models. Common simplifications include replacing the stochastic model with a deterministic model, assuming spatially homogeneous systems, ignoring interactions with native species, and employing simple nearest-neighbor dispersal models. Analysis of such simplified models has resulted in many papers that suggest that landscape management should focus on preventing or limiting the spread of the IS at its frontier (e.g., Sharov, 2004). Recent work has developed methods for directing the invasion's pathway when spread cannot be prevented (Epanchin-Niell and Wilen, 2012).

In this chapter we describe our work on applying Markov decision processes (MDPs) to formulate and optimize IS problems. A MDP is defined by the set $\mathcal{X}$ of states, the set $\mathcal{A}$ of actions, the cost $C(X, A)$ of taking action A in state X, the initial state S_0, the discount factor ρ, and the transition probability distribution $P(X_{t+1}|X_t, A_t)$. In an IS model, it is customary to divide the landscape into a set of cells. Each cell may be occupied by some mix of species (native and invasive), and it may also have some other properties (index of invasibility, distance to highways, distance to towns, etc.). The state X_t of the ecosystem at time t specifies the state and properties of every cell in the landscape. An action typically affects only some of the cells in the landscape. For example, a typical IS action attempts to eradicate the IS in one or more cells of the landscape. The "dynamics" of the MDP, $P(X_{t+1}|X_t, A_t)$ describes the effects of each possible action A_t on the state of the ecosystem, as well as the ongoing biological processes (reproduction, dispersal, mortality, etc.) of the system.

Our computer science algorithms are quite straightforward, but they provide a valuable new tool for economists. Economists have customarily formulated their bio-economic models in terms of table-based MDPs. In a table-based MDP, the economist must provide a probability transition matrix $T_A(X, X')$ for each management action A that specifies the conditional probability $P(X'|X, A)$ that the system will move from some state X to state X' when action A is performed. This representation is not very "user friendly," and it can be very difficult to determine each of the transition probabilities in the matrix. A simulator-defined MDP, in contrast, is defined by a stochastic simulator that, given the current state X of the landscape and the chosen management action

A, generates a new state X' according to the stochastic bio-economic model. Simulators are much easier to write and validate.

Even with our algorithms, there are tight limits on the size of the problem that can be solved – specifically the number of states and actions. Our method is suitable for "modest-sized" problems having fewer than 50,000 states and 10 actions. Although our IS model contains considerable simplifications in the ecological model and in the landscape size, the model still incorporates the critical aspects of concern to IS managers: uncertainty, species/habitat characteristics, and complicated spatial dispersal of species.

After describing the economics IS literature and the computational spatio-dynamic optimization literature, this chapter sets up an economic cost min-imization model for a riverscape facing a bio-invasion and describes the computational methods used to solve that model. The subsequent section characterizes the IS management results from this model, with emphasis on the spatio-temporal characteristics and the ecological features of the setting. Then, the chapter describes the types and importance of results that derive from the key characteristics of the model that the computational methods were developed to solve. The final section of the chapter discusses general lessons from stochastic spatio-dynamic optimization and identifies needs for further computational methods to address other aspects of IS management.

Background and Related Work

Within economics, the aspects of when and how much IS management action (e.g., surveillance, prevention, removal) is optimal has been a predominant focus of analysis. However, space is a critical dimension in developing bio-economic models that accurately represent landscape heterogeneity and IS spread and dispersal. One approach is to treat space as implicit, which simplifies the analysis by ignoring the spatial arrangement of the system, and informs a general per-unit area effort to expend on management or depending on how quickly the IS expands. Economic analyses that represent space explicitly often use deterministic methods and make simplifications to the system to make the problem tractable.

The ecological literature uses a variety of models to explicitly represent the existence and spread of IS across space. Reaction-diffusion models represent short-distance IS dispersal using partial differential equations. Integrodiffer-ence models describe spread using kernels and allow for changing rates of spread and small jumps. Cellular autonoma models define a landscape as a matrix of cells, where transition rules dictate interactions and IS spread in a "neighborhood" of each invaded cell. Gravity models define the flow of a species from location i to location j in terms of the "propagule pressure" (density of seeds) at i and j and the distance between the two locations. These models have been used to address long-distance IS dispersal for cases in which the IS moves by hitchhiking on human activity and where human movements can be predicted based on the distance between locations (e.g. Baxter and Ewing, 1981; Bossenbroek et al., 2001), as compared to diffusion models that emphasize the rate of movement rather than the attraction between locations. Any of these modeling frameworks can be used in development of a bio-economic model of IS management.

A smaller literature within economics focuses on the spatio-dynamic aspects of IS management, and addresses the "curse of dimensionality." Epanchin-Niell and Wilen (2012) develop a model of IS spread deterministically and choose a functional form for the nonlinear model that can be transformed into a system of linear equations, and solved using integer programming. Similarly, Aadland et al. (2015) develop a linear approximation for a nonlinear model of timber harvest decisions to manage a forest pest. The authors simplify the problem by only controlling the IS through timber harvest rather than through direct management effort. Chalak et al. (2017) develop a stochastic spatio-temporal model of IS management by assuming the IS population is in a steady state.

Model and Solution Method

We developed a bio-economic MDP for the tamarisk IS problem with four components: the state space (Figure 12.1); the action space; the dynamical model that specifies the processes of mortality, seed production, seed dispersal, and seed establishment; and the cost model that quantifies management costs and IS damage and includes an annual budget constraint. All of the parameter values for these components, and their sources, are provided in Table 12.1. The bio-economic model and results are described in more detail by Hall et al. (2017), while the computational methods are the focus of Taleghan et al. (2015). The discussion here is drawn from those articles.

State Space

The river network is a binary tree in which each edge is known as a "reach" (Figure 12.1). Each reach can be viewed as a site at which one plant (either native or invasive) can live. We denote the number of reaches by U. The state

Table 12.1. *Base case parameter values*

	Parameter	Value	Source
ρ	Discount rate	0.95	
$d(0)$	Degraded site cost	0.05	
$d(1)$	Invasive species cost	20	
$d(2)$	Native species cost	0	
$c(a_e)$	Control/removal cost per reach	1	Tamarisk Coalition 2009
$c(a_p)$	Restoration of degraded reach	1	Tamarisk Coalition 2009
$c(a_r)$	Restoration of invaded reach	1.8	
q	Probability of action failure	0.2	Tamarisk Coalition 2009
C	Budget constraint	2	
α_2	Mortality rate of native	0.2	Muneepeerakul et al. 2007
α_1	Mortality rate of invasive	0.2	Muneepeerakul et al. 2007
f_2	Invasive fecundity	2000	Stevens, 2002; simulator
f_1	Native fecundity	100	Schopmeyer, 1974; simulator
u	Upstream dispersal rate	0.1	Muneepeerakul et al. 2007
d	Downstream dispersal rate	0.5	Muneepeerakul et al. 2007
V_1	Exogenous arrival count, invasive	200	Simulator, relative to fecundity
V_2	Exogenous arrival count, native	0	Simulator, relative to fecundity
p_1	Exogenous arrival probability	0.1	Simulator, chosen to be within range of dispersal matrix
β	Relative competitiveness of invasive species seeds	1.3	Stromberg, 1998; simulator
e_s	Establishment probability	0.13	Sher & Marshall, 2003

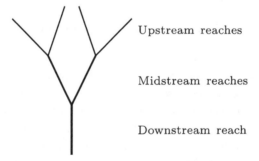

Figure 12.1 Schematic of the stylized river network assumed in the simulations.

of the network is described by a U-element vector $X_t = (x_{1,t}, \ldots, x_{U,t})$, where $x_{i,t}$ denotes the state of reach i at time t. Each $x_{i,t}$ can take on three possible values, $\{0, 1, 2\}$ corresponding to the ecological characteristic of the reach: degraded ($x_{i,t} = 0$), occupied by the IS ($x_{i,t} = 1$), or occupied by the native species ($x_{i,t} = 2$). A degraded reach is currently unoccupied but is available for colonization by either a native or an IS if seeds arrive at that reach. Ecologists refer to it as "degraded" because the reach is not biologically productive (i.e., it is not producing biomass). In our base case, there are 7 reaches and $3^7 = 2,187$ possible riverscape states. A stylized riverscape of this size could readily be examined for a one-period spatial optimization, but optimizing over an infinite horizon poses computational difficulties for the backward-induction methods typically used in economics. In addition, many IS economic models consider only a few initial state conditions for the landscape, but our computational methods define the optimal management actions and locations for every possible state of the riverscape.

Actions

At each time step, the manager can perform an action A. The action is a vector of length U: $A_t = (a_{1,t}, a_{2,t}, \ldots, a_{U,t})$, where each $a_{i,t}$ is one of four possible single-reach actions: {do nothing, eradicate, restore, eradicate+restore}. The "do nothing" action makes no change in the reach. If the reach is occupied by the IS, then the "eradicate" action kills the invasive plant with probability q. If the reach is degraded, the "restore" action attempts to plant a native plant. This succeeds with probability q. Finally, the "eradicate+restore" action first attempts to kill the IS and then plant a native species. This either fails entirely with probability $1 - q$ (leaving the site occupied by an invasive plant) or succeeds with probability q (with the site occupied by the native plant).

Transition Model

After the actions have been performed, the remainder of the state transition process is simulated through a series of four subprocesses. First, each of the currently living plants (native or invasive) may die according to a Bernoulli mortality probability α_1 (for invasive) or α_2 (for native). Second, each surviving plant produces seeds. The number of seeds is f_1 (for invasive) and f_2 (for native) plants. The third process – dispersal – is the most complex. We employ the model developed by Muneepeerakul et al. (2007). It defines a $U \times U$ dispersal matrix $\mathbf{B}$ where each element, b_{ik}, represents the probability that a seed from reach i will disperse to reach k, defined as

$$b_{ik} = Ru^{\mu_{i,k}}d^{\delta_{i,k}} \text{ with } R = \frac{(1 - 2u)(1 - d)}{1 - ud}. \tag{12.1}$$

To reflect the fact that seeds are less likely to travel long distances than short distances, exponents $\mu_{i,k}$ and $\delta_{i,k}$ specify the number of reaches between

i and k upstream (μ) or downstream (δ). To reflect the difference in seed movement upstream versus downstream, the arrival rate of seeds dispersing from i to k is controlled by parameters u (upstream) and d (downstream). The quantity R is the probability of seeds remaining in the reach where they were produced (corresponding to $\mu_{i,k} = \delta_{i,k} = 0$). When u and d are both greater than zero, there is a non-zero probability that a seed can travel from any reach i to any other reach k. If there are n seeds of species s at reach i, then their locations after dispersal have a multinomial distribution with parameters n and $(b_{i,1}, \ldots, b_{i,U})$. Hence, the number of seeds of species s arriving at reach k is the sum of U different multinomially distributed random variables, one corresponding to each source reach i. The use of the ecological simulator permits our examination of this complex dispersal model rather than relying on assumptions about neighborhood spread.

This is very different from many IS economic models that assume that the IS moves radially at some rate of spread or, in a discrete setting, can only move to nearest neighbors – or short-distance dispersal. We can capture such models in our simulator by setting $b_{i,k} = 0$ for all pairs of reaches i and k that are not immediate neighbors.

In addition to seeds arriving at reach k from other reaches, we also model external sources of seeds (e.g., birds, anglers, etc.). These are known as "exogenous arrivals," For each reach, the number of exogenous seeds arriving for species s has a binomial distribution with number of trials V_s and probability of success p_s in each trial. Together, the seeds dispersing within the system and arriving from outside of the system combine to create a total number of seeds $z_{s,k}$ of species s arriving at reach k.

The fourth subprocess in the state transition model is the competition for establishment. If a seed of any species arrives at an occupied reach, the seed simply dies and no change occurs to the ecological state of that reach. But if the reach is degraded, then all of the seeds that arrive there compete to determine which species will become established. Following the ecological model in Muneepeerakul et al. (2007), species compete to establish based on the number of seeds from each species that arrive at the reach, $z_{s,k}$, and on the species' relative competitive advantage, β. The species that wins that competition changes the state of the reach from degraded to native or invaded. The probability that species s outcompetes the other species is

$$\Psi(x_k = 1) = \frac{\beta z_{1,k}}{\beta z_{1,k} + \beta z_{2,k}}, \tag{12.2}$$

$$\Psi(x_k = 2) = 1 - \Psi(x_k = 1). \tag{12.3}$$

The combination of dispersal and competition means that from the perspective of probabilistic modeling, the state of each reach at time $t + 1$ depends on the state of every other reach at time t. Hence, the states of all reaches are coupled, and the corresponding probabilistic graphical model is fully connected. This makes it impractical to derive a closed-form expression for the state transition matrix.

Cost Model

Each action $a_{i,t}$ incurs a cost $c\left(a_{i,t}\right)$ as follows. Taking no action has a cost of 0. The "restore" and "eradicate" actions each cost one unit. Finally, the "eradicate+restore" action costs 1.8 units. The cost of the entire action vector A_t is the sum of the costs of the individual within-reach actions. We impose a budget C on the total cost of management actions in each time step t, which reflects the reality of limited resources available to managers for IS management (Januchowski-Hartley et al. 2011; Visconti et al. 2010).

In addition to the action costs, there are also "damage costs" $d\left(x_{i,t}\right)$ for each state. A degraded reach incurs a cost of 0.05; an invaded reach costs 20 units; and a reach occupied by the native species costs 0 units. The total cost of the state vector X_t is the sum of the costs of each reach.

Optimization Objective

The overall objective is to find a policy π that minimizes the expected infinite-horizon cumulative discounted cost:

$$J\left(\pi\right) = \mathbb{E}\left[\sum_{t=0}^{\infty} \rho^t \left(\sum_{i=1}^{U} d(x_{i,t}) + c(a_{i,t})\right) \middle| X_0\right], \qquad (12.4)$$

where

$$A_t = \pi(X_t), \qquad (12.5)$$

$$\sum_i c\left(m_{i,t}\right) \le C \quad \forall t. \qquad (12.6)$$

The discount factor is denoted by ρ. The expectation is taken with respect to the probability transitions $P\left(X_{t+1}|X_t, A_t\right)$, which are implemented by the simulator according to the processes described above. This incorporates the stochasticity resulting from the management actions and from the four processes of mortality, reproduction, dispersal, and competition for establishment.

To explore the tradeoffs between control and restoration and their locations across a riparian network, the base case parameter set was chosen to mimic the aggressive riparian invader, tamarisk (*Tamarix* sp.), which has established extensively in the southwestern USA and is spreading northward. Tamarisk is highly fecund, and its seeds are able to out-compete native vegetation for establishment in degraded riverscapes. When available, parameter values for the base case are based on those found in the literature, as noted in Table 12.1. To populate the unknown ecological parameters, we calibrated the ecological simulation model to approximate the timing of tamarisk expansion in the western USA (Tamarisk Coalition 2009). Economic parameters for treatment costs were chosen using information supplied by the Tamarisk Coalition on the average treatment costs of a tamarisk invasion. Ecological costs or damages were chosen such that the marginal social costs of the invader are greater than the marginal costs of management when the budget constraint binds (Epanchin-Niell and Hastings, 2010). Information on the economic and ecological costs of a tamarisk invasion indicates the validity of this assumption (Zavaleta, 2000). Additional parameter sensitivity analysis can be found in Hall (2014) and Hall et al. (2017).

Solution Method

We apply the value iteration method (Sutton and Barto, 1998) to compute the optimal value function and the corresponding optimal policy. There are two major challenges to applying value iteration to this problem. The first challenge is the size of the probability transition matrix. A river network with seven reaches, each with three possible states, has $3^7 = 2187$ possible system-wide or spatial states. At each time step, there are four management actions that can potentially be performed in each of the seven reaches, so there are $4^7 = 15384$ possible action vectors A. A naïve formulation of the transition probability distribution $P\left(X'|X,A\right)$ would require $2,187 \times 2,187 \times 15,384 \approx 7.3 \times 10^{10}$ entries. Fortunately, the budget constraint and the fact that only some state–action combinations are permitted ("restore" applies only to "degraded" reaches; "eradicate" and "eradicate+restore" apply only to "invaded" reaches) greatly reduces the size of this table.

The second challenge is that the probability transitions cannot be computed directly from the model in closed form. We address this by computing Monte Carlo estimates of the transition probabilities as follows. For each possible system-wide state X and each legal action vector A (after accounting for the budget constraint and symmetries), we perform repeated simulations of single time step transitions to estimate the distribution over result states X' : $P(X'|X,A)$. First, we allocate a vector N with one entry for each possible result state and initialize it to zero. Then, we perform a sequence of simulations, all starting in a particular state X and applying a specified action vector A. Each simulation produces a result state X', and we increment the corresponding element $N_{X'}$. After S simulations, the probability $\theta_{X,m,X'}$ of the transition $P\left(X'|X,A\right)$ can be estimated as $\hat{\theta}_{X,m,X'} = N_{X'}/S$. We determine S adaptively by accumulating sample transitions until a 95 percent confidence interval on the value of $\theta_{X,m,X'}$ has width less than 0.01, as computed by the Clopper–Pearson method (Clopper and Pearson, 1934). This computation does not need to be performed in all 2,187 possible landscape states. Many sets of states are symmetrical because the position of any pair of left-and-right river branches can be swapped. Hence, we perform this computation for one state X of each equivalence class of symmetrical states and copy the computed probabilities into the transition matrix entries for all of the symmetric states.

Once the transition matrix has been computed for every possible pair of state X and action vector A, we apply the value iteration algorithm to compute the optimal value function V^* and policy π^*.[1]

Main Results of the Model

To study optimal IS management, we computed the optimal policy for several different MDP parameter configurations. Table 12.1 shows the "base case" parameter values. Table 12.2 describes the other MDP configurations that we evaluated.

An open question in IS management is the relative merit of eradication (also known as "control") versus restoration. To study this, we examined the behavior of the optimal baseline policy by summing over all possible riverscape states, the frequency with which control (eradication) or restoration (including the eradicate+restore actions) is applied in each reach. The results are summarized in Figure 12.2. Not surprisingly, the answer is not uniform, but instead depends on the location of the site within the river network. The base case demonstrates that control, the less expensive treatment tool, is employed more often than restoration. The midstream reaches receive the most treatment per reach, with an emphasis on restoration. The upstream reaches receive the

---

[1] Hall et al.'s (2017) text and appendix and Taleghan et al. (2015) contain more description and discussion of this computational solution method.

Table 12.2. *MDP configurations analyzed*

Name	MDP Configuration
A	Base case
B	No upstream dispersal
C	IS long-distance dispersal advantage
D	High IS fecundity
E	High IS seed competitiveness
F	High exogenous arrivals of IS seeds
G	No IS mortality
H	No exogenous arrivals of IS seeds
I	Short-distance dispersal only

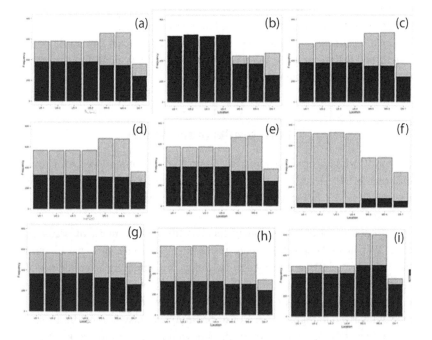

Figure 12.2 Management action type (gray: control; black: restore) and location (upstream: US, midstream: MS, or downstream: DS) and frequency of restoration and control policies (y-axis) under different ecological assumptions: (a) base case; (b) no upstream dispersal; (c) IS with long-distance dispersal advantage; (d) high IS fecundity; (e) high IS seed competitiveness; (f) high exogenous arrivals of IS seeds; (g) no mortality (IS only); (h) no exogenous arrivals; (i) short distance dispersal.

most treatment overall, with a focus on control. The downstream reach receives the least treatment, with control dominating restoration.

Spatial Arrangement of the System

The computational methods used here allow us to examine more complex IS dispersal and interactions across the entire spatial setting than are found in most IS economic analysis. Note that the management attention that any individual reach receives depends on that reach's spatial relationships to other reaches and the state of all other reaches. Control actions are applied more frequently as we move upstream. This reflects the strength of downstream propagation – eliminating an upstream plant eliminates a source of downstream seeds. Restoration actions are applied more frequently at midstream and least frequently at the downstream reach. This reflects two factors. First, planting a native plant in a midstream reach serves to occupy a degraded site and thereby protect it from invasion. Second, the native plant becomes a source for sending native seeds downstream. It might appear that the midstream native plants also serve as a "barrier" to invasive propagation, but that is only partly true. Invasive seeds can travel from upstream to downstream in a single time step, so native plants at midstream do not stop this. However, the probability of downstream propagation is exponentially less than propagation from upstream to midstream, so in this sense, planting natives midstream is exponentially more useful for preventing invasive establishment than planting them downstream. Planting natives upstream has virtually no preventive effect, because it only prevents rare upstream propagation of invasive plants. However, upstream natives do provide a seed source for mid- and downstream sites. In the base case parameterization, the invasive plants produce many more seeds than the natives, so the role of native plants as a source of downstream native seeds is not as important as the role of native plants in occupying reaches to prevent invasive establishment.

River Directionality

As compared to the base case, a river network that allows no upstream dispersal leads to optimal decisions that focus more management in the upstream locations overall (Figure 12.1(b)) and with a complete reliance on control and no use of restoration. This makes sense because without upstream propagation or exogenous arrivals, upstream eradication is permanent. These also explain why there is less treatment midstream and markedly lower levels of restoration. Once upstream sources of invasive seeds are eliminated, midstream eradication also becomes permanent. Finally, under model (b), the downstream reach is treated more often and with more restoration. It seems that occupying the downstream reach with a native plant is a useful first step before eradicating the invaders from upstream-to-downstream.

Ecological Characteristics

The ecological simulation-based methods also enable the analysis to incorporate a range of IS species characteristics rather than simplifying to rates of spread. IS can use various different mechanisms to dominate ecosystems. They can produce more seeds, disperse seeds further, compete more successfully for establishment, and have higher rates of exogenous arrivals than native species. For each of these mechanisms, the model parameters were varied to explore the effect of the mechanism on the optimal choice of management actions and locations (Figure 12.2(c)–(i)).

Dispersal

When IS can disperse across longer distances than can natives, optimal management includes more restoration in the upstream reaches as compared to the base case (Figure 12.2(c)). The manager also chooses more restoration and control overall in the upstream reaches, and places less restoration and control in the mid- and downstream reaches. Restoration can be used in upstream reaches to prevent IS establishment there, and to prevent the potential for the IS to spread from that location to anywhere in the river network in future time periods. These aspects of restoration are particularly important when the invader can disperse more widely than the native species, because the limitation on dispersal of native species implies that fewer native seeds will be available to compete with the IS in distant dispersed-to reaches. When an IS is only capable of short-distance dispersal, control is used fairly uniformly across upstream and midstream reaches, and restoration is focused on the midstream reaches (Figure 12.2(i)).

High Fecundity (Propagule Pressure)

Management of highly fecund IS employs more restoration in the upstream and midstream reaches than with low-fecundity species (Figure 12.2(d)). Restoration upstream places natives there, which reduces the risk of invasion throughout the network by creating a native seed source – and preventing an IS seed source – in these high-dispersal locations.

Seed Fitness

High seed fitness (competitive advantage) for the IS increases the importance of restoration, because if a site is occupied by a native plant, then it cannot be invaded, regardless of the number of seeds. The optimal policy prefers to restore the midstream reaches (Figure 12.2(e)) for the same reasons we have discussed above.

Exogenous Arrivals

When there is a high chance that IS can arrive from outside of the system, restoration is preferred as a management strategy (Figure 12.2(f)). This is because eradication is likely to be rapidly reversed by exogenous arrivals, whereas restoration protects a site no matter how many seeds arrive. Despite the equal probability of exogenous arrivals across all network reaches, the location of management actions differs across levels of the arrival risk. The upstream reaches are the least "dispersed to" reaches in the network, which means that exogenous arrivals of IS upstream face little competition from dispersing native seeds, as compared to the more highly dispersed-to reaches midstream and downstream. Restoration in those upstream locations both prevents invasion by exogenously arriving IS and provides native seeds to disperse throughout the system to compete with exogenous arrivals elsewhere, which combines with the budget constraint to lead to more restoration upstream with higher levels of exogenous arrivals of IS seeds. Allowing for no exogenous arrivals reduces the benefits of healthy native habitat in all reaches and the effort spent on restoration (Figure 12.2(h)).

Mortality

When we modify the model so that the native species can die a natural death but the invasive species cannot, the invasive's establishment is irreversible without management action to eradicate. In that case, optimal management involves more upstream restoration and more downstream control than the base case in which both species can die (Figure 12.1(g)). With no natural reversibility to an invasion through death, removing the invasion becomes more important overall. Because control is less expensive that restoration but creates a degraded – and therefore re-invadable – reach it is applied in downstream reaches that will benefit from upstream native seeds dispersing downstream.

Results Possible through this Computational Method

A major advantage of being able to use a highly complex simulator to specify the MDP is that it enabled us to look at two factors of importance to managers that particularly complicate standard analysis: decisions under uncertainty for a highly stochastic ecological system and the long-distance dispersal by IS.

Uncertainty

Although stochasticity itself presents only limited difficulty for purely dynamic analysis, the spatially explicit setting greatly increases the dimensionality of the state space and makes the traditional table-based approach much more difficult to apply. To determine the importance or necessity of accounting for uncertainty, we conduct two types of analysis. First, we compared the optimal choice of action types and locations for cases with and without exogenous arrivals of both native and invasive species. Second, we analyzed the difference between the optimal policies for a deterministic version of the simulation with the baseline stochastic version.

The exogenous arrivals case reflects a concern for managers that species – both native and invasive – can arrive in the managed system from afar. The introduction of seeds from outside the system can occur through large-scale ecological processes or as hitchhikers on animals, humans, or vehicles. Here, we model those arrivals as being equally likely on any reach in the system. As compared to the base case with no such arrivals of either species, exogenous arrivals of both species shift the location of management or treatment actions to upstream reaches (Figure 12.2(h)). This change in emphasis of treatment to upstream reaches derives from the additional risk of invasion in those reaches, which face limited risk of invasion through within-system dispersal due to the prominence of downstream directionality in the dispersal process. In addition, the choice of treatment shifts toward restoration, which prevents IS from establishing in those locations even if many IS seeds arrive. That change reflects a desire to avoid invasions in the now-vulnerable upstream reaches because invasions there readily disperse IS seeds throughout the river network. Incorporating this type of uncertainty in the decision framework reveals that managers of riverscapes with potential for IS arriving from outside the system should modify the management policy toward restoration and shift the locations of restoration to upstream reaches.

Reflecting the riparian ecology literature, our ecological model contains many points at which ecological outcomes are simulated by draws from random variables, including plant mortality, number of seeds generated, dispersal locations of seeds, and which species establishes in degraded reaches. Previous studies in economics and ecology, including the original Muneepeerakul paper (Muneepeerakul et al. 2007), replace the stochastic model with a deterministic model. To mimic that deterministic approach, we insert the expected value for each random variable and then compute the optimal policy for the resulting deterministic MDP. For example, plants no longer die, because the mortality outcome is less likely than the survival outcome. The number of seeds arriving at each site is replaced by the expected number of seeds, and so on. For the base case with no exogenous arrivals, the deterministic optimal policy differs from the base case in 15 percent of the riverscape states. In particular, in states where only one reach is invaded, the policy changes in 24 percent of those states. In invasions where six out of the seven reaches are invaded, the optimal policy is different in 21 percent of the states. The changes tend to shift toward increased restoration and to taking more actions in the midstream reaches.

Widespread Dispersal

The most common simplifying assumption in the spatio-economic analysis of IS is that the invasion spreads only to the nearest neighbors of any invaded parcel or reach. In many settings, that assumption is perfectly appropriate, but many IS are capable of more distant dispersal that may include discrete jumps beyond the invasion's frontier. To compare our base case to a model with only nearest-neighbor dispersal, we modified the dispersal matrix to maintain strong downstream dispersal but to set all dispersal beyond the nearest-neighbor reaches to zero. Of course, this dramatically decreases the size of the transition matrix, which reduces runtimes and could permit analysis of larger riverscapes. But, this simplifying assumption leads to changes in the location and type of management. When only short-distance dispersal occurs, the optimal policy employs less restoration overall and more eradication. It shifts the location of management actions toward the midstream reaches (Figure 12.2). In short-distance dispersal, restoration next to the invaded sites creates a barrier beyond which invasion cannot spread. Conversely, restoration in upstream reaches is less useful because downstream invaded reaches can act as a barrier to prevent the native species seeds from dispersing. Without long-distance dispersal, degraded reaches without invaded neighbors face no immediate risk of invasion, so restoration of such reaches can be deferred. These factors reduce the relative value of restoration as compared to control, which shifts the portfolio of management tools toward control.

These experiments suggest that previous analyses based on nearest-neighbor spread and deterministic dynamics are producing misleading and biased results. Of course, there is a computational tradeoff between analyzing larger landscapes and employing stochastic, complex dispersal dynamics. Our results suggest that it is better to understand a smaller landscape with a more accurate dynamical model than it is to consider larger landscapes with simplified models. An important goal for future computer science research is to develop methods that can handle high-fidelity models on larger landscapes.

Discussion and Concluding Remarks

By exploiting a complex simulator-defined MDP, the analyses here incorporate more ecological aspects of bio-invaders, including a higher level of stochasticity and spatial complexity, than many economic optimization models. The MDP is still highly stylized, but the inclusion of some types of interactions between native species and invasive species also enables examination of restoration – especially the planting of native species – as a management tool. Sensitivity analysis of the relative strength of an invader's ability to produce an abundance of seeds, disperse long distances, and establish in a degraded site demonstrates the differences in both location and types of treatment that managers should optimally use for each of these ecological mechanisms that enable invasive species to dominate a riverscape. In particular, riverscapes with highly fecund invaders require midstream and upstream treatment; those with widely dispersing invaders need upstream treatment; and those with high seed fitness/strong establishment invaders do best with midstream treatment. In addition, the inclusion of uncertainty in the ecological system leads to different optimal management choices from the deterministic case in nearly 20 percent of the relevant states. Because both the type and location of treatment differ between deterministic and stochastic settings and across invasion biology, incorporating these aspects into the analysis provides unique insights for managers.

Economists are not systems modelers, but instead seek to build and solve decision problems that capture policy-relevant, salient characteristics of the system to produce generalizable results. Given the relevance of different aspects of the ecological system and its stochasticity for management outcomes, these aspects appear important to incorporate in spatio-dynamic optimization for many settings. The issues of dimensionality, long-distance spread, and spatial heterogeneity, however, present considerable challenges to solving such models because they require large transition matrices, tracking the state of the entire landscape, and limit the ability to exploit symmetries to reduce computation. The computational methods employed here generate solutions to these complex models by estimating the probabilities in the transition matrix by running a large number of Monte Carlo simulations. These methods enable us to examine issues of importance to managers, including uncertainty and long-distance dispersal of invaders, and to investigate which model simplifications prove important in determining optimal spatial and dynamic treatment in the riverscape.

A shortcoming of the computational approach described in this chapter is that it does not provide a confidence guarantee on the optimality of the computed policy. The Clopper–Pearson confidence intervals are satisfied for each estimated transition probability, but these need to be combined to obtain a confidence interval on the value of the computed policy. This can be accomplished through extended value iteration (Strehl and Littman, 2008). In related work, Taleghan et al. (2015) present methods for integrating the Monte Carlo simulations with extended value iteration to greatly reduce the number of required simulations. Future studies should consider applying these methods, as they will give greater confidence that the computed policies are optimal.

Future collaborations between ecologists, economists, and computer scientists could examine several other aspects of bio-invasions that our computational methods cannot readily address. First, this model does not permit invasive species to invade reaches that are healthy and dominated by native species, but that situation occurs in many settings. One way to extend these methods to address that scenario would be to define a relationship between the number of invasive seeds arriving at healthy reaches and the probability of the native surviving that invasion, which this method could accommodate as long as the transition from healthy to invaded occurs as a function of the seeds arriving rather than some time-based characteristic of the native species, such as their age. Second, some species can alter the characteristics of a site even after they are removed. For example, tamarisk changes the salinity of the soil, which decreases the success of native species thereafter on that site. Modeling this in the MDP would require an additional state variable for each location to track the soil salinity. Third, in real river systems, more than one plant can grow along a river reach. This could be modeled by introducing multiple habitat sites within each reach. That would enable analysis of species competition within a reach as well as modeling treatment costs that depend on the number of invasive plants growing within a reach. Increasing the number of habitat sites per reach would, however, exponentially increase the number of states in the MDP.

From a computer science perspective, other approaches might permit examination of larger landscapes. In particular, an alternative to applying value iteration to the tabular MDP is to apply policy search methods. These methods start by defining a space of policies as a function of a vector θ of parameters. Then, search algorithms seek to find the value of θ that maximizes the expected return of the corresponding policy. There are two major challenges to this approach. First, the most popular policy search methods require that the policies be stochastic – that is, they select action a according to a probability distribution $\pi(a|s;\theta)$ – whereas decision-makers (and economists) prefer deterministic policies. Second, the search methods generally find policies that are only locally optimal and cannot provide guarantees of global optimality. From the point of view of policy analysis, this means there are two reasons why we might not find the optimal policy. First, the optimal policy might not exist in our parameterized policy space. Second, even if it does exist, the policy search might not find it. To address these problems, an interesting direction for future research is to combine a very flexible policy space with a global search method, such as Bayesian optimization. Deep neural networks and related representations make it possible to create extremely flexible policy spaces, and these are highly likely to contain the optimal policy. Bayesian optimization can guarantee finding the optimal policy, provided that the policy space is sufficiently smooth.

Summary

The problem of optimal management of IS can be modeled as an MDP. However, the biological processes of mortality, reproduction, dispersion, and competition can be very complex, which makes it difficult for economists to calculate the probability transition matrix that is required for applying standard value iteration MDP solvers. Fortunately, it is quite easy to write a simulator that incorporates these biological processes. In this chapter, we have presented a simple algorithm that estimates the transition matrix by making thousands of calls to the simulator. This method allows us to solve spatio-temporal optimization models without resorting to simplifications such as nearest-neighbor spread or deterministic state transitions.

We refer to our approach as a "whole landscape" approach because it explicitly models the state of the entire landscape. This contrasts with approaches that treat space as implicit. The resulting optimal policies differ from those computed from simplified dynamics (deterministic transitions and only local dispersal). In particular, it reveals the value of restoration as an important management tool in many situations. The whole landscape approach also reveals how the optimal action choice depends on the location of each site within the river system. Although not discussed in this chapter, the whole landscape approach suggests interesting sequencing of actions. Under some conditions (e.g., no upstream propagation and no exogenous arrivals), the optimal plan is to eradicate from upstream to downstream. But when there are many exogenous arrivals, the optimal approach shifts to restoration from the middle-outwards. In summary, our IS management case study demonstrates the usefulness of a simulator-defined MDP approach in capturing complex spatial system dynamics, which characterizes a wide range of economic decisions of interest to managers and economists.

Acknowledgments

This material is based upon work supported by the National Science Foundation under grant numbers 0832804, 1331932, and 1521687. Any opinions, findings, and conclusions or recommendations expressed in this material are those of the authors and do not necessarily reflect the views of the National Science Foundation.

References

Aadland, D., Sims, C., and Finnoff, D. (2015). Spatial Dynamics of Optimal Management in Bioeconomic Systems. *Computational Economics*, **45**(4), 545–577.

Baxter, M., and Ewing, G. (1981). Models of Recreational Trip Distribution. *Regional Studies*, **15**(5), 327–344.

Bossenbroek, J. M., Kraft, C. E., and Nekola, J. C. (2001). Prediction of Long-Distance Dispersal Using Gravity Models: Zebra Mussel Invasion of Inland Lakes. *Ecological Applications*, **11**(6), 1778–1788.

Chalak, M., Polyakov, M., and Pannell, D. J. (2017). Economics of Controlling Invasive Species: A Stochastic Optimization Model for a Spatial-Dynamic Process. *American Journal of Agricultural Economics*, **99**(1), 123–139.

Clopper, C. J., and Pearson, E. S. (1934). The Use of Confidence or Fiducial Limits Illustrated in the Case of the Binomial. *Biometrika*, **26**(4), 404–413.

Di Tomaso, J. M. (1998). Impact, Biology, and Ecology of Saltcedar (*Tamarix* spp.) in the Southwestern United States. *Weed Technology*, **12**(2), 326–336.

Epanchin-Niell, R. S., and Hastings, A. (2010). Controlling Established Invaders: Integrating Economics and Spread Dynamics to Determine Optimal Management. *Ecology Letters*, **13**(4), 528–541.

Epanchin-Niell, R. S., and Wilen, J. E. (2012). Optimal Spatial Control of Biological Invasions. *Journal of Environmental Economics and Management*, **63**(2), 260–270.

Hall, K. M. (2014). Optimal Spatial-Dynamic Resource Allocation Facing Uncertainty: Integrating Economics and Ecology for Invasive Species Policy. Oregon

State University. Retrieved from http://oatd.org/oatd/record?record=%22handle
%5C%3A1957%2F52661%22

Hall, K. M., Albers, H. J., Taleghan, M. A., and Dietterich, T. G. (2017). Optimal
Spatial-Dynamic Management of Stochastic Species Invasions. *Environmental
and Resource Economics*, **70** 1–25.

Januchowski-Hartley, S. R., Visconti, P., and Pressey, R. L. (2011). A Systematic
Approach for Prioritizing Multiple Management Actions for Invasive Species.
Biological Invasions, **13**(5), 1241–1253.

Muneepeerakul, R., Weitz, J. S., Levin, S. A., Rinaldo, A., and Rodriguez-Iturbe,
I. (2007). A Neutral Metapopulation Model of Biodiversity in River Networks.
Journal of Theoretical Biology, **245**(2), 351–363.

Sharov, A. A. (2004). Bioeconomics of Managing the Spread of Exotic Pest Species
with Barrier Zones. *Risk Analysis: An Official Publication of the Society for Risk
Analysis*, **24**(4), 879–892.

Stewart-Koster, B., Olden, J. D., and Johnson, P. T. J. (2015). Integrating Landscape
Connectivity and Habitat Suitability to Guide Offensive and Defensive Invasive
Species Management. *Journal of Applied Ecology*, **52**(2), 366–378.

Strehl, A. L., and Littman, M. L. (2008). An Analysis of Model-Based Interval
Estimation for Markov Decision Processes. *Journal of Computer and System
Sciences*, **74**(8), 1309–1331.

Sutton, R., and Barto, A. (1998). *Reinforcement Learning: An Introduction*. Cambridge,
MA: MIT Press.

Taleghan, M. A., Dietterich, T. G., Crowley, M., Hall, K., and Albers, H. J. (2015).
PAC Optimal MDP Planning with Application to Invasive Species Management.
Journal of Machine Learning Research, **16**, 3877–3903.

Tamarisk Coalition (2009). Appendix H: Riparian Restoration. Assessment of
Alternative Technologies for Tamarisk Control, Biomass Reduction, and
Revegetation. In: *Colorado River Basin Tamarisk and Russian Olive Assessment*.
www.tamariskcoalition.org/sites/default/files/files/TRO_Assessment_FINAL
%2012-09.pdf. Accessed December 16, 2017.

USDA (2013). Forest Service national strategic framework for invasive species management. www.fs.fed.us/foresthealth/publications/Framework_for_Invasive_Species_
FS-1017.pdf

Visconti, P., Pressey, R. L., Segan, D. B., and Wintle, B. A. (2010). Conservation
Planning with Dynamic Threats: The Role of Spatial Design and Priority Setting
for Species' Persistence. *Biological Conservation*, **143**(3), 756–767.

Zavaleta, E. (2000). The Economic Value of Controlling an Invasive Shrub. *AMBIO: A
Journal of the Human Environment*, **29**(8), 462–467.

Glossary

(Artificial) neural network (machine learning) A system of processing input features based on multiple layers of nonlinear processing units, called artificial neurons. Each artificial neuron receives input signals from neurons connected to it in the previous layer, processes them, and then send an output signal to artificial neurons connected to it in the next layer.

Classification (machine learning) The problem of identifying to which class an instance belongs, given a training set of instances whose class is known. Classification is an example of supervised learning (Bishop, 2006).

Convolutional neural network (CNN) An artificial neural network with multiple layers of conceptual neurons, each completing some basic computation with assigned weights. Further, in some layers, the neurons share the weights and the computation is restricted to a region of a spatially connected field (Krizhevsky et al., 2012).

Covariate (statistics) A variable that is possibly predictive of the outcome under study. A covariate may be of direct interest, or it may be a confounding or interacting variable (Everitt and Skrondal, 2002). In many contexts, it has the same meaning as *Feature (machine learning)*.

Deep learning A class of machine learning methods that are based on a cascade of multiple layers of nonlinear processing units, each successive layer using the output from the previous layer as input. Each processing unit is referred to as an artificial neuron, and the cascade of layers of neurons is referred to as an artificial neural network (LeCun et al., 2015).

Digital elevation model (DEM) A digital elevation model is a digital model representing height information of a terrain's surface created from terrain elevation data (Peckham and Gyozo, 2007).

Feature (machine learning) A measurable attribute or characteristic of a problem instance (Bishop, 2006). Features can be categorical or real-valued. Extracting or selecting features is often challenging.

Game (game theory) A formal description of a strategic situation in which there are multiple players, and each player can choose from a set of actions, and the outcome and payoffs to the players are determined by their joint actions.

Game theory The study of decision-making in games.

Geographic information system (GIS) A system that captures, creates, stores, edits, manipulates, integrates, analyzes, manages, presents, and displays spatial or geographic data (Maliene et al., 2011).

Expected payoff The payoffs of all possible outcomes weighted with their probabilities when the outcome is random.

Expected utility See *Expected payoff*.

Label (machine learning) In machine learning, a label of a data point is a meaningful and informative tag of the data point. For example, in classification, a label of an instance is the class it belongs to.

Law enforcement A system whose members act in an organized manner to enforce the law. It mostly applies to those who directly engage in patrols or surveillance to dissuade and discover criminal activity or non-criminal violations of rules and norms, and those who investigate crimes and apprehend offenders (Germann et al., 1970).

Leader–follower game See *Stackelberg game*.

Linear program (LP) A mathematical program in which the objective function is linear, and the feasible region is defined by a set of linear equalities and inequalities (Schrijver, 1998).

Markov decision process (MDP) A discrete time process that is partly controlled by nature and partly controlled by a decision-maker. At each time step, the process is in some state, and the decision-maker may choose an action that is available in the current state. The process moves into a new state in the next time step in a stochastic way and gives the decision-maker a reward. The probability of moving to a new state is only dependent on the current state and the decision-maker's action. In an MDP there is a state transition function that prescribes a probability distribution over all states for each combination of the current state and the decision maker's action (Howard, 1960). MDPs provide a mathematical framework for modeling decision-making in situations in which outcomes are partly random and partly under the control of a decision-maker. MDPs are useful for studying a wide range of optimization problems.

Mathematical program An optimization problem of finding the values of a set of real-valued decision variables that are within a given feasible region (often defined by a set of equality and inequality constraints) to optimize a given objective function of the variables (Dantzig, 2010).

Mathematical programming The study or use of the mathematical program (Dantzig, 2010).

Mixed integer linear program (MILP) A mathematical program in which some of the decision variables are restricted to be integers and the objective function, and the constraints other than the integer constraints are linear (Schrijver, 1998).

Mixed strategy A randomization over pure strategies or actions in a game.

Nash equilibrium A solution concept in game theory. It consists of a list of strategies, one for each player. For a player in the game, if all other players are playing the strategies described in the equilibrium, then also playing the strategy described in the equilibrium leads to the highest payoff. That is, in Nash equilibrium, no player can unilaterally change their strategy and get a better payoff (Myerson, 2013).

Optimal solution The optimal solution of a mathematical program is the best value of the decision variables.

Optimal value The optimal value of a mathematical program is the optimal value of the objective function.

Optimization problem In computer science, an optimization problem is a problem of finding a solution that optimizes an objective among all feasible solutions.

Payoff (game theory) A number quantifying the desirability of an outcome to a player. It is also called utility (Turocy and von Stengel, 2001).

Player (game theory) An agent who makes decisions in a game.

Rationality (game theory) A player is said to be rational if he or she tries to maximize his or her (expected) payoff.

Satellite imagery Images of Earth or other planets collected by imaging satellites (Hand 2015).

Spatial Monitoring And Reporting Tool (SMART) A software tool for monitoring efforts to tackle poaching and other illegal activities. It is used in many conservation sites around the world (SMART 2017).

Stackelberg game A game with a leader and one or more followers. The leader moves first, and then the followers move. It is also called a leader–follower game.

Strategy (game theory) A deterministic or random way of choosing one of the available actions of a player.

Supervised learning The learning task of inferring a function from labeled training data (Mohri et al., 2012).

Test dataset A set of examples used to assess the performance of a machine learning model. The test dataset is independent of the training dataset but follows the same probability distribution (Ripley, 2007).

Training dataset The training dataset is a set of examples. Each example is a pair of problem instance and a label or value associated with it. It is used to train a machine learning model, i.e., to determine the mapping from the problem instance to the label or value.

Utility (game theory) See *Payoff*.

Zero-sum game A game in which the sum of the payoffs to all players is zero for any outcome. When the game has only two players, the game is zero-sum if and only if one player's gain is the other player's loss.

References

Bishop, C. M. (2006). *Pattern Recognition and Machine Learning*. Springer.

Dantzig, G. B. (2010). The nature of mathematical programming. *Mathematical Programming Glossary*. https://glossary.informs.org/second.php?page=nature.html.

Everitt, B., & Skrondal, A. (2002). *The Cambridge Dictionary of Statistics* (Vol. 106). Cambridge University Press.

Germann, A. C., Day, F. D., & Gallati, R. R. (1970). *Introduction to Law Enforcement and Criminal Justice*. CENGAGE Delmar Learning.

Hand, E. (2015). Startup liftoff. *Science*, **348**(6231), 172–177.

Howard, R. A. (1960). *Dynamic Programming and Markov Processes*. MIT Press.

Krizhevsky, A., Sutskever, I., & Hinton, G. E. (2012). Imagenet classification with deep convolutional neural networks. In *Advances in Neural Information Processing Systems*. Curran Associates, Inc.

LeCun, Y., Bengio, Y., & Hinton, G. (2015). Deep learning. *Nature*, **521**(7553), 436–444.

Maliene, V., Grigonis, V., Palevčius, V., & Griffiths, S. (2011). Geographic information system:old principles with new capabilities. *Urban Design International*, **16**(1), 1–6.

Mohri, M., Rostamizadeh, A., & Talwalkar, A. (2012). *Foundations of Machine Learning*. MIT Press.

Myerson, R. B. (2013). *Game Theory*. Harvard University Press.

Peckham, R. J., & Gyozo, J. (2007). *Development and Applications in a Policy Support Environment Series: Lecture Notes in Geoinformation and Cartography*. Springer.

Ripley, B. D. (2007). *Pattern Recognition and Neural Networks*. Cambridge University Press.

Schrijver, A. (1998). *Theory of Linear and Integer Programming*. John Wiley & Sons.

SMART (2017). Overview brochure. http://smartconservationtools.org

Turocy, T. L., & von Stengel, B. (2001). Game theory*. Draft prepared for the Encyclopedia of Information Systems. London School of Economics.

Index

AI: Artificial Intelligence
  AI and Improving the Effectiveness of
    Ranger Patrols, 26
  History, 6
  Law Enforcement for Wildlife
    Conservation, 27
  New Era of AI, 7
  Partnership of AI and Conservation Science,
    8
  Subfields of AI, 7
  What is AI?, 5

Bagging Ensemble Model, 46, 47
Bio-Invasions, 227
Black-Box Attackers, 59, 61
BoostIT, 33–35, 37, 41
Bootstrap Aggregation Technique, 67

CAPTURE, 30–34, 37, 39
Conservation Biology, 3, 4, 9, 12, 47
Convolutional neural network, 81
Coral Reef Ecosystems, 103, 104
Covariates, 44

Dataset Preparation, 46
Defender Strategies, 59, 74, 103, 104, 107,
  112, 115, 124, 144

Expected Utility, 109, 126

Field Tests, 26, 29, 30, 32
Forestry, 151, 152, 174

Game (game theory), 33
GREED, 71, 73
Green Security Games (GSG), 59, 60

INTERCEPT, 30, 35, 37, 39, 41

Law Enforcement, 12, 21, 26
  Law Enforcement for Wildlife
    Conservation, 17, 27
  Law Enforcement Practice in Africa: An
    Example from Uganda, 18
Linear Program (LP), 104, 115, 124, 140
Logistic Regression, 37, 39

Markov decision process (MDP), 8, 137, 210,
  211
Mathematical Program (MP), 63
Mixed Integer Linear Program (MILP), 63
Mixed Strategy, 61, 62, 65, 107, 109–110
Model Free Monte Carlo (MFMC), 158

NECTAR (Nirikshana for Enforcing
  Compliance for Toxic wastewater
  Abatement and Reduction), 136–137,
  143–145, 147, 149

OPERA (Optimal Patrol Planning with
  Enhanced Randomness), 58, 59, 67, 73,
  74
Optimal Patrol Planning, 71
Optimal Solution, 126, 218, 219
Optimization Problem, 8, 122, 124, 126, 203

Policy Search, 152, 168, 227, 228
Population Models and Estimation, 179
Predictive Model, 6, 9, 10, 29, 31, 32, 47, 53, 67, 70, 205

RAND, 71, 73
Reward Functions, 154, 155, 203

Satellite Imagery, 11
Scalability, 112, 114, 130, 141
Simulations, 7, 152, 154, 218, 219, 224, 227
SMAC, 167–169, 171
Spatial Monitoring And Reporting Tool (SMART), 9, 22
Stackelberg Security Game (SSG), 58, 103, 104, 106, 109, 115
Stakeholder management, 151, 155, 169

Test Dataset, 41
Testing, 30, 39, 59, 70, 71, 96

Timber, 21, 23, 151, 213
Training Dataset, 9, 37, 46

Uniform Random (UR), 144
Unmanned Aerial Vehicle (UAV's), 77–79, 82

Visual Analytics, 155, 156

Wildfire
　Adding Interactivity to WildFire Assistant, 158
　Building a Wildfire Assistant, 151
　WildFire Assistant for Forest Managers, 155
　Wildfire Assistant Process, 153
　Wildfire Suppression Decisions in Context, 152
Wildlife Crime Dataset: Features and Challenges, 32
Wildlife Poaching, 3, 12, 29, 30, 33, 39, 45